A MARITIME HISTORY OF
NEW YORK

SANDY HOOK LIGHTHOUSE

Dedicated to the Twin Towers of the World Trade Center
which shown as beacons to all reaches of New York Harbor, 1970-2001

"PORTS ARE NOT ONLY interface between land and water. They are sources of national wealth, pride and concern. They are, or have been, points of interaction between cultures and peoples. But above all they are places; places have history and the past of a place affects its present. For ports, in short, history matters.

History matters in another sense, too, because taking a longer view of port development enables us to understand what is going on now rather better. In particular, it helps us to distinguish between genuinely fresh developments, which require new ways of explaining things and novel responses, and developments which are really old problems in a new form."

Prof. Sarah Palmer, 'Current Port Trends in a
Historical Perspective,' *Journal of Maritime Research*,
(jmr.nmm.ac.uk, December 1999)

NEW YORK POST

The New York Post, now the nation's oldest continuously published newspaper, was founded at a time when the city's commercial and economic development was inextricably tied to the waterfront.

In its first issue - Nov. 16, 1801 - the paper's editor, William Coleman, promised to devote special attention to the needs of the merchant class (many of whom were recruited by Alexander Hamilton to be among the paper's initial investors) and pledged to "industriously collect and report the earliest Commercial Information," which at the time meant chiefly arrivals and sailings of trade ships.

The Post was an early advocate for safer ferryboats and devoted much attention to the dangers in the crossings from Manhattan to Brooklyn and to Paulus Hook (Jersey City). Coleman was a particularly strong backer of Robert Fulton's steamboat: "The experiment of this day removes every doubt of the practicability of the Steam Boat being able to work in rough weather," he wrote following an 1807 trip to Albany. Indeed, just a few weeks after Fulton began regular service to the state capital, he called for mail service to be transferred to Fulton's steamboat.

In 1970, the paper moved into its last downtown home: the old Journal-American building, which had been built on Catherine Slip by William Randolph Hearst in the 1930s specifically because of its waterfront location, which was meant to speed up the delivery of newsprint.

Today, The Post - part of the international News Corporation media empire - has left the waterfront area for midtown and the steamboat era for cutting-edge publishing technology. The paper's $300 million, 430,000-square-foot printing plant in the Port Morris section produces state of the art color production that has helped spur The Post's record circulation growth in recent years.

The Journal of Commerce

Covering the Waterfront Since 1827

The Journal of Commerce and New York Harbor grew up together. The JoC was founded in 1827, only two years after the completion of the Erie Canal made New York the nation's top port. The JoC's original investors included Samuel F.B. Morse, who later gained fame as inventor of the telegraph.

The JoC was an innovator in news-gathering techniques. It had the fastest "news boats" - the harbor schooners that that carried reporters out to meet incoming ships off Sandy Hook and get cargo manifests and the latest news from Europe. In 1847, the JoC's David Hale led New York publishers in founding the Associated Press. The first three AP presidents were from the JoC.

The newspaper earned recognition as "the Bible of the Maritime Industry." It has continued to change with the times, embracing Internet distribution of news with JoC Online while publishing The Journal of Commerce as a weekly magazine.

Since 2001, the JoC has been a division of Commonwealth Business Media, whose other publications include Shipping Digest, Pacific Shipper, Florida Shipper, Gulf Shipper, Canadian Sailings, Traffic World and Air Cargo World.

Drawing shown is of a schooner employed by The Journal of Commerce to gather news in the 1820s and 1830s.

Acknowledgements

GOING COASTAL, INC. wishes to express our appreciation and acknowledge those companies and individuals whose generous support helped to restore to print A Maritime History of New York:

> Maersk Sealand
> The Port Authority of New York and New Jersey
> Sandy Hook Pilots Association
> Reinauer Transportation Companies
> The New York Post
> Journal of Commerce

Special thanks to everybody who helped us in our efforts:
Stroock, Stroock & Lavan LLP; Norman Brouwer; Patricia Redding Scanlon; The Navy League; Municipal Archives of the City of New York; Marine Log; Jim Crowley; and Benjamin Miller.

A MARITIME HISTORY

OF

NEW YORK

COMPILED BY

WORKERS OF THE WRITERS PROGRAM OF THE

WORK PROJECTS ADMINISTRATION

FOR THE CITY OF NEW YORK

ORIGINAL INTRODUCTION BY THE HONORABLE FIORELLO LA GUARDIA

WITH NEW PROLOGUE BY NORMAN BROUWER
AND EPILOGUE BY BARBARA LA ROCCO

PUBLISHED BY

GOING COASTAL, INC.

Library of Congress Control Number 2004112487

ISBN 0-9729803-1-8

This Going Coastal edition of *A Maritime History of New York* is a re-publication of the original edition written by the New York City Unit of the Federal Writers' Project, sponsored by the Mayor of City of New York, and published by Doubleday, Doran and Company, Inc. in 1941. The illustrations and cover design are based on the original. The original manuscripts and related research materials are in the WPA Federal Writers' Project collection at the New York City Municipal Archives.

Production by Barbara La Rocco and Zhennya Slootskin

PRINTED IN THE UNITED STATES BY GOING COASTAL, INC., BROOKLYN, NEW YORK

Going Coastal
Coastal Classics™

WWW.GOINGCOASTAL.ORG

Publisher's Note

T HE CONTENTS of this book are those of the New York City Unit of the Work Projects Administration Federal Writers' Project published under the same title in 1941. The writer's provide a concise and insightful description of the Port of New York's 400 year history—and the resilience of the people, the city and the port through changing times. This volume provides the "big picture"—how the global city of today was an international one from the time the first trading post was established on its shore; how the city's fortunes, industry and standing rested on its vast and vastly successful Port.

We first came across *A Maritime History of New York* while doing research for *Going Coastal New York City,* a guide that portrays the city's waterfront today and explores the relationship between the city and its coastal environment. It struck us that so much of the old "sailor town" and traditional waterfront have survived, albeit in a recycled form. The original text has been supplemented to include a prologue that provides an anthology of the book; a foreword which offers a tour of the port today; and an epilogue that gives an overview of activity in the port from the close of the book in 1941 to modern times, as well as historical information about some of the companies that helped to establish the seaport. This volume is presented in the hope of generating renewed port-consciousness.

GOING COASTAL, INC.

Going Coastal, Inc. is a 501(c)3 nonprofit volunteer organization dedicated to connecting people and coastal resources through publishing, media, and outreach programs. All sales support these programs.

The Port Authority of New York & New Jersey
Marine Terminal Facilities

New Jersey

Newark

Port Newark

Elizabeth-
Port Authority
Marine
Terminal

Elizabeth

Newark Bay

Bayonne

Kill van Kull

Arthur Kill

Howland Hook
Marine Terminal

Staten Island

Jersey City

Auto
Marine
Terminal

Hudson River

Manhattan

East River

Brooklyn
Piers

Red Hook
Container
Terminal

Upper
New York Bay

Brooklyn

New York

Lower
New York Bay

Contents

Illustrations

PROLOGUE

By NORMAN BROUWER

THE YEARS 1935 through 1943 were very productive in the fields of research and publication on America's maritime heritage. During this period the Federal Writers Program, a New Deal depression relief effort intended to aid out-of-work writers, produced over fifty guide-books to the then forty-eight states, three territories, and several major cities. Teams of researchers went out into communities large and small to collect information about their histories, folklore and current activities. Many of these communities were involved in maritime commerce or various aspects of the fishing industry.

In 1935 poet and historian Constance Lindsay Skinner interested publishers Ferrar and Rinehart in a series of books on the "Rivers of America." The first volume, Robert P. Tristram Coffin's history of Maine's Kennebec River, came out in 1937. By the time Ferrar and Rinehart's successors, Rinehart & Winston, ended the series in 1974, sixty-four rivers had been documented.

It was apparently in part as a response to their competitors that Doubleday Doran embarked on the "Seaport Series." Their first study of an American seaport was *The Port of Gloucester* by James B. Connolly published in 1940. A year later Doubleday Doran brought out the original edition of *A Maritime History of New York*. The Seaport Series was not as long lived as the Rivers of America, but it did outlive the Federal Writers Project, which was ended on April 27, 1943. At least twelve volumes were produced in the Seaport Series, including on the two Canadian west coast cities of Vancouver and Victoria which came in 1948.

The Federal Government also provided a brief, but productive, "Historic American Merchant Marine Survey." From March 1936 to October 1937 teams of out-of-work draftsmen and naval architects were employed recording surviving evidence of ship design and construction, through measured drawings and photographs of the vessels themselves, laid up or abandoned around the country or in some cases still working, and by taking lines off shipbuilders' half models.

Why was so much attention being paid to America's maritime past in the late 1930s? In the case of federal support, the fact that the current occupant of the White House, Franklin D. Roosevelt, had a lifelong interest in maritime and naval history may have played a role. But, this revival of interest in American maritime history can be traced back to the early 1920s, and the great optimism over the future of the country's merchant marine that grew out of the massive World War I shipbuilding program.

The "Golden Age" of American seafaring had peaked in the clipper ship era of the 1850s. The Civil War, and the decades that followed, saw only steady decline. By World War I, less than ten per cent of America's foreign commerce was being handled by American-owned ships. When the Untied States entered the War of 1917 it embarked on the most ambitious shipbuilding program the world had ever seen. It also began recruiting men to crew these ships throughout the country, and bringing them to major ports to receive their training. Recruitment was encouraged by extolling the glories of America's maritime past, particularly the clipper ship era, and by painting a rosy picture of the coming "new Golden Age" of the country's merchant marine. With its ample fleet of modern vessels America fully expected to dominate ocean commerce in the post-War years.

This did not happen. The ships were completed too late to play a significant role in the War. They were employed for a few years resupplying Europe with the goods it had been cut from during the conflict, and the materials it needed to rebuild. Great Britain and Germany, that had dominated shipping before the War, rebuilt their fleets. By the early 1920s American ship owners were finding it as difficult to compete as they had a decade earlier. It was only possible to maintain American flag vessels on certain "vital trade routes" through the payment of government subsidies.

The interest in America's maritime past that had been stimulated by wartime optimism survived. The first major historian of the era to get into print was Samuel Eliot Morison. In his *Maritime History of Massachusetts 1783-1860*, published in 1921, he articulated the popular view of the past Golden Age. "Never in these United States, has the brain of man conceived, or the hand of man fashioned, so perfect a thing as the clipper ship. In her, the long-suppressed artistic impulse of a practical, hard-worked race burst into flower. The *Flying Cloud* was our Rheims, the *Sovereign of the Sea* out Parthenon...".

More works followed. In 1926-1927 Octavious T. Howe and Frederick C. Matthews completed their two volume *American Clipper Ships 1833-1858*, published by the Marine Research Society of Salem. Three years later Carl C. Cutler produced *Greyhounds of the Sea: The Story of the American Clipper Ship*. In 1931 the *Journal of Economic and Business History* published Robert G. Albion's article "New York Port and its Disappointed Rivals, 1815-60," which he later expanded into the book *The Rise of New York Port 1815-1860,* published in 1939.

The clipper ship became an American icon. During the 1920s and 1930s paintings of clipper ships by Gordon Grant, Frank Vining Smith, and others, were frequently reproduced on calenders or magazine covers. In 1927 there was even a brief effort to save the last clipper ship *Glory of the Seas,* before her wooden hull was burned for its metal sheathing and fastenings on a beach in the Puget Sound.

Later sailing ships that resembled clippers, though lacking their grace and speed, were subjects of other efforts. The British-built iron bark *Star of India* was preserved in San Diego in 1927, where she survived long enough to be fully restored in the 1960s. The Maine-built *Benjamin F. Packard* of 1883 was the subject of a preservation effort in New York, but ended her days as an attraction at a shorefront amusement park before being scuttled in Long Island Sound in 1940. In November 1941, just days before Pearl Harbor, the whaling ship *Charles W. Morgan* was rescued from a beach in Massachusetts and towed to the shore of a maritime museum in Mystic, Connecticut founded ten years earlier through the efforts of historian Carl C. Cutler.

The preservation of historic ships in this country was put on hold through the war years. It revived in the 1950s with the expansion of the fleet at Mystic, and the restoration of the sailing ship *Balclutha* in San Francisco, followed by the creation of a fleet of historic vessels on the waterfront of the port. In the 1960s similar fleets were created in other parts, including New York, and communities throughout the country took on one or more vessels to represent their maritime heritage.

With the general interest in history that developed in the 1960s and continues to the present day, many of the classics of American maritime history that appeared in the 1920s and 1930s have now been reprinted, while original editions have become sought after by collectors. We are indebted to Going Coastal for taking on this reprint and updating of *A Maritime History of New York*, the first work to provide an overview of the history of our greatest seaport from prehistoric times to the moment it was published.

NORMAN BROUWER is a nautical historian and author of T*he International Register of Historic Ships* and co-author of *Mariner's Fancy: The Whaleman's Art of Scrimshaw* with Nina Hellman. For 30 years Mr. Brouwer served as curator and marine historian at the Melville Library of South Street Seaport Museum. He is currently in the process of restoring the 1933 steamship *Lilac* at Pier 40 in New York City.

"CRIES OF WONDER"

A Short Waterside Tour of New York Harbor

WHEN Giovanni da Verrazano—the first European explorer to see what would one day be called New York Harbor—anchored there in 1524, he noted in his log: "We found a very beautiful port. We saw about 20 barges of natives who came with various cries of wonder round about the ship. All together, they uttered a loud shout, signifying that they were glad."

Today, nearly 500 years later, the people of New York and New Jersey are still gladly welcoming ships from both near and far—but those ships are entering what is now one of the world's most famous ports, and they carry much more diverse cargo than the inconsequential "little bells" and other "trinkets" mentioned by da Verrazano in his log: automobiles; shoes, toys, and machinery—usually packed in containers; and a mind-boggling spectrum of other items such as beverages, lumber, wood pulp, plastic, coal, chemicals, and oil. The Port of New York and New Jersey is also the largest petroleum- importing port in the United States.

Although the Port of New York and New Jersey is no longer the busiest in the world (a distinction it held throughout most of the 19th and 20th centuries), it is today the largest port on the U.S. East Coast and the third largest in the United States. And it is still growing both in size and in throughput capacity, thanks primarily to its favorable location at the hub of a highly concentrated and affluent consumer market and its immediate access to the most extensive interstate highway and rail network in the region.

Cargo volumes in and through the port are at record highs, according to Richard M. Larrabee, commerce director of the Port Authority of New York and New Jersey, a public agency that promotes trade and commerce in the greater New York and New Jersey port area.

A Polyglot Port of Call

There are actually several terminals in the port area—all of them on the shores of Newark Bay and Upper New York Bay. A tour of the terminals reveals an interesting maritime complex. All ocean vessels entering the port must pass under the Verrazano Narrows Bridge, which separates Upper and Lower New York Bay and connects the borough of Brooklyn with Staten Island. Ships entering the port come from almost every country in the world—about half of them are from Europe; most of the others are from the Far East and Latin America. All major U.S. trading partners are represented in the hundreds of thousands of tons of exports and imports that enter and leave the port each year: China, France, Germany, Italy, Japan, South Korea, Taiwan, Thailand, the Netherlands, and the United Kingdom.

On the Staten Island side of the Verrazano Narrows Bridge is historic Fort Wadsworth, now the headquarters of U.S. Coast Guard Activities, New York, where Coast Guardsmen operate the Vessel Traffic Services (VTS) system, without which the management of ship traffic in and through the port would be virtually impossible. The VTS system coordinates vessel movements through all areas of the port, principally through the use of a VHF-FM radiotelephone network, augmented by radar and low-light closed-circuit television, to gather the information needed to visually track and continuously monitor the more than 5,000 ships moving through the port each year. Chief Radarman Harold Williams, a VTS watch supervisor, likens the work to that of an air traffic controller—"but at a little slower pace."

The captain of any ship operating within the port area must file a sailing plan (similar to a flight plan) with VTS prior to entering port (or, when departing, before getting under way). The report must include the following information: vessel name and type; current position; destination and estimated time of arrival; intended route; and such other information as deepest draft, any dangerous cargo being carried, and tow configurations. Coast Guardsmen match the data received with current weather conditions, tide tables, and vessel traffic levels, then advise ship captains on what marine traffic they can expect to encounter.

After sailing through The Narrows, the first terminal one comes to is the Red Hook Container Terminal, located on the Brooklyn waterfront just across the water from Governors Island and the Statue of Liberty. A relatively small terminal—but with a 40-foot deep channel that can safely accommodate most deep-draft vessels—Red Hook, which is operated by American Stevedoring Inc., offers the shortest sailing time in and out of the harbor.

Cocoa Beans, Locomotives, And the Statue of Liberty

Red Hook also is home to the New York Cross Harbor Railroad, last of the rail carfloat operations in the New York City area. Red Hook has the distinction of handling more cocoa beans—175,000 tons a year, 100,000 tons of them packed into 8,000 freight cars—than any other port in the United States. A typical crossing between Red Hook and Jersey City, N.J., takes just 40 minutes, versus several days to carry freight across the Hudson via Selkirk, N.Y., near Albany. The operation has essentially remained the same as it was at the turn of the 19th century, when thousands of floatbarges dotted New York City's waterways on any given day. Cross Harbor, which uses diesel-electric locomotives built in the 1940s, is the last marine rail operation in the New York City area; officials say the future appears bright, though, and plans already are underway to expand the railroad's routes and cargo capacity.

The next terminal on this sea-level "cruise" is Brooklyn Marine Terminal, which extends for two miles along the East River between

Red Hook and the Brooklyn Bridge. The Port Authority developed the terminal in the 1950s and today uses five of the terminal's piers for warehousing and three for bulk cargo-handling and storage and for the berthing of transient ships.

Battery Park comes into view as one crosses the East River and rounds the lower tip of Manhattan. Here is where passengers board the famed Staten Island Ferry as well as other ferries going to the Statue of Liberty, Ellis Island, and the New Jersey terminals of Weehawken and Port Liberte. The several ferries collectively transport about 40 million passengers a year in the port.

Pirates, Spirituals, And Speedboat Cruises

Also on the Battery is the Coast Guard's AMVER public relations office. AMVER, or the Automated Mutual Assistance Vessel Rescue System, is the only worldwide computerized ship reporting system routinely used by the Coast Guard in the hundreds of search-and-rescue missions launched annually to assist merchant vessels in distress at sea (or aircraft that are downed and/or reported missing). Merchant ships voluntarily provide AMVER with their sailing plans and current positions no matter where they are in the world. When the AMVER system receives a distress signal, Coast Guardsmen determine which AMVER-participating ship is in the area and request its assistance.

About 12,000 oceangoing ships, or 40 percent of the world's merchant fleet, participate in the AMVER program, which is credited with saving more than 2,000 lives since 1990. Richard T. Kenney, AMVER public relations officer, said that the number could be higher, and that he wants to get the word out to mariners who do not now use the system that AMVER can benefit them as well. If AMVER personnel already have a vessel's sail plan, he pointed out, they can locate the vessel much more quickly if it is in distress and/or loses radio communications or even, perhaps, is boarded by pirates—not an uncommon event in certain parts of the world.

After passing the Battery and Chelsea Piers, one sees a number of cruise ships tied up along the North (Hudson) River piers of midtown Manhattan. Most of the bigger cruise ships berthing at the Passenger Ship Terminal at piers 88 to 90 are headed for the Caribbean or other overseas destinations, but some cruises are strictly local. A cruise circumnavigating Manhattan takes about three hours. Among the several unusual local cruises available are the "Harlem Spirituals Gospel Cruise" and a number of somewhat adventurous speedboat cruises—which make the Coast Guard's VTS operations both more exciting and more difficult.

A Short Shift West

At one time, freight vessels of all types called in Manhattan. As recently as 1959, 23 percent of all of the port area's general cargo imports and exports came through Manhattan terminal. Today, the figure is less than 1 percent. In that same period of time, general cargo traffic through Brooklyn dropped from 46 percent to about 7 percent. The lack of terminal space in the high-rent New York City area was the main reason for the shift in traffic. Today, nearly all of the port area's freight traffic—90 percent—has shifted to New Jersey. A defining moment in the shift came in 1956, when Malcom McLean's converted WWII tanker, the *Ideal X*, carrying 58 containers, sailed from Newark to Houston on the first-ever containership voyage.

Container imports and exports, which are measured in TEUs (20-foot equivalent units—i.e., containers 20 feet long), increased from 1.8 million TEUs in 1991 to more than three million TEUs in 2000.

The two big New Jersey terminals handling most of the container traffic are Port Elizabeth and Port Newark. To reach them, one must navigate the narrow waterway called the Kill Van Kull, between New Jersey and northern Staten Island. What nature did during the last ice age, man is now trying to improve upon. The KVK—as locals call the waterway—was formed by the Earth's shifting plates many millennia ago and then scoured to a depth of 42 feet by the slow but inexorable movement of rock-encrusted glaciers. As recently as 10 years ago, 42 feet was deep enough to accommodate almost any oceangoing vessel. However, since then, a growing number of larger container vessels have been built that require shipping channels 45 or even 50 feet deep.

A key work item in the Port Authority's $1.8 billion five-year improvement plan is the dredging of channels and berthing spaces, particularly in the KVK, which connects the port's busiest terminals. The Port Authority's goal is to create a channel 50 feet deep by 2009. Currently, the biggest (6,000–TEU capacity) container ships can traverse the waterway, but only when carrying a reduced load. Today, dredges from five companies can be seen scooping rock and sediments from the bottom of the KVK near the Bayonne Bridge. Because the bottom in some areas is mostly bedrock, workers must first blast their way through granite.

Finding disposal sites for the rock and sediment has proved to be a challenge. Myron Ronis, deputy director of port commerce for the Port Authority, said that New Jersey developers are using some of the dredged material to reclaim land for new uses such as shopping malls and golf courses. He added that studies are being conducted to determine if the material also might be used as an additive for making concrete and other building compounds.

Reason for Optimism

Looming against the New Jersey skyline are the massive container gantry cranes of the Elizabeth and Newark terminals, and of the Global Terminal in Bayonne, N.J. The cranes can reach out 200 feet to lift containers off a ship and gently place them on trucks or rail flatcars waiting dockside. Maher Terminal in Elizabeth, N.J., the largest terminal in the port, is investing $300 million in improvements, including bigger container cranes, according to M. Brian Maher, the terminal's chairman and CEO. A number of warehouses will be demolished to provide more paved area for containers. Maher has just signed a new 30-year terminal lease with the Port Authority, reflecting his optimism for the long-term growth of the facility.

That optimism is bolstered by recent statistics provided by the Port Authority showing the following:

* In 2003, container volumes grew by eight percent over 2002.

* For the first time in the Port of New York and New Jersey's history, the total value of all cargo surpassed the $100 billion mark, an increase of almost 12 percent.

* New York continues to be the No.1 ocean-borne auto-handling port in the nation. Motor-vehicle imports and exports increased 5.9 percent in 2003, from 590,777 units in 2002 to 625,798 in 2003.

* The number of ships entering and leaving the port increased by 6.5 percent —5,280 ships in 2003, compared to 4,955 ships in 2002.

* The port now supports more than 230,000 jobs and contributes an estimated $25 billion to the regional economy, according to Port Authority officials, who expect cargo volumes to double from current levels in 10 years.

* China continues to be the port's largest trading partner, accounting for 18.6 percent of the port's activity. Trade with China grew 27.9 percent in 2003. In addition, for the first time, Asia has become the Port's largest origin and destination for containerized cargo with a 41 percent share of the region's market.

* Italy, Germany, India and Brazil round out the top five trading partners with the Port. In 2003, trade with Russia grew by 49.8 percent and trade with Turkey grew 31 percent.

* The top three import categories on a tonnage basis, were beverages, vehicles and plastic. The top three general cargo export commodities were wood pulp, plastic and machinery.

Such rapid growth, combined with space limitations and an aging transportation infrastructure, poses a challenge not only for port users but also for the Port Authority. "This year we begin to undertake the most ambitious maritime construction program since [the building of] the Erie Canal," Larrabee said. In addition to the KVK dredging, the $1.8 billion in improvement money is earmarked for, among other things, the purchase of 124 acres of industrial property adjacent to Howland Hook; the construction of a 13-acre 40 double-stack railcar storage facility serving the Newark and Elizabeth terminals; and the previously mentioned improvements at the Maher Terminal.

A Synergistic Solution

The Port Authority also hopes to take more trucks off the road, thereby improving air quality, easing congestion, and increasing energy efficiency all at the same time. Ronis said he envisions the creation of an inland distribution network serving the dense urban trade "clusters" where most container-carrying trucks now tend to collect. Urban planners say that using rail or barge to carry containers to and from these clusters would be more cost-effective and, not incidentally, kinder to the environment.

William G. M. Goetz, assistant vice president of CSX Railroad, the largest rail user of the port area, shares Ronis's vision and said that the track is already in place to serve such cluster cities in Pennsylvania as Harrisburg, Pittsburgh, and Reading. He is optimistic about the potential growth in rail-sea shipments. Container shipments through the port have, in fact, already increased significantly—from 27,000 containers in 1991 to 178,000 in 2000. Because most of the balance of the three million containers transported to and through the port last year were carried by trucks, Port Authority officials point out, there is almost unlimited room for further growth in the shipment of containers by rail and/or barge.

Wrapping up the tour of the Port of New York and New Jersey is a short cruise from New Jersey across Newark Bay to the Howland Hook Marine Terminal on Staten Island. Howland Hook, which is much smaller than the Elizabeth and Newark terminals, is also designed to handle container traffic and, with a 72 percent growth rate from 1999 to 2000, is now the fastest growing terminal in the port. Access to Howland Hook is from Lower New York Bay through the KVK and then through Arthur Kill.

At the end of this short tour through New York Harbor to the various terminals of the Port of New York and New Jersey one can only reflect on da Verrazano's own description of this "beautiful port"—and perhaps suggest that the "cries of wonder" that greeted the great Florentine explorer and his crew almost 500 years ago have echoed down the years and continue to the present day.

"Cries of Wonder" was written by David Vergun and originally was published in the May 2001 issue of *Sea Power* magazine. It is reprinted with the permission of the Navy League of the United States. The article has been updated with new Port information provided by The Port Authority of New York and New Jersey.

Introduction

By FIORELLO H. LA GUARDIA, Mayor

AS A CITY of skyscrapers New York is widely known. Because of the rise of industrial and financial New York, many Americans overlook the fact that their largest municipality is also a great seaport; that its tremendous expansion can be traced to the growth and dominance of the Port; that, lying between ship docks and railroad terminals, the city's development was the natural corollary of its growth as a maritime center. This is the growth principle of any seaport city.

Here is an account that is more than a recital of facts: it is a dramatic tale peopled with colorful, vigorous characters ranging from pirates, smugglers, and slavers to sea captains, great merchants, shipbuilders, and city officials—the men who made municipal history. It is a story, furthermore, of typical American growth, nation and city; of men and goods from every land arriving in the Port; of commodities, ever increasing in extent, flowing into the Port for distribution to every part of a great country; and of an endless procession of American exports being shipped out of that same Port to all parts of the world. It is impossible to treat the history of the City of New York apart from the history of the Port of New York.

Especially does the Port of New York have an intimate relation to the country as a whole: it is likely that the majority of Americans today are the descendants of immigrants who arrived by sea and who entered the United States through the Port of New York. New York it was, then, that introduced these men to the United States; for them it was a city symbolizing both the vitality of a new nation and the opportunities offered by that nation to peoples of every race and creed.

The dominant part the sea has always played in the affairs of New Yorkers gains in dramatic importance in our own time because of a great war whose prosecution depends so directly and vitally on the exchange of materials between countries separated by oceans. Today, in 1941, darkened freighters slip out of port bound for the waters of Europe's combat zone in almost the same manner that American privateers slipped out past Sandy Hook to run the blockade during the War of 1812. The wonder in the eyes of Verrazano's men, and in the eyes of Henry Hudson's men as they entered the Lower Bay in 1609, has been and still is reproduced in the eyes of seafarers, immigrants, and refugees arriving for the first time at America's premier seaport.

It is hoped that a reading of this history of the Port will result in a better understanding of the City of New York—its present as well as its past, its problems as well as its accomplishments.

1941

A PROFILE OF THE PORT

New York Harbor—America's Water Gate

An ILLUSTRATED account of the growth of the Port, this *Maritime History of New York* traces the evolution of New York Harbor from an early geologic period, through Verrazano's traditional discovery more than four hundred years ago to the present day; proposes plans for its great future development; reviews its colorful past from times of Indian dugouts to the modern epoch symbolized by streamlined transatlantic liners, sleek-bodied oil tankers, sturdy cargo carriers, and graceful flying clippers. This book marks a reawakening of port-consciousness on the part of progressive New Yorkers, harks back to a period a century past when the life of the city centered about South Street—New York's "street o' ships," forecasts America's future on the seven seas and in the upper air.

The significance of the role played today by what is, not only America's premier port, but also the world's greatest harbor has been expressed by the Honorable Fiorello H. La Guardia, who declared in 1940:

> It is important for our citizens to realize that one-half of our country's foreign commerce enters and clears the Port of New York and that nearly three-fourths of the travelers by sea to and from foreign countries pass through the city. In these troubled times it is of paramount importance to the world to continue and perpetuate the peaceful commercial relations and contacts between the United States and other countries.

The Port of New York, with its constantly improved deep main channels, capacious and well-defined anchorages, specially constructed piers, tremendous floating dry docks, seven hundred and seventy-one miles of protected waterfront,[1] trunkline railroad[2] and motor-truck terminals, fast-growing airports, its unsurpassed freight handling and warehousing facilities, continues to hold its pre-eminent position among the ports of the world; receives and ships a large part of the goods and people of our planet. The Port's unique geographical position, in the past at least, was largely responsible for the great metropolis that gives it its name—New York.

The rise of New York from seaport town to world metropolis is reflected in the pages that follow. The immensity of New York Harbor can be grasped only when seen from the air. Aloft one can look down and across its sprawling profile delineated by eight major bays—the Upper and Lower, Newark, Raritan, Sandy Hook, Gravesend, Jamaica, and Flushing; four river mouths—the Hudson, Hackensack, Passaic, and Raritan; one large sound, Long Island, connecting the open ocean with the Harlem and East rivers; two straits, Kill van Kull and Arthur Kill, connecting Newark Bay and the Upper and Lower bays. From the air can be seen the extent of the harbor's inland waterway and canal connections with the interior—a feature shared with few other ports— together with its protected inside route to New England via Long Island Sound and the Cape Cod Canal.

This vast port area encompasses an economic unit which, when circumscribed within a twenty-five-mile radius from the Statue of Liberty, encloses nearly fifteen hundred square miles, numbers a population of more than eleven million, contains some forty thousand industrial establishments, which annually produce goods valued at about eight billion dollars. The circumference of this area extends northward to Tarrytown, eastward farther than Jamaica Bay, southward beyond Perth Amboy and Sandy Hook, and up Long Island Sound as far as Port Chester.

To the Port of New York move the ships of more than one hundred and fifty lines, bearing the flags of at least twenty-five countries and carrying to and fro the peoples and products of more than seventy nations.

[1] Five hundred and seventy-eight miles of waterfront in New York City.
[2] Twelve trunk lines now enter the Port of New York.

This vast maritime complex is presented in the eleven chapters that follow; its rapid growth traced; its spectacular development described; its future, as outlined by port planners, forecast.

CHAPTER I

Discovery and Foundation—1524-1626

GLACIERS, INDIANS, EXPLORERS, FIRST SETTLERS

NEW YORK HARBOR took form when vast glaciers melting in slow retreat scoured out the great rift of the Hudson River Valley. Through hundreds of thousands of years these ice masses, sweeping seaward in four successive waves, ground down the rugged slopes of the Adirondacks, rounded the Catskill sandstones to friendly hills, and dredged the harbor site.

Rolling toward the distant sea, the glacial river cut out a rock-walled chasm through the eroded mountains—a chasm not as wide but almost as deep as the Grand Canyon of the Colorado. During the ice ages the level of the Atlantic Ocean was far lower than it is today, and the site of Manhattan was one hundred and fifty miles inland. Beyond this point the now submerged Hudson River Gorge dipped sharply to the ocean. Today at a distance of one hundred and twenty-five miles from the coast, it gapes seven miles from rimrock to rimrock. Here soundings plumb a depth of seventy-five hundred feet—four thousand feet of this below the canyon brim—and the canyon continues sloping toward the dark deeps of the Atlantic.

Within comparatively modern times, geologically speaking, the waters of the ocean rose to cover the slowly sinking land, and Manhattan, once situated on a plateau at least thirty-five hundred feet above the old sea level, became a low-lying island with tidewater on every side.

19

Indians and Wampum

Postglacial man roamed North America and reached the Atlantic seaboard. As the climate moderated, he was supplanted by Mongoloid tribes that probably reached this continent from Asia by way of Alaska. These people were hunters and fishermen, living in sparse, seminomadic communities. They had no metal except raw copper, which they used like stone, and they neither cleared lands nor built towns.

Winter brought snow, but the hardwood forests of beech, oak, and maple gave a never-failing supply of fuel. In addition to bitter beechnuts and acorns, hazel, hickory, walnut, chestnut, and butternut trees provided good food. In season the briars were bright with ripe berries. Wild deer drank from every stream; small game was abundant. There were very few dangerous beasts of prey. Quail and partridge found shelter in the woods, and the adjacent swamplands were teeming with clamorous waterfowl. The spring run of shad filled the great river with glistening silver. Summer or winter, in stream or sea, many kinds of excellent fish abounded. Clams could be taken from any sandy beach or mud flat. Huge shell mounds attested the abundance of oysters. Planted maize, squash, pumpkin, and tobacco, harvested with little labor, provided more than sufficient store for the year. Though they grew maize and pumpkin, these Indians had not learned to rotate crops—they simply rotated Indians. After each harvest had been gathered, they moved their plantings to fresh fields. They did not clear forests but made use of natural clearings. At most they girdled tree trunks, in order to kill the heavily foliated standing timber and permit the sunlight to nourish their crops.

The Indian name for the island was *Manna-hata*—variously translated as isle of hills, and place of surpassing beauty—which the Dutch corrupted to Manhattan. Here lived various groups of the Algonkian-speaking Indians. There were other groups on Long Island, giving to its different sections their strangely musical names, many of which are retained today in their original, or in slightly altered, forms. Every

Long Island commuter knows of Manhasset, Rockaway, Setauket, Patchogue, and Montauk. The north shore of Long Island Sound was occupied by the Siwanoy (who also penetrated inland as far as what is now White Plains); while Staten Island and the Jersey shore nearest Manhattan served as camping grounds for Leni-Lenape groups.

Generally these people lived at peace with one another. Occasional tribal wars were as likely as not to end in yelling contests with little damage done to the warriors. It was the fierce painted braves of the Five Nations (called Iroquois by the early French explorers) who supplied most of the excitement, visiting fire and destruction on the harbor villages.

Peacetime occupations, such as hunting, fishing, and primitive agriculture, dominated Indian life on the island and outlying territory. Trade, of course, was in its most rudimentary stage, an affair of individual caprice rather than of organized competitive effort. Transference of commodities might be effected on the spur of the moment, by a pair of Indians (they usually traveled in pairs), visiting a neighboring tribe. Impressed with the colorful beads which the chief was wearing, they would offer in exchange a piece of buckskin, or some eagle feathers, which, by all the rules of Indian etiquette, were invariably accepted.

To a greater extent than is often realized, the barter system prevailed. Mediums of exchange were infrequent. Despite a popular notion of wampum, or sewan (seashell beads), as Indian money, the fact is that wampum had a number of other, and more important, uses. It served as ornamentation, and as a means of communication between tribes, particularly to indicate friendly greetings, or to express condolence over the death of a chief. It also symbolized power: the chief who proudly displayed his shell necklace was bound to be a man of prominence, revered by his people, and feared by his enemies. And, equally important, it was woven into "treaty belts," the exchange of which signified the sealing of contracts between tribes.

In the days of the Indian, the southernmost end of Manhattan Island was a flat formed of mud, silt, and swamp. Cattails and tall grasses swayed in the wind. Occasionally a canoe would glide from a near-by shore into the harbor waters. For the most part, however, there was little sign of human life. It was a peaceful, desolate spot, without history. And thus it remained until the white man came.

Early European Explorers

Thirty-two years after Columbus' discovery of America the first Europeans dropped anchor in New York Harbor. Giovanni da Verrazano, a Florentine navigator in the service of Francis I, King of France, left Madeira January 17, 1524, in command of the *Dauphine*, and sighted land at Cape Fear (North Carolina) in March. In quest of a route to Cathay, he sailed north and is believed to have found in our Lower Bay "a pleasant place below steep little hills," from which "a mighty, well-guarded river runs into the sea." The ship anchored and some of the crew rowed upstream in a small boat. Feathered Indians put out in canoes to meet them, but the wind turned and the small boat scurried back to the *Dauphine*, which put out to sea. Verrazano made another stop, possibly at the site of Newport, before abandoning his northern quest and returning to Europe.

The next year Esteban Gomez, a Portuguese sailing under Charles V of Spain, explored a good part of the American coast from Nova Scotia to the Caribbean. Gomez charted the mouth of the Hudson, and, by him or in his time, the river was first named Rio de San Antonio. Maps of New York Harbor began to appear in Europe. A Paris library has one dated 1570, cartographer unknown. An Englishman, Thomas Hood, signed a "platte" of "Cape de las Arenas," or Sandy Hook, in 1592, probably after a visit by some Virginia colonists. If others came here before 1609, their names have been lost to posterity.

Henry Hudson, who rounded Sandy Hook on September 3, 1609, was the first navigator to realize the commercial possibilities of New

York. "This territory," he wrote, "is the finest for cultivation that I ever in my life set foot upon and the situation well adapted for shipping." Hudson had tried to reach China via the Arctic in 1607 and 1608. With other explorations, these two attempts made him famous, and the Dutch East India Company employed him to take the *Halve Maen* (*Half Moon*) on a similar search. He set out through the Zuyder Zee April 4, 1609, trying the eastward passage first and then doubling back around North Cape to cross the Atlantic.

Portrait of a Mariner

After three months at sea the *Halve Maen* came within sight of the Newfoundland coast. Hudson proceeded south from his landfall as far as the James River in Virginia. Finding no ready northwest passage in this direction, he turned back and on September 2 "anchored probably off what are known as the Navesink Highlands to the south of New York Bay." Continuing north, he found "a fruitful, pleasant region of islands and great rivers." The voyage continued inland up the "great river," and Hudson traded with the Indians. "Many brought us Beaver skinnes, and Otters skinnes which we bought for Beads, Knives and Hatchets," wrote Robert Juet, first mate of the *Halve Maen*. About one hundred and forty miles from the river mouth sand bars and shallows convinced the navigator that, despite the tides of this straitlike inlet, it was indeed a river, and he had again missed the long-sought northwest passage. He turned back and shortly thereafter returned to Holland.

Hudson's charts refer to the river that now bears his name as the Great River of the Mountains. Subsequent Dutch traders called it variously the Mauritius, the River of the Manhattees, the Rio de Montaigne, and the North River, the last because it marked the northern limit of the Dutch territorial claims in America. This name distinguished it from the South or Delaware River. It was not until fifty years later that the name Hudson's River was first used on the charts of the encroaching English. The North River designation still holds for the lowermost reaches of the Hudson.

First White Traders and Shipbuilders

Between the years 1610 and 1612 two Dutch mariners, Hendrik Christiaensen and Adriaen Block, visited the island of Manhattan in a ship, which presumably they had chartered, loaded with articles suitable for barter with the Indians. The exact date of the voyage is uncertain, but the fact is established that they returned to Holland with a cargo of valuable pelts and were engaged by a group of Dutch merchants to make a second voyage. Accordingly in the fall of 1613 there sailed into New York Bay two small high-pooped sailing vessels, the *Tigre* and the *Fortyn*, commanded by Captains Block and Christiaensen.

While Captain Christiaensen proceeded up the Hudson in the *Fortyn* and founded Fort Nassau, the first Dutch trading post in America of which there is absolute record, Captain Block remained with the crew of the *Tigre* to winter on Manhattan Island. It was during this time (winter of 1613-14), while the *Tigre* was riding at anchor in the Upper Bay, that Captain Block and his crew had to fight a fire which broke out aboard ship. This disaster, unfortunate in itself, resulted in the genesis of a great industry that was in centuries to come to breed the sturdy packets and the romantic clipper ships of the New York shipyards.

After building log cabins for shelter, these first shipwrights of the New York area set to work constructing a new ship, using materials hewn from the virgin forest for the hull which had been destroyed and fitting it out with the sails and rigging salvaged from the *Tigre*. In the following spring they were able to launch the "long yacht" *Onrust* (*Restless*). The first ship built in the region, the *Onrust* was forty-four and a half feet long, of eleven and a half feet beam, and of sixteen tons burden. Block's shipyard, if it could be called such, was probably on the bank of a creek which still flows beneath the pavement of Broad Street.

The *Onrust* is credited with being the first vessel to brave the dangerous rip tides of Hell Gate. Captain Block's own chart, prepared after an exploratory voyage as far north as Cape Cod Bay, shows a fairly accurate knowledge of both shores of Long Island Sound. Landings were made at Visschel's Hoek, now Montauk Point, and on Block Island, which bears the navigator's name.

Block returned to Holland in July 1614. On the basis of his explorations, the States-General granted a charter to the United New Netherland Company, giving it a three-year monopoly in the "aforesaid newly discovered countries in America between New France and Virginia, the seacoast whereof lies in the latitude of from forty to forty-five degrees, now named New Netherland, as is seen by a Figurative Map, hereunto annexed."

A series of voyages to New Netherland by many little ships, including *Vosken* (*Little Fox*) and *Nachtegael* (*Nightingale*), as well as the *Fortyn* (*Fortune*) and others, were made between 1615 and 1618, although no permanent colony had as yet been established.

The charter of the United New Netherland Company was not renewed, presumably because more powerful merchants became interested in the new fur trade. In 1621 an act of the States-General made exploitation of New Netherland a monopoly of the Dutch West India Company, newly organized with a capital equivalent to about five million dollars—a company which was to figure for years to come as the dominant factor in the life of the colony. Trading continued as usual, but nearly three years elapsed before the directors of the company felt that a permanent settlement was necessary if they were to protect their investment. This belated decision arose from their alarm over the increasingly possessive attitude adopted by the English toward the new colony. In 1609 King James I had openhandedly made a grant to the Plymouth Company of all land in North America between 41° and 45° north latitude.

Dutch Settlers

In the spring of 1624, the two-hundred-and-sixty-ton *Nieuw Nederlandt*, with Captain Cornelis Jacobsen Mey in command, sailed from Amsterdam with the first Dutch colonists. There were aboard thirty families of Protestant Walloon refugees who had fled from the Spanish Netherlands to escape the Inquisition. They were required to be loyal

Reformed Calvinists, to obey orders, to convert the heathen, to live where they were told for six years, and to lend a hand in all communal enterprises. The vessel carried one hundred and ten men, women, and children, with farming implements, livestock, seeds, household effects, and trading goods. In May the ship entered the mouth of the Mauritius.

On her return voyage to Holland the *Nieuw Nederlandt* carried seven hundred otter and four thousand beaver skins valued at twenty-seven thousand guilders. Captain Mey remained with the colony. During the following summer (1625), while Willem Verhulst was director of the colony, Pieter Evertsen Hulft, one of the directors of the Dutch West India Company, sent over from Holland more than one hundred head of cattle. The expedition embarked on three ships, furnished by Hulft, and an armed yacht provided by the Dutch government accompanied it. That the cattle were well cared for is proved by the fact that of the one hundred and three head aboard only three died on the voyage. The transportation of a herd of this size was of the greatest service to the colonists and gave them considerable advantage over the Plymouth colonists of the same period.

Willem Verhulst was recalled to Holland within the year, and on May 4, 1626, the *Meewtje* (*Little Sea Mew*) brought Pieter Minuit to replace him. On the new Governor's orders Kryn Frederycks, an engineer, made plans for a stockade, Fort Amsterdam, not far from the moldering log huts originally built by Captain Block. Some settlers who had come with Minuit cleared fields and built their homes near the stockade.

Before the first frost appeared in 1626 the guns of Fort Amsterdam commanded the narrow entrance to the East River and the broader sweep of the Hudson. It was at this time that Director Minuit consummated his famous real-estate deal with the Indians. An extract from a letter sent by one P. Schaghen to his colleagues back in Holland reported the matter with commendable brevity:

> . . . they have bought the island Manhattes from the wild men for the value of sixty guilders, it is 11,000 morgens in extent. . . .

CHAPTER II

New Amsterdam—1627-74

PATROONS, TRADE, SMUGGLERS

No GIFT of prophecy, however great, could have foreseen the future of the Port of New York at the time of its beginnings in the 1620s. To a lookout perched high on one of the two-masted galleons of that era, little that met his eyes would have been impressive. As his craft pushed slowly up the Lower Bay toward the island of Manhattan, he might have seen, far off to port, the desolate stretches of beach along Staten Island. He would have progressed through the Narrows and into the Upper Bay before he caught sight of an island famous in Dutch history for its nut trees—the one hundred and seventy acres of land known today as Governors Island.

Finally he would have arrived off the lower tip of Manhattan, which, like a gigantic arrowhead, splits the harbor into two parts. The jutting rocks of the corrugated shore line contained the area that was to emerge as Battery Park many years later.

Fort Amsterdam added an element of security to the ragged row of some thirty-odd rude huts which were strung along the edge of the East River. Somewhat later a reed-thatched roof topped the warehouse whose walls were constructed of Manhattan stone. A windmill stood close to the fort.

The island, narrower than it is today, was covered at its southern extremity with low wooded hills and grassy valleys. Where the Tombs prison now casts its shadow was a fresh-water lake, which drained into the East River by a stream the Dutch called the "Fresh Water" and into the North River by a stream that, in more modern times, gave Canal Street its name.

Beyond the modest settlement the virgin forest screened the view of Manhattan's twenty-two thousand acres of rock, lakes, and rolling tableland, which rose in spots to an altitude of one hundred and thirty-seven feet. In its early days the visiting sailor might have landed, by flatboat used to discharge crews and cargoes, by Indian canoe, or by one of the ship's dinghies, at a small dock at the end of the rudimentary street that began at the fort. Here the commercial center of the town had been established—with hardly a shift of the historic locality up to the present day.

The geographic uniqueness of the Port gave it an advantage at the outset, as the logical place for the shipment of furs collected in the interior. Creeks, bays, rivers, and inlets afforded inland commerce with the Indian settlements. The East River joined the Upper Bay with Long Island Sound. Long Island offered a shelter from the full brunt of the ocean waves, all along the Connecticut coast, and was to afford an ideal "back door" to New England.

The sweep of the North River was such that it was less protected than the landlocked lower reaches of the East River, the infant community's main anchorage. For more than two centuries the North River was to be limited mainly to traffic with the upper Hudson region, while incoming ships sought the natural protection of the smaller waterway. Ocean fogs seldom penetrated the inner harbor.

At the beginning the Dutch West India Company gave only grudging attention to the primitive trading outpost. Progress generally was slow, although by 1628 a wind-driven sawmill was being built at the water's edge, and a windmill north of the fort furnished power for a gristmill. By 1639 the number of farms on Manhattan Island had increased from seven to thirty.

Nieuw Amsterdam, 1650-53

The Carolus Allard view of New York, 1673

Coastwise Traffic

In 1627 Director-General Minuit had the provincial secretary, Isaac de Rasiere, write to Governor Bradford of the Plymouth Colony, offering to barter Dutch goods "either for beaver or any other wares or merchandise you should be pleased to deal for." In reply, Governor Bradford warned Minuit of "divers others besides" the New England colonists who would not hesitate to expel or "make prize of any, either stranger or English, which shall attempt either to trade or plant within their limits." "Yet for our parts," he wrote, "we shall not go about to molest or trouble you in anything," although "we desire that you forbear to trade with the natives in this bay and river of Narragansett and Sowames, which is (as it were) at our doors." Minuit answered in a friendly letter but firmly maintained their "right and liberty to trade in those parts" and pointed out that, if the English had their authority from the King, the Dutch had a similar right from the States-General of Holland and would defend it. Three months later, having received no answer from Bradford, Minuit dispatched a messenger with another letter, inviting Bradford to send a special representative to New Amsterdam to confer on the trade problem. As a further evidence of good will he sent along a "rundlet of sugar and two Holland Cheeses." Governor Bradford, in a letter acknowledging the presents, requested that Minuit send a delegate to Plymouth, saying that "one of our boats is abroad and we have much business at home," and therefore he could not send a representative at the time. Accordingly Minuit dispatched De Rasiere, who, Bradford wrote, was " a man of fair and genteel behavior." De Rasiere won over the Puritans by his polished manners, and his efforts led to the first regular coastwise traffic out of the Port of New York.

The passing of ships trading between New England and Virginia brought English visitors to the settlement. In order to accommodate them, a stone tavern was built in 1642 at the head of Coenties Slip; in 1653 this became the Stadt Huys or City Hall. It was a three-story structure, higher than the surrounding houses, which could be seen by all incoming ships from the anchorage at the foot of Whitehall Street.

The fort was replaced in 1635 by a larger fortress, two hundred and fifty by three hundred feet, which enclosed the Governor's house, the barracks, and the church. In 1653 a palisade was erected on the outskirts of the town, which later gave its name to Wall Street. Thirty years after the founding of the settlement the first census showed one hundred and twenty houses and one thousand inhabitants.

Waterfront—Harbor

In the seventeenth century the shore line was naturally quite different from that of today. What are now Front, Water, and South streets were then covered with water at high tide. At one time high tides threatened the foundations of the Stadt Huys, so a protecting stone wall was placed before the structure. What is now Broad Street in the early days was an inlet used as a canal, named by the Dutch De Heere Gracht. Extending from the East River to Wall Street, it was crossed by several footbridges and one broad bridge at Hoogh Straat.

In 1654 the shore, from the Stadt Huys to the "corner of the ditch" (De Heere Gracht), was planked up and filled in with earth and rubbish—probably the first land fill made for the improvement of the city's waterfront. It is not surprising that colonists from Holland, where land fill is almost a tradition, should have extended the shore line and widened the island, even at this early period.

The Patroons

To stimulate the growth of population in the colony, the directors of the Dutch West India Company devised the patroon system. A charter of liberties and exemptions granted the patroons freedom in trade except for furs and eternal possession of "fruits, rights, minerals, rivers, and fountains." Any director could become a patroon by subscribing a million guilders (about four hundred thousand) and agreeing "to plant there a colony of fifty souls upwards of fifteen years old" and "may where they wish to settle their colonies" purchase from the Indians land extending "sixteen miles along the coast on one side of a navigable river, or eight miles along both sides of a river, and as far inland as the situation of the occupants will permit." Although the patroons were restricted to the parts of the colony outside Manhattan Island, their influence extended into the life of New Amsterdam.

For the most part the directors presented the gifts and blessings of the patroon system to themselves. Through his agent in New Netherland, Kiliaen Van Rensselaer secured large grants of land on both sides of the North River, above and below Fort Orange, which stood a few miles north of the abandoned Fort Nassau. This venture prospered and became a sort of government within a government. Kiliaen remained in Holland, but his factors cleared land for farms, built flour mills with wind sails, and carried on a profitable trade with friendly Iroquoian tribes. For more than a century they were able to control traffic on the upper Hudson by their imposts and restrictions.

Closer to the port, Michael Pauw purchased Staten Island from the Indians. Later other purchases of the same land were made by one David Pietersen de Vries, known as a mariner, and by Cornelis Melyn. After a dispute over rights of possession, Governor Kieft persuaded De Vries to allow Melyn to establish a plantation on a large tract of land near the Narrows. Still later Melyn received a patent from the West India Company, granting him the patroonship over the whole of Staten Island, except for the portion reserved for De Vries.

Van Rensselaer was so influential that when Pieter Minuit was disposed in 1632 he was replaced by the patroon's nephew, "tippling, potbellied" Wouter Van Twiller. Van Twiller, who arrived from Holland in 1633 (Bastiaen Jansz Krol having served as Director- General from 1632 to 1633), soon became the richest landowner on Manhattan and purchased Indian rights to Governors, Wards, and Blackwells (Welfare) islands, where he grew tobacco and raised cattle.

Fur Trade

The *Wapen van Amsterdam* (*Arms of Amsterdam*), sailing September 23, 1626, left the first-known manifest of a vessel clearing from the Port. Listed were 7246 beaver skins, 853 otter, 48 mink, 36 wildcat, 34 muskrat pelts, and "many logs of oak and nut wood." The whole cargo was valued at around $25,000, according to today's monetary standards.

The Dutch West India Company, chiefly interested in furs, maintained a strict monopoly on all trade and fixed prices on exports and imports.

Although New Amsterdam had been founded as a fur-trading post, this trade proved less profitable than the directors had expected. While the annual exports of the colony had more than doubled between 1624 and 1635, the total trade of 705,000 guilders barely paid a profit on the company's investment. A peak figure for the fur trade had been given as 85,000 skins a year. This was a poor enterprise when compared with the company's lucrative ventures in Brazil and elsewhere. The capture in 1628 of seventeen Spanish galleons alone brought them loot worth 12,000,000 guilders.

The company was sharply criticized both in Holland and in New Netherland. The militant clergyman, Everardus Bogardus, who had come over on the same ship with Van Twiller, now turned on the Governor and attacked him from the pulpit. Discontent became general, and prominent citizens wrote to the company, accusing Van Twiller of using his office to promote his own interests while he neglected those of the colonists.

Van Twiller was recalled in 1637, but his successor, Willem Kieft, was not appointed until 1638. Kieft arrived in New Amsterdam aboard the *Harnick* (*Herring*). He wrote to his superiors that the fort was unfit for defense; the mills were idle; the warehouse disintegrating; cattle escaped to the woods, and "every vessel unserviceable, the yacht *Prince Willem* alone being fit for use, and only one new one on the stocks."

In an attempt to remedy conditions, Kieft introduced sumptuary laws—a nine-o'clock curfew and a prohibition against "the harboring of sailors on shore overnight"—assuming apparently that the devastation he found was the work of drunken seamen. Two outraged sailors, who tore the proclamation from the mainmast of their ship, were sentenced to three months at hard labor.

Smuggling

Because of the unreasonably strict maritime regulations imposed by the various governors, most of the colonists were engaged in smuggling. British vessels, Dutch sloops trading in Virginia, and even the company's own ships, without knowledge of their owners, carried on an illicit trade. Drastic but ineffectual regulations were also drawn up against "Scotch traders" and others who sought profit at the company's expense. Smuggling, a direct result of the monopoly in fur trading, always remained.

The company directors complained in 1638 that "several persons" were in the habit of acquiring the best furs for themselves and reserving those of inferior quality for shipment to the company. The guilty persons then exchanged their own furs for merchandise, which they sent out "in the Company's own ships clandestinely, secretly and without knowledge of the Company."

A law was passed providing that no resident of New Amsterdam was to export any merchandise not properly declared, "on pain of confiscation." But all laws remained ineffectual so long as the company officials shut one eye. Trading sloops continued to ply stealthily between New Amsterdam, Plymouth, and Virginia. Even Negro slaves got tobacco money by bootlegging furs.

Kieft tried without success to halt the smuggling with a new code of laws. Soon the Amsterdam chamber voluntarily relinquished its trade monopoly. In 1639 the fur trade was "thrown free and open to everybody." All merchants of Holland and other friendly nations were invited to convey to New Netherland any cattle or merchandise they desired, provided they used the company's ships.

Slave Trade

As a final inducement to the patroons, in efforts to increase colonization, the company undertook to supply them with "Negro servants." This seems to have been the origin of the New Amsterdam slave trade. The first Negro slaves were introduced into the colony about the year 1626, but it was not until the 1640s, when the colonists began to take up agriculture in a serious way, that large numbers of slaves were required. Negroes were purchased for the equivalent of sixty dollars in Curacao and sold here for one hundred to one hundred and fifty dollars apiece, although Van Twiller paid forty guilders each for three Negroes in 1636. Later the price of slaves rose to a figure as high as two hundred and seventy dollars. The first were reported as sold for "pork and peas."

Most of the slaves were Negroes, but a few Indians were taken from foreign shores and pressed into service. In 1641 Dutch men-of-war took Loango Sao Paolo in West Africa from the Portuguese, and the company became increasingly active in the world's slave markets. Three years later Governor Kieft granted manumission to nineteen elderly slaves and their wives because of their eighteen years of faithful service to the company. In 1646 the first cargo of Negro slaves to be sold in New Netherland arrived from Brazil; the first cargo imported directly from Africa arrived in 1655.

This traffic in the early period did not prove profitable. Colonists who had rashly invested in slaves, in the belief that they "could work more and at less expense than farm servants," soon had cause for complaint. "Great things were to be done with these slaves," they wrote to the States-General, "but where are they? They have slipped through our fingers." Many slaves had escaped to the woods; some were welcomed into Indian communities.

Indians

During Van Twiller's administration Raritan Indians attacked the colonists. The warfare thus begun soon became chronic. When Kieft

was Governor his chief innovation was to tax the Indians "for protection"—a curious analogy to the present-day rackets of New York City.
Even his language has a contemporary ring: "If there be any tribe that
will not willingly contribute, we shall induce them to do so by most
suitable means." His means, including the massacre in 1643 of eighty
upriver Indians who had taken refuge at Pavonia (site of Jersey City),
were so "suitable" that for the next two years the colony enjoyed little
peace. During this time nearly all the outlying white settlements were
wiped out. More than once the entire population of New Amsterdam
was forced to remain within the fort.

Peter Stuyvesant

The peg-legged Peter Stuyvesant, a former Governor of Curacao
appointed to succeed Kieft, arrived in New Amsterdam during the
month of May 1647, with a fleet of four vessels. "I shall govern you as
a father governs his children," said the stern old martinet.

The new Director-General spent a large part of his time fighting the
constant smuggling. He forbade all vessels, "Dutch, English, French,
Swedish, and others," to use "other roadstead than in front of the City
of New Amsterdam between Capske Point and Guide Board near the
City Tavern" or "to land, remove, or transship any wares until the
vessels are visited and the goods entered with the Honorable General."
No vessel might clear "without first being visited." No cargo might be
unloaded "after sunset and before sunrise." It became a crime "to
conceal, carry away, or transport" out of the colony any of the colony's
servants, free traders, or inhabitants without a pass signed by the director. Each year saw a new set of edicts, the contents of which only prove
that the inhabitants continued to engage in smuggling on a large scale.

Stuyvesant and the Slave Trade

In 1648 a committee appointed by the States-General made a report
on the affairs of the West India Company, in which they referred to the

slave trade as having "long lain dormant to the great damage of the company." "With a view to encouraging agriculture and population," the committee declared, "we should consider it highly advantageous to allow them to export their produce even to Brazil in their own vessels, under certain duties and conditions, to trade it off there and to carry slaves back in return; which privilege of sailing with their own ships from New Netherland to Brazil should be exclusively allowed to patroons and colonists, who promote the population in New Netherland, and not to interlopers who only carry goods to and fro, without attending to agriculture." But the New Amsterdam slave trade was beset with difficulties. It was seven years before another slave ship, the *Witte Paert* (*White Horse*), brought a new cargo. These slaves were sold at public auction and shipped out of the colony. Outraged by this interference with his plans to increase the colony's population, Stuyvesant declared that, whereas "the negroes lately arrived here from the bight of Guinea in the ship *Witte Paert* have been transferred hence without the Honorable Company or the Inhabitants of the Province having derived any revenue or benefit there from, there shall be paid at the General Treasury ten per cent of the value or purchase money of the negroes who shall be carried away or exported from here elsewhere beyond the jurisdiction of the New Netherlands."

In the years that followed four slavers discharged cargoes at New Amsterdam. Typical of conditions aboard slavers at that time is an account of the slave ship *St. Jan* (*St. John*), which sailed from Almina, on the African Gold Coast, to Rio del Rey, a port on the African Slave Coast, where two hundred and nineteen Negroes were taken aboard. Although there is no account of the accommodations provided for the Negroes on this ship, it may be assumed that they were similar to those aboard other slavers. Negroes were usually consigned to the hold, where they were chained to the deck and made to lie shoulder to shoulder in rows, in order to conserve space. Hatches were battened down in bad weather; the air was foul, and, even when no epidemic of cholera, plague, or blackwater fever broke out, a captain expected to lose twenty-five or fifty per cent of his cargo by death. Aboard the *St. Jan* foul water and lack of food brought on the bloody flux. Before the vessel was wrecked and captured by an English privateer, one hundred and ten men, women, and children died, "the greater portion of the slaves having died from want and sickness."

Although the slave trade never became the source of real profit at this period, and Dutch farmers were unwilling to pay the price a good plantation hand would command in the Southern market, slaves were always considered good currency in trading for Virginia tobacco or West India rum.

Shipbuilding

The great years of Manhattan's shipbuilding lay far ahead, but in 1631 a timid beginning was made when the *Nieuw Nederlandt* was constructed on the banks of the East River. Prior to that only a few sloops and shallops had been built, the timber having been brought down from the upper Hudson. Captain Block's *Onrust* was an exception and a product of circumstances rather than a planned attempt.

Compared with those of other nations, all Dutch vessels were small, owing to the shallow canals and coastal waters of the mother country for which they had been constructed. The builders of the *Nieuw Nederlandt* (called Belgians by some authorities, Swedes by others) decided to build their vessel bigger and better than was customary at the time. Accounts disagree as to the actual size of the ship; one gives six hundred tons, another eight hundred. When the *Nieuw Nederlandt* reached Holland, she was greatly admired for her soundness and beauty of construction, but the company directors complained that her great size led to excessive operating costs. The builders did not repeat the venture.

Once, about 1658, Dutch shipbuilders refused a contract to build a galiot, saying: "We are not yet in condition to build such a craft here." But along Pearl Street, which then fronted the East River, there were a number of yards building smaller craft. A twenty-eight-foot canoe was built for the equivalent of eleven dollars, while a sloop cost five hundred and eighty dollars.

Save for vague tradition and a few rude engravings, there is little detailed knowledge now obtainable as to models or rigs of the American merchant craft of the years before the Revolution. Among the venturesome traders, the ketch and the sloop predominated. The sloop had a one-masted rig, carrying sometimes on the larger craft a square topsail. The ketch was a two-master but very different from the two-masted rig of a later period. One square-rigged mast was stepped aft from the bow, and a smaller mast, sometimes square-rigged, was erected near the stern. The schooner came into vogue in the first half of the eighteenth century. It was the characteristic vessel of American coasting trade for one hundred and fifty years and supplanted the ketch and brig for coastwise voyages. The size of ships in 1641 was comparatively small. The *Mayflower* was only one hundred and eighty tons; a ship built in Salem was three hundred tons; and of more than twelve hundred in the British navy, only two hundred and seventeen were of more than eighty tons. But altogether not more than five were over two hundred tons.

Port Improvements

A great many improvements in the equipment of the Port came with the increase of trade. Before Stuyvesant's term all incoming ships had anchored in the East River roadstead under the guns of the fort. Passengers were transferred to small boats and scows, then rowed to a small floating dock on De Heere Gracht, which was navigable for small boats as far as the present Exchange Place. In 1647 Stuyvesant's council recommended the construction of a small wharf, and in the next year the first pier in New Amsterdam was erected on the East River at Schreyer's Hook. A second and larger pier, called the "Bridge," was built in 1659 near the foot of the present Moore Street.

In the spring of 1654 a weighhouse, with scales for the proper regulation of weighing and measuring, was built upon the wharf; and a collector was appointed to collect the duty, which was paid always according to weight. In 1656 Isaac de Foreest, the brewer, was appointed "Master of the Weigh House." When New Amsterdam was surrendered to the British in 1664, this weighhouse was confiscated, and the building became the customhouse of the new administration. By an edict of 1656 farm produce, formerly hawked through the streets, was concentrated on a beach at what is now the intersection of Pearl and Whitehall streets. This inaugurated the first city market. Another Port improvement was the first "marine telegraph" on a hill opposite the Narrows. A white flag hoisted on a pole informed New Amsterdam merchants that a vessel was approaching.

The company wanted a solid town, easily defended, and gardening on city lots where houses might otherwise be built was discouraged. The inhabitants were urged to live close together like the New Englanders, who were concentrated within comparatively small areas and "who do not suffer these horrible massacres." The company declared that no houses were to be built outside the city walls until all the lots within had been occupied. However, a number of colonists were engaged in farming in the outlying settlements in Long Island, Staten Island, and New Jersey, whose market was in Manhattan. This meant ferries. The first ferry was established sometime between the years 1638, when the Brooklyn colony was begun by Governor Kieft, and 1642. The first ferryman, Cornelis Dircksen, ferried passengers from the foot of the present Fulton Street in Brooklyn to Peck Slip on the Manhattan shore. Rowboats, canoes, and other small craft were used at first; later flat-bottom boats for the accommodation of passengers and cattle were propelled by sail. In 1661 provisional permission was granted to William Jansen by the schouts and schepen of the village of Bergen in New Jersey "to work a ferry between Bergen and the Island of Manhattan." There was a Harlem River ferry in 1667; its price card for meals and lodgings decorates many a museum and history book. The South Ferry-Stapleton (Staten Island) run did not open until 1713, but there is a clear record of a rowboat service to New Jersey, soon to be supplanted by horsepower (using windlass and sweeps), that began in 1661, crossing the Hudson squarely at South Ferry.

At this time there were many different types of ships and many new types of cargoes coming into the Port. More and more vessels anchored in the East River roadstead. Sloops, yachts, and ketches brought tobacco from Virginia and fish from New England. Pinks laden with sugar and molasses came from Barbados. Galiots from Curacao carried rum, dyestuffs, and salt. From Holland, often by way of the West Indies, came settlers, cotton prints, liquor, wine, and cattle; while the colony exported grain, timber, pelts, and pot ashes.

New Fortunes

Several fortunes were made in the coastwise trade and in that with the West Indies and Brazil. Among the leading merchant traders were Isaac Allerton, an Englishman from the Plymouth Colony, whose trading ventures brought him to New Amsterdam in 1638, where in the year 1647 he built a great warehouse at the present site of Fulton Fish Market; Pieter Cornelissen van der Veen, and Gouvert Loockermans, who made a fortune in gun running, selling liquor to the Indians, and, when necessary, in legal trade.

Colorful figures around the Port in the 1650s were Jan Peeck, an Indian trader, and his wife, Long Mary, who kept a tavern on the Great Highway at Smit's Valey. She was the widow of Cornelissen Volkertsen, one of the owners of the ship *Fortyn*, and married Peeck shortly after the death of Volkertsen in 1650. The list of their conflicts with the New Amsterdam authorities is interminable. On one occasion Peeck was charged with maintaining at his house "drinking clubs on divers nights . . . with dancing, jumping, and entertaining of disorderly people; also tapping during preaching, and that there was a great noise made by drunkards." Peeck was fined and his license annulled, but shortly afterward tapping privileges were restored in consideration of his being an "old burgher" and "burthened with a houseful of children and more besides." Locked up two years later for felonious assault on a soldier in his tavern, he protested that he was illegally held, as he had "only defended his house and wife against the soldier's violence." In 1664 Long Mary was fined five hundred guilders and sentenced to banishment for selling liquor to the Indians, an offense "for which she had long been famous."

Seafaring Stock

The ebb and flow of commerce fortunately devolved upon the Dutch, who both by inheritance and environment were sailors and shipbuilders from the world's best seafaring stock. Conditions were such as to intensify this maritime instinct. The sea played a large part in the thought of the early settlers. In these times the sea was the best and surest highway between the colonies. For passenger or freight traffic between New York, Massachusetts, and Virginia, the main reliance was the handy ketch or pinnace. Their stout shallops had nothing to fear from the fragile canoe of the Indians. The perils of the ocean then were far greater than now—coasts were not charted and buoyed, and the waters were always dangerous to small ships navigating among reefs in fogs and storms. When the English were ready to dominate New York, they found that the sturdy Dutch had laid solid foundations upon which to rear a mighty maritime superstructure.

English Rule Begins

Since the founding of the Plymouth Colony, the English had theoretically laid claim to New Netherland. During the term of Willem Kieft, English settlers had drifted into the vicinity of New York. Englishmen had occupied farms at Heemsted (Hempstead) on Long Island, and some had established themselves in the Connecticut River Valley.

In 1635 a company bark was sent out to dislodge several Englishmen from the Virginia Colony who had settled at Fort Nassau on the South (Delaware) River, and the settlers were taken prisoners. In the next year Charles I of England issued a patent to the Earl of Stirling, granting him the whole of Long Island.

When in 1664 four British men-of-war, under the command of Colonel Richard Nicolls, entered the harbor, the people of New Amsterdam, chafing under Stuyvesant's harsh rule, had little desire to defend the city. The English immediately changed the name of the fort to Fort James. When Nicolls was proclaimed deputy Governor for James, Duke of York, he ordered that the city's name be changed to New York.

Governor Nicolls kept his promise not to interfere with the trade of the Dutch colonists with Holland, although from the start commerce was encouraged with England and the British colonies.

A persistent legend has it that James, Duke of York, attempted to define the boundaries between New York and New Jersey and ruled that all islands in New York Harbor which could be circumnavigated in a day should belong to New York. Captain Christopher Billopp resolved to win Staten Island, geographically part of New Jersey, for New York. He lightened the sloop of nearly all ballast, to avoid running aground on the Raritan River sandbanks, and covered the deck with empty barrels, to catch the least breath of breeze. He completed the circuit in twenty-three and one half hours. Yet, despite Captain Billopp's feat, Staten Island remained a subject of intercolonial dispute until the American Revolution.

In 1673, when England and Holland were at war, a Dutch fleet appeared in New York Harbor, and the Dutch regained temporary control. But New Orange, as the colony was renamed, was to survive for less than a year. In October, 1674, the *Muyll Tromp* (*Jew's Harp*) brought the news that hostilities had ceased and that the Treaty of Westminster had ceded the province to England. The new Governor, Major Edmund Andros, arrived in November of the same year.

CHAPTER III
New York under British Rule—1675-1763
FLOUR, PIRATES, SLAVES

GOVERNOR EDMUND ANDROS took the best visions of his predecessors and the best single attempts to develop world trade at the Port of New York and coordinated them. He instituted a drive for colonial prosperity through exports, a well-organized and successful campaign under which the whole area throve—and the City of New York was its gateway. His one blind spot blacked out the customhouse; he never learned that high duties bred smugglers.

Andros in 1675 procured the adoption by his council of resolutions urging the creation of a "harbour . . . before ye City of New York," the prohibition of casting anchors or grapnel at the Battery sea wall, and of throwing refuse into the harbor waters, the last an important sanitary innovation. On his orders the pestilential canal, De Heere Gracht, was filled in, and the resulting highway, wider than the usual street of the time, was named Broad Street. Of more importance was the new city dock, built of stone, which extended along the shore front from White-hall Slip to Coenties Slip and the City Hall. This was finished in 1675. Andros also made the usual preferential tariff (ten versus two per cent) for English and against other imports.

The colony was already realizing a quick cash income in the milling of wheat and its export, either as flour or hardtack. Farmers, especially those in the Hudson Valley, were presaging Yankee ingenuity in the kinds of wheat they could adapt to the moist Eastern climate, and the blends of flour, not to say the varieties of packing they could evolve and profitably export. Andros quickly realized that even the most honest and farsighted miller could not possess the skill, the variety of wheats, or the machinery to grind, sift, and blend the proper kinds of wheat at the proper seasons and in the proper and requisite states of ripeness and dryness. The alternative, he also realized, was that the term "New York flour" would soon become either meaningless or worse. Quality was necessary then as now, but uniformity was almost more important. He resolved to achieve uniformity at the bottleneck, where the wheat comes to mill and where, being ground, it passes through screens of fine sifting cloth. This, the final process, is bolting, and in the bolting laws Andros identified pure-food legislation as a necessary adjunct of profitable world trade. Such legislation involved monopoly of one manufacturing process. There were complaints from individuals whose business the acts harmed, but in the long run the colony benefited.

Though various laws in the series of bolting acts were repealed, amended, or ignored, the long-range effect was regularity of process and uniformity of product. The beneficial effect upon the Port itself appears statistically: in 1678 the city had three ships, seven sloops, and eight small boats; in 1694, when criticism of the monopolistic features of the bolting acts was at its height, the city had sixty ships, sixty-two sloops, and forty boats. Eventually Andros brought about six hundred families out of a total of nine hundred and eighty-three into the flour industry.

Shortly after he had been recalled Andros wrote a justification of his administration. He claimed that on his arrival he found New York "poore, unsettled, and without trade, except a few small coasters; hardly any went or came from beyond seas;" but he left the town "greatly increased in people, trade, buildings, and other improvements; new townes and settlements lately built. ...A market house (the only one in all those parts) . . . and the navigation increased at least ten times to what it was; and plenty of money (hardly seen there before) . . . and noe disaster happened in any part of the government during my command there.. . .”

One can fairly balance Andros' achievements against even his conspicuous and dramatic blunders: the emphasis on high duties, the unwarranted invasion of New Jersey and arrest of Governor Carteret, his administrations' failure to act forcibly against smuggling or against piracy.

Pirates Spread on Troubled Waters

The last quarter of the eighteenth century saw a general state of war in Europe in which England, Holland, Spain, France, and Portugal took part. The conflict, periodically interrupted by short-lived peace treaties, became a desultory kind of naval guerrilla war, with the individual ship captains not too discriminating about whom they attacked and plundered. The commissioned privateers of each country were granted the right to capture enemy vessels and sell their cargoes as prizes of war. This privilege proved too strong a temptation for many of the privateer captains. With huge profits in sight, they made "mistakes" with alarming frequency. In most cases the captain and crew shipped for a voyage on the basis of "no plunder, no pay;" in other words, they took on the adventure at the risk of their lives for what they could get out of it through attacking enemy ships. Another inducement to piracy was the voiding of a privateer's commission after each peace treaty, leaving captain and crew without employment.

A surprising number of privateers who began in what was officially a legitimate occupation soon became out-and-out pirates under these conditions. Many of them felt to the end, which was often the end of a rope, that what they had done was right and proper.

The important Red Sea trade had its inception many years before the beginning of the eighteenth century, but it reached its peak about that time. On the huge unsettled island of Madagascar, off the East African coast, privateers and pirates of all nations established a haven of refuge for themselves.

Although pirates roamed all the chief trade routes of the world, most of their recorded activities centered around the West Indies, the east coasts of North America, and the Red Sea. Ships bearing Red Sea commerce at the time had to reach Europe by the long route around the Cape of Good Hope, and the Madagascar pirates were in a strategic position to raid the richest and probably the most exotic commerce the world then knew.

New York merchants soon discovered that here was a source of handsome profit, and the Red Sea trade flooded the markets of the city with looted fabrics, spices, jewels, and Arabian gold. The Port of New York became a pirate center.

Murderous pirates, some of them notorious figures, walked the streets of the city with impunity. The goods they brought ashore filled the counters of merchants. Fashionable women bought the silks and brocades, the jewels, and the porcelains; gentlemen about town strolled the Bowery in embroidered waistcoats and silver shoe buckles, carrying jeweled swords.

The Man Higher Up

Piracy became so common that it was accepted by a large section of the public as a near profession. It is necessary to understand this state of mind in order to account for the amazing condonation of robbery and murder at sea as legitimate endeavor. For one thing, the public seldom heard the bloody details—and when they did the stories were told in a manner calculated to evoke applause for the pirates' wit and courage; for another, the game was made respectable to many by its open or covert tie-up with the names of some of the most influential and respected citizens and officials of New York.

The case of Frederick Philipse is illustrative of the wealth, influence, and respectability that often lay behind pirate ventures. The

founder of the Philipse family was of Dutch descent, the name originally having been Vrederyck Felypsen. He is believed to have reached
New Amsterdam in 1658. Poor at first, he became a fur trader. His real
success came after he married, in 1662, Margaret Hardenbroch, widow
of the rich fur trader, Pieter de Vries. Philipse immediately entered a
number of enterprises and gathered great wealth in a few years. His
best-known operations were in real estate. Eventually the Philipse
estate ranged all the way from the Croton River to Spuyten Duyvil. The
manor house still stands in Yonkers, while a Dutch church, built in
1699 by Philipse and his second wife, Catharine Van Cortlandt, remains
in service at Tarrytown.

Surrounded by the evidence of his respectability at Philipse Manor,
Philipse bought and sold pirate vessels, outfitted smugglers, and
arranged for the exchange of goods and money in such far-off pirate
strongholds as Madagascar. History is definite about Philipse's place in
the life of at least one pirate, Captain Samuel South Burgess.

Burgess, of good education, was a purely local product, having been
born in New York City. His early experience included privateering in
the West Indies. Philipse liked him and decided to use him as a trader
with the pirates in Madagascar, where Philipse and other owners sent
ships to trade liquor, guns, ammunition, and money for the cloths,
spices, and jewels of the East.

Captain Burgess committed several acts of piracy on this first voyage
for Philipse; in Madagascar he proved a good trader and sailed back to
New York with a full hold. Off Sandy Hook he unloaded the cargo and
then wrecked the ship, landing in New York as an honest shipwrecked
mariner. Meanwhile the goods were smuggled into the city sans tax.
After marrying a relative of his employer, he made two voyages in
legitimate trading. He then had the misfortune to be captured off Good
Hope and was taken to England, where he was charged with piracy.
Burgess was tried twice; the second time he received the death sentence
but was pardoned by Queen Anne.

He then shipped as mate on *H.M.S. Neptune*, which sank two pirate ships. However, when the *Neptune* was in turn taken by pirates, he cast his lot with them. His subsequent career was usual for the type, ending with violent death—in Burgess' case, by poisoning.

Bonded Pirates

Benjamin Fletcher received the appointment as Royal Governor of New York in 1692. He soon became friendly with the pirates of New York City and was accused of selling them permission to land at the Port for the price of one hundred dollars a man. In 1697 the Lords of Trade wrote from London, warning him not to protect "marauders," who, they had been informed, used New York as a place of refuge. Fletcher defended himself by declaring that he never gave protection without his council's approval and that the pirates had given bonds for good behavior. He claimed further, in apparent seriousness, that he could not be blamed if the privateers he commissioned later became pirates and that he only associated with pirates for the purpose of reforming them.

Captain Kidd

Lord Bellomont, who succeeded Fletcher in 1698, made the first large dent in buccaneering activities, although, curiously enough, he was responsible for the vivid career of one of the most famous of them all—Captain William Kidd.

During Fletcher's regime many pirates sailed from the Port of New York, among them such rogues as Richard Glover, John Evans, Thomas Wake, John Ireland, and Edward Coates. It was for the purpose of rounding up such pirates that Bellomont and the British Admiralty made an agreement in 1695 with Kidd, whereby he as a privateer was to protect English ships.

The government of King William III would not furnish a ship for Kidd to command, so Bellomont, Philip Livingston of New York, and some friends raised money for the *Adventure Galley*—287 tons, 34 guns. Kidd and his crew sailed in 1696 under the "no plunder, no pay" agreement. When the captain found no pirates in more than a year, the crew was on the verge of mutiny. When Kidd allowed a Dutch vessel to go free because its papers were in order, one William Moore, a gunner, protested vehemently. In the ensuing argument the captain smashed a bucket over his gunner's head, killing him. This act later became the basis of murder charges against Kidd.

Not long afterward the captain seized the *Quedagh Merchant*, an Armenian ship sailing under French registry. He changed ships and put in to Ste. Marie, Madagascar, for provisions. Here all but thirteen of the crew deserted, but with these and a few new men Kidd sailed homeward. Meanwhile it had become known in New York that Kidd, instead of taking pirate ships and French merchantmen, had himself become a pirate.

King William III had commissioned Bellomont Governor of New York and Massachusetts on June 18, 1697. When he arrived in New York to begin his administration on April 2, 1698, he carried orders from the Crown to arrest Kidd if he returned to North America.

Captain Kidd cruised the West Indies and there learned he was wanted as a pirate on complaint of the Mocha fleet merchants of India. Deciding to straighten out things with Bellomont, he sailed to New York but found the Governor's answers to his emissary ambiguous. He thereupon sailed for Boston and, on the way, buried what treasure he had on Gardiners Island; but it was soon recovered by Bellomont's men.

When Kidd reached Boston in July 1699, he was immediately seized on a warrant by Bellomont. Since piracy had never been a hanging offense in the colonies, he was transported to England for trial. The trial took place at the Old Bailey in 1701. Captain Kidd was found guilty of murder and piracy and was accordingly hanged at Execution Dock. This seems strange justice after the leniency accorded Burgess, who deserved the title of pirate far more than did Kidd.

Under Lord Bellomont the Port was fairly well cleared of pirates. In 1699 warships were stationed off Sandy Hook. In 1700 Bellomont was instructed to give clearance only to those vessels posting bond not to call at Madagascar or other outlaw gathering places. The high tide of piracy had been reached; the ebb had begun; yet for more than a hundred years these sea marauders remained in existence.

Some Pirates Died in Bed

A few of the pirates turned respectable or bought immunity. Joseph Thwaites, incomparably more homicidal than Kidd, began his career in 1763 by entering the Turkish service as commander of a forty-four-gun frigate. He roamed the Mediterranean for some years, building a fortune, which he secreted in England and New York. He adhered to the theory that "dead men tell no tales," making a practice of drowning his prisoners. When pressure for his capture became too insistent, he took his valuables to New York, built a mansion near the city, and settled down to life as a country gentleman. A year later he died of snakebite.

John Avery made a specialty of preying on the Mocha fleets, his largest haul being the *Gunsway*, which belonged to the Great Mogul himself. He seized one hundred thousand pieces of eight (roughly one hundred thousand dollars) and a treasure in diamonds. Avery arrived in America in 1696 with the diamonds and what was left of the money. Unable to dispose of the diamonds in America, he found willing merchants in England, settling then in Devon. The English merchants accepted the diamonds, promising to send him money as they disposed of the gems. The money came slowly and in small amounts, then not at all. Avery became ill and died a pauper.

A pirate named Charles Vane enjoyed a few years of local respectability, although eventually he was hanged in Jamaica. During all this time it is probable that a majority of the sailors who frequented the Port had, or had once had, intimate acquaintance with the "free citizens of the world," answering that wild cry, "All up and board!" Many of them lived to pull a rope or strain at a windlass on the later privateers.

Slave Traders

Like the Red Sea traffic with pirates, the slave trade was an important contributing factor in the life of the Port. New York, a melting pot of goods as well as men, found the two synonymous when the unfortunate blacks began to arrive. But those newcomers who survived the horrors of the voyages early formed a habit of disappearing shortly after their arrival. This is small wonder when it is considered that, in transit and during the "seasoning" period, the death rate among slaves "sardined" into this country averaged as high as fifty per cent.

It is most astonishing and impressive to look over the list of those engaged, in one way and another, in the slave traffic. Some of New York's foremost families diverted their capital or ships to this commerce. Between 1715 and the Revolution the Port's merchant-ship owners went in for the highly profitable traffic quite extensively, transporting thousands of Negroes to the West Indies, to Southern colonial markets, and additional hundreds to Manhattan.

Light is thrown on the operations of the slave traders by the contents of a letter written March 30, 1762, by John Watts of New York to a Salem shipowner:

> For this market they must be young the younger the better if not quite Children, those advanced in years will never do. I should imagine a cargo of them none exceeding thirty might turn out at fifty pounds a head gross Sales. Males are best. . . . Our duty is four pounds a head from the West Indies forty shillings from Africa. New Jersey pays none at all for which reason the Master might lay a mile or two below the Town and send up word.

This sending up word was apparently in the best tradition of the Port. Behind the scenes, "below the Town," contraband and slaves were constantly being slipped into the province, unrecorded and duty free.

Smuggling flourished primarily because of the shortsightedness of Britain. Through the series of Navigation Acts the Crown had said to its colonial merchants, in effect: "You must buy all your manufactures through us or from us; you may not establish your own plants; because we must protect our own farmers we'll buy only a fraction of the produce raised by yours; and since we must defend the profits of our own merchants at all costs, you may export certain 'enumerated' commodities only, in British ships only, and only to British ports." What but smuggling on a vast scale could possibly result?

In one respect, however, the British held the trump card: the manufactures of Great Britain were cheaper and better than those of the Continent. The inevitable outcome was a trade balance unfavorable to the colonials.

Cadwallader Colden, later Lieutenant Governor of the province and prolific writer on colonial affairs, observed in 1723 that mercantile profit "seldom continues in the province six months before it is remitted for England."

Under these circumstances, and to square accounts with the British, the merchant shippers of New York established and fostered the foreign West Indies trade as a ready market for surplus colonial commodities. The West Indies needed North American timber, fish, and flour; they could furnish unlimited quantities of sugar, rum, and molasses. Molasses meant rum; rum meant slaves; slaves meant cash.

War Clouds with Silver Linings

Privateering, near the middle of the century, was highly profitable for those engaged in it. During 1744, to take one isolated year as an example, the New York *Post-Boy* devoted considerable space to a listing of prize ships brought into New York Harbor by privateers, to the great enrichment of captains and crews. One privateer, the *Launceston*, was reported as arriving with the French ship *St. Francois Xavier*, three hundred tons; the *Post-Boy* recorded:

> This is the fifteenth vessel taken from this ship. She was saluted by all our Privateers, and several other vessels, and the general Acclamation of the People, as a Testimony of the Sense they have of the signal Service done by this gentleman during the continuance of the war.

The gentleman referred to was "the brave Commodore Warren," the same Sir Peter Warren who played a decisive part in the siege of Louisburg and whose three-hundred-acre Manhattan farm covered much of the site of Greenwich Village.

An impression of the times is given by the many advertisements appearing in the weekly papers, of which the following from the *Post-Boy* is a good example :

> For a Cruize on a Privateering Voyage,
> against His Majesty's Enemies
> The Ship, TARTAR, JOHN MACKY, Commander,
> Burthen 300 tons, 18 Carriage and 20 Swivel
> Guns, 120 men. Flush Fore and Aft; being
> completely fitted and equipped as a Ship of
> War for said voyage, and will sail in 20 Days

> All Gentlemen, Sailors and Others, inclined to go
> on said Cruize, may repair to the Sign of the
> Crown & Thistle, in Front Street, where the Officers
> Attend, and the Articles are to be seen and signed.

Thus, anomalously, the Port grew strong because of wars rather than in spite of them. Wars, therefore, were not unpopular, and there was always plenty of action for the fighting men. And for those with no liking for arms, there was the flag of truce which could be used for personal protection without foregoing possible profits.

Theoretically the flag of truce was an eighteenth-century custom designed to facilitate the exchange of prisoners. But when a ship sailed out with prisoners to he exchanged in some of the French islands for "such of our countrymen as may have fallen in the enemy's hands," there was nothing to prevent cargoes of foodstuffs from being taken on board as well as prisoners.

That these practices were condemned by many is gathered from an indignant letter to the editor of the *Post-Boy*, dated June 6, 1748, and significantly signed "Free Trader:"

Can it be unknown to you that scarce a week passed without an illicit Trader going or coming into this Port, under the specious name of Flags of Truce, who are continually supplying and supporting our most avowed enemies, to the great loss and damage of all honest traders and true-hearted subjects? . . . Let me beg you to sound the alarm . . . that all may know how the whole community, for the private benefit of a few mercenaries, must soon be engulfed in ruin and destruction.

It soon became clear that the New York "mercenaries" were doing much better for themselves than Free Trader suspected. In 1754-63, during the French and Indian War, a fleet of one hundred and twenty-eight privateers brought home eighty prizes valued at a million pounds sterling, and this figure did not include the attractive penny turned by the local merchants in transporting food supplies to the French armies.

Trade with the enemy flourished particularly during the first five or six years of the French and Indian War. Governor Hardy had tried to stop it almost as soon as hostilities began. He embargoed "all ships clearing out with provisions, but such as are loading, or to be laden for His Majesty's Islands or Plantations."

But this drastic measure, like others of its kind, failed rather signally, to judge by the fact that many New Yorkers promptly found means of establishing trade with the foreign islands. This is confirmed by Hardy himself in a letter to the Lords of Trade, written at Halifax on July 10, 1757 (after his resignation as Governor of the province). Hardy inveighs against the introduction of:

> . . . tea, canvas, Gunpowder and arms for the Indians and many other Articles from Holland that render to His Majesty no Duty in Europe, and almost totally discourage the Importation of these commoditys from Brittain. When I first arrived at New York I found this iniquitous trade in a very flourishing state, and upon inquiry was informed that it had been a common practice for Vessels to come from Holland, stop at Sandy Hook, and smuggle their Cargoes to New York and carry their Vessels up empty; this I was determined to put an end to, when this trade took another course by sending their Vessels to the ports of Connecticutt, from whence it is not very difficult to introduce their goods thro the sound to New York, and

even to Philadelphia . . . Another method the Importers take is to stop at some of the Out ports of Britain (in their outward bound passage from Holland) and make a report and enter only half of their cargo, by which the King is defrauded of his Duty on the other half. In short My Lords, if some effectual means are not used, the greatest part of the commerce of the American Colonies will be withdrawn from the Mother Country, and be carryed to Holland.

It was not long after Governor Hardy's departure that Lieutenant Governor De Lancey reported deals by the colonials with the enemy, "having had credible information that there were some vessels (two in particular I had proof of) that had been trading with the French at Cape Francois in Hispaniola."

Colonial shippers intensified rather than lessened their treasonable traffic with the French during the following months. Reliable estimates put the number of provision-laden vessels that docked at Monte Christi in 1760 at more than five hundred. This illegal provision trade with the French West Indies helped to prolong the English-French wars. Thoroughly aroused by such flagrant disregard for the British law, the government of the newly crowned George III went into action, and Prime Minister William Pitt ordered the commanders of His Majesty's fleets in North America to take action against the illegal trade. Ships of the Royal Navy began raiding Dutch and French island ports in the West Indies. Revenue agents, armed with blank search warrants, were prodded into something approaching enforcement of the Molasses Act, which placed prohibitive duties on the importation of that commodity from other than British sources. Seizures, arrests, and confiscations increased sharply, but not for long and not for much. During 1761 duties were collected amounting to £1189, as against the £259 collected in 1755.

But the American coast was a long patrol, and with Britain at war only a limited number of ships were available for enforcement. Furthermore, American skippers not only were naturally adept, but had had decades of practice at navigating in the dark of the moon. They knew all the bars and channels, the secluded inlets and landing places. And revenue officers could still be induced to wink when occasion warranted.

Colonials Keep "Connections"

Another obstacle to enforcement was lack of convictions. New York merchants still retained their "connections" with the courts—a factor which prompted Colden, on one occasion, to demand the removal of Judge Robert Livingston, "since no cause of any consequence can come before him in which . . .he or the Livingston family are not interested." Finally—and fatally—Britain was dealing with a lawlessness that enlisted the support and sympathy of a large section of the populace. By the middle of the century smuggling in our young and struggling country had advanced from an expedient to a virtue, and compliance with the tariffs had become a quixotic eccentricity.

Just as the Molasses Act of 1733 was "more honour'd in the breach than the observance," so the high-tariff Sugar Act of 1764 came to be of little moment, although the creaking machinery of English law enforcement moved to enforce it. This may be said to be the turning point of colonial history, marking the final phase of a revolt that had been brewing for nearly a century. Always profitable, smuggling now assumed the color and fervor of patriotism.

Barter and Exchange

At the beginning of the eighteenth century New York appears to have had about half as much trade as Boston, and about one third of it was in direct violation of the navigation laws. The West Indies trade was handled so intelligently that it grew steadily, and throughout the remainder of the colonial period rivaled the fur trade in its profits. Provisions were shipped from New York and exchanged for West Indies products, which were taken to England and then again exchanged for manufactured goods. These were brought back to New York and sold, and thus there were three profits on each transaction. The bulk of this

The Stadhuys, 1679, corner of Pearl Street and Coenties Slip

New York (City) about 1793-96 seen from the North (Hudson) River
opposite Battery Place by Archibald Robertson (Engraving)

traffic was with the British islands; there was more trade with Barbados than with any of the other islands, as provisions were taken there, not only for the local supply, but also for transportation to the Spanish coast and the French islands. Most of the trade was merely an exchange of products, but a considerable cash balance resulted, which was remitted at once to England to pay for manufactured goods.

New York did not neglect ordinary trade, but it grew slowly. From 1717 to 1720 imports averaged £21,000 and exports £52,000 annually. From 215 to 235 vessels cleared yearly, the figures being about the same for Philadelphia. The city lived almost wholly on trade with Indians, Great Britain, and the West Indies. To England the traders sent mostly beaver, whale oil, and some tobacco; to the West Indies flour, bread, peas, and pork, and sometimes horses, and they brought back "rum which pays duty, and molasses which does not."

The middle years of the century brought a vast increase in docking facilities, shipping, shipbuilding, and commerce generally. Despite the severity of British restrictions, the Port made mammoth strides. From 1747 to 1762 the number of ships owned by residents of New York increased from 99 to 447, and the number of employed seamen from 755 to 3552. Ten years later 709 vessels were owned in the city, and exports had risen to £150,000 annually, with £100,000 as the figure for imports. It must be remembered that official figures on imports and exports take no cognizance of the value of goods handled by smugglers and therefore represent only a fraction of the trade which was actually entering and leaving the Port. How small a fraction can only be guessed, but it has been estimated that, for every cargo seized by the customs authorities, a dozen were discharged surreptitiously.

Shipbuilding and Growth

An increase in shipbuilding followed the growth of trade. From the modest beginnings of Mynheer Rip van Dam, toward the close of the seventeenth century, three busy shipyards had sprung up between

Beekman Street, northern limit of the town, and the Catharine Street docks. John Dally, John Rivers, and the brothers Joseph and Daniel Latham were, until William Walton eclipsed them all, New York's notable shipwrights.

By the time of the Treaty of Paris, 1763, the city's population had passed the thirteen-thousand mark (it had been 4476 in 1700); its wealth had increased tremendously, and a new class of mercantile capitalists—pushing aside or absorbing the earlier landowner-merchants—- was figuring in the river, coastal, inland, and ocean trades. These men could see that the old cycle of molasses, rum, slaves, smuggling, and an unfavorable trade balance had little connection with the changed conditions, and that the new approach which was called for was necessarily one antagonistic to the interests of Great Britain.

The interior was increasing its shipments of agricultural products to New York, calling for increased varieties and quantities of the city's merchandise, and trade generally was vigorous, but Great Britain's restrictions were increasing in severity. Further taxation, with or without representation, was the last thing the merchants wanted.

Commerce had become the battleground of power. Whereas monarchs had once ruled, simply and without hypocrisy, through naked force, now they governed by customs percentages. If the Molasses Act proved ineffective, there was the Sugar Act; if the Stamp Act failed of its purposes, there were the other Acts of Trade.

A new sequence was beginning and new forces gathering. The colonials' traditional answer to tyranny was to boycott.

CHAPTER IV

Revolution and Reconstruction—1764-83

SUBMARINE, TORIES, TEA PARTY

FOR THE GRIEVANCES cited in the Declaration of Independence there was a maritime background. Large bodies of armed troops came to New York by sea, and the Port's world trade was cut off by marine blockade. The "taxes . . . without our consent" were dramatically focused upon two items Americans refused to buy: tax stamps, carried by water from England; and tea, twice water-borne from China, as it was reshipped from Great Britain.

In 1764 warships carrying troops from England arrived to enforce collection of customs. Great Britain was determined to stop smuggling; the colonials were to import nothing except in British ships, unless the British had inspected it en route; exports were to be sent to Great Britain alone, and no wool could be exported or even sent to other colonies. There was a heavy duty on sugar from the non-British West Indies and a low duty on molasses used in the manufacture of rum for export. These were some of the Acts of Trade around which controversy centered.

In the following year the ship *Edward* brought New York its first stamps, consigned to James McEver, newly appointed distributor, who hastily resigned his position in fear of his life. The conservative merchants proposed a Stamp Act Congress, to which the Provincial Assembly quite properly sent delegates. Working for the same ends but in different fashion, the Sons of Liberty, who had forced McEver's resignation, burned Governor Colden in effigy and presented such a show of strength and purpose that Colden removed the supply of stamps from the *Edward* to his own residence inside Fort George.

While the merchants met in Burns' City Arms Tavern to vote on a boycott resolution, the Sons of Liberty were drafting these words for Colden:

> ... we can with certainty assure you of your fate, if you do not this Night solemnly make oath before a Magistrate, and publish to the People, that you will never . . . endeavor to introduce or execute the Stamp Act.

With this threat, delivered November 1, they added that if necessary they would hang him "upon a signpost, as a memento to all wicked governors."

The agitation was successful, and on March 18, 1766, Parliament repealed the Stamp Act but left the Acts of Trade in effect. The Sons of Liberty celebrated repeal by erecting a liberty pole in The Fields—the open land which is now City Hall Park—while the Assembly ordered the erection of two statues, one of Pitt and the other an equestrian figure of George III.

It was not until the passage of the Townshend Acts (reaffirming those broad and almost limitless powers of taxation that had been strangling colonial trade) that the conflict was renewed on specific issues. This was in 1767, and again boycott followed immediately the news of the enactment. In one year, 1768-69, the Port's official imports from Great Britain dropped from nearly half a million pounds to a negligible figure whose custom duties were estimated at forty shillings. The Provincial Assembly was forbidden to pass any other act whatever until it had appropriated funds to support His Majesty's armed forces. The colony had to submit to Parliament's taxation and also had to consent to taxing itself and giving up money for the army of occupation. For the second time Parliament sought to cure boycott with repeal (1770), while retaining—in affirmation of the monarch's prerogatives—a token tax of threepence on a pound of tea.

Bostonians expressed their resentment through a tea party. New York had its own tea party on April 22, 1774. Captain Lockyear's ship, the *Nancy*, just missed the party, arriving in port on the eighteenth and leaving on the twenty-third, tea still aboard. Lockyear knew his errand was dangerous but had a trick in reserve. On arrival he asked permission to go ashore to buy provisions for the return crossing. Once on land he visited agents and discussed deliveries. Militant citizens rushed him back on board ship, where he stayed, virtually incommunicado, until the *Nancy* sailed.

The decks of the *London*, Captain Chambers, were a poor setting for an international incident. She had only eighteen cases of tea on board, and Chambers, after first denying that they were there, claimed them as his own. Although this ruse failed, the attempted deception so angered the citizens that they caused Chambers to be held at Fraunces' Tavern while they boarded the *London*. Watched by a large number of spectators, including bandsmen who chose "God Save the King" as a suitable musical accompaniment, they then threw the eighteen cases of tea into New York Harbor.

Congresses and Committees

The First Continental Congress met in 1774 at Carpenters' Hall, Philadelphia. To this the Provincial Assembly of New York sent accredited delegates. Then followed the battles of Lexington, Concord, Bunker Hill, and a second Congress. The Assembly, whose political elements were always nearly balanced, veered Royalist for a time and voted military supplies for the British troops garrisoned in the colonies. It also refused to accredit delegates to the Second Continental Congress, one of whose purposes was the creation of the Continental Army.

The Assembly then lost its remaining popular support, and many of its functions were taken over by independent bodies. In New York City there was always an active local group: first the Committee of 51, which merged with the Committee of Mechanics to form the Committee of 60, and then the cumbersome Committee of 100; all reminiscent, in name at least, of civic groups that had functioned in Kieft's and Stuyvesant's administrations. The local steps matched the national progress; lacking delegates to Philadelphia, the people of New York Province met in popular conventions, elected delegates, and accredited them to the Second Continental Congress.

In the City of New York there was a "general insurrection of the populace" in April 1775. The city was in a "state of confusion and anarchy," but a confusion so methodical that when the citizens broke into an armory, six hundred muskets went to the most reliable and trustworthy among them, who formed a voluntary corps and set up a local government. As Great Britain was now the official enemy, her mails were seized and opened; her supplies for Halifax and Boston were unloaded from two sloops in port, and her sympathizers in the Committee of 100 were thwarted by the suspension of that committee in favor of the New York Congress, entirely patriot in membership.

The Second Continental Congress established the Continental Army in 1775 and appointed Washington commander in chief. The New York Provincial Congress, focus of all local committees and governing bodies in the province, became the de facto government in May 1776 by the seizure of the powers and functions of His Majesty's Provincial Assembly. On June 29 General Howe arrived at Sandy Hook with nine thousand British soldiers. Early in July this force was joined at Staten Island by Admiral Howe and a body of Hessian troops. In August another force of British soldiers under General Clinton was added. With nearly thirty thousand representing the Crown, the resultant clashes with the patriot forces extended across Brooklyn, up the length of Manhattan Island, and on into New Jersey, leaving the Port at the mercy of enemy occupation. The patriots controlled all of inland New York, except as expeditions from Canada threatened it, and the stretches of the Hudson River, as well as most of the Sound and the north shore of Long Island. The British controlled the harbor, the ocean coast of Long Island, and the city.

First Submarine in New York Harbor

While Washington was still in possession of Manhattan Island and the British held Brooklyn and the harbor, the British forces on Governors Island were undoubtedly the first soldiers in history to witness a submarine engaged in the maneuver of attacking a battleship. This occurred on August 17, 1776.

The submersible in question was David Bushnell's invention which has since been called the *Turtle*, and the one-man crew was Sergeant Ezra Lee of the Continental Army, whom Bushnell had chosen to operate his odd craft. That the object of the attack, the fifty-gun frigate *Eagle*, was not sunk was due more to bad luck than bad management.

Bushnell, a Yale classmate of Nathan Hale, described his ingenious vessel as looking like "a hardshell clam wearing a hat." The *Turtle* was composed of oak timber scooped out and fitted together in such a manner that the operator, sitting or standing in a very small space, could manipulate it with comparative facility. The top or head was made of a watertight metallic composition on hinges, which permitted the "crew" to get in and out—but that was about all. Nevertheless, the craft could submerge or rise to the surface at will and managed a top speed of about three miles an hour in still water.

Two force pumps by which water could be ejected from the hold, a foot spring which permitted the intake of water, and two hundred pounds of detachable ballast as part of the seven-hundred-pound keel effected submersion and rising. Six small pieces of thick glass in the head supplied light—enough, it is recorded, so that the operator "could see to read in clear water at a depth of three fathoms." The navigator steered by a rudder, the tiller of which passed through the back of the machine at a water joint, and with his other hand he cranked a crude propeller with twelve-inch wooden blades. This amazing craft also had a glass tube, twelve inches in length, which enclosed a piece of cork. The cork rose with the descent of the craft and fell with the ascent, an inch rise denoting a depth of one fathom.

The submarine's torpedo was a "magazine . . . shaped like an egg and itself composed of oak scooped out, with 130 pounds of gun powder, a clock and a gun lock with a good flint that would not miss fire." This was attached to the back of the submarine, papoose fashion, and could be detached when a "sharp iron screw was made to pass out of the top of the machine . . . and adhere to the ship's bottom ... a line leading from this screw to the magazine kept the latter in position for blowing up the vessel."

In the daring and unprecedented attempt to attack the British ship, the submersible was towed by a whaleboat during the night to a position near the *Eagle*. There Sergeant Lee entered it and at slack water, "after two and a half hours' cranking," managed to get beneath his prospective victim. But, "owing probably to the ship's copper and a lack of pressure" (in the screw which was designed to attach the magazine to the hull), the attempt failed.

Lee came to the surface and once more submerged, but morning was beginning to dawn, and he decided that it was strategic to withdraw. It was during his furious cranking to cover the not inconsiderable distance back to the Battery that the British soldiers on Governors Island saw him bobbing along on the surface, boarded a barge, and went out to investigate. Lee released the magazine in hopes of blowing up the barge, but discretion conquered the soldiers' curiosity, while the deadly "egg" the sub had laid drifted past and into the East River, where it exploded. The explosion was witnessed by General Putnam, who was waiting near the Battery for Lee's return.

George Washington described the undertaking as "an effort of genius." Had Lee succeeded in destroying or damaging one British man-of-war, it is conjectural that he might have shortened the war and augmented the victory. As it was, Washington, about a month after this attempt, left the Port in British hands, where it remained for seven years.

New York's Privateers

As the interior of the province remained in the hands of Whigs, or patriots, the invaders depended for supplies on Long Island, other colonies, and Great Britain. This shipping offered splendid objectives for Whig privateers. The Tories, or Royalists, also engaged in privateering, aided by British occupation of the Port itself.

Most of the privateers operated from Long Island, New Jersey, or Connecticut inlets, thus avoiding the British blockade of the Port. Some were small craft intent on seizing a few bales of goods or heads of livestock; others made important captures. It was more advantageous to reap the profits of privateering from Britain's merchant fleet than to confine their operations to those of an organized navy.

However, one privateer, the armed sloop *Montgomery*, under Captain Rogers, "seemed," Rogers wrote, "to be damned unlucky. It is hard to think that we have cruised so long and have got nothing." In 1780 two whaleboats captured a British schooner and were in turn taken by the British, twenty-eight of their crew eventually suffering imprisonment.

Governor Trumbull of Connecticut was accused of allowing privateers to exceed the provisions of their commissions, and some of his men outraged the feelings of local Whigs by making New York their headquarters. The Connecticut marauders were not always careful whose property they seized—or perhaps had their own standards in distinguishing between Whig and Tory. After a sharp exchange of letters between Governor Clinton of New York and Trumbull the latter made an investigation and ordered his citizens to return Whig property.

While private citizens competed to afflict the British through privateering, the Continental Congress was fighting them, through other ports, with an aggressive force of armed fishing craft and merchantmen. Because of the seven-year occupation by the British, New York had little share in this story.

East River Treasure

New York Port holds one of America's oldest treasure-ship myster-
ies, dating from 1780 when the British frigate H.M.S. *Hussar* foun-
dered in Hell Gate, East River, with a fortune in gold allegedly aboard.

The *Hussar*, a new frigate of the British navy, mounting twenty-
eight guns, was dispatched to the colonies to act as paymaster for the
British troops. Its treasure room was said to have held approximately
four million dollars in gold. Naturally, considerable official secrecy
surrounded the transportation of such a sum, and exact verification has
never been obtained, either of the amount or that it was actually sent.
However, most historians accept the story, and the later costly salvage
operations show that wide credence was given it.

The frigate's orders were to proceed through Hell Gate and to meet
the British army paymaster at a rendezvous on the Connecticut shore
sometime after the ship's arrival in New York on September 13, 1780,
but the ever-dangerous Hell Gate added the *Hussar* to its tidal trophies.
The ship struck Pot Rock, since removed, and her hull began to fill. The
captain tried to gain a point off Port Morris in order to run the frigate
aground, but he failed, and the *Hussar* sank in seventy-five feet of
water, only her topmasts showing.

Although the British Admiralty stated during the War of 1812 that
there was no gold aboard the *Hussar,* this was discounted as a ruse. The
East River location of the treasure, with a great city's facilities at hand,
offers almost unlimited opportunities to treasure hunters, but Hell Gate
has kept its secret to the present day. In 1880 Captain George Thomas,
an eccentric character who organized a corporation called Treasure
Trove, obtained permission from the United States Treasury Department to conduct salvage operations. The attempt succeeded only in
amusing the public. In the present century Simon Lake, the submarine
inventor, made a protracted effort to retrieve the treasure. Lake had
developed a special caisson diving tube, which he planned to have
lowered to the wreck at an angle so that a man might walk down to the

sunken ship from the surface. He made the attempt in 1937 but failed because, as he later explained in his autobiography, the shore line had changed completely since the sinking and he could not locate the hulk.

Union Jack Struck

The Revolutionary War ended in 1783, and on November 25 of that year the Continental Army took formal possession of New York. Washington and Governor Clinton, with their suites, on horseback entered the city and were met at the Bull's Head in the Bowery and escorted to Cape's Tavern. Before leaving the fort the British had cut the halyards under the British flag and had greased the flagpole. An American sailor, John van Arsdale, then climbed the pole by nailing cleats to it as he ascended; he reached the top, detached the British flag, and replaced it with the American standard. The last of the British military embarked that same day, but the fleet did not sail until December 5.

On December 4 Washington bade farewell to his officers at Fraunces' Tavern and set out to resign his commission before the Continental Congress assembled at Annapolis. A great crowd saw him off at Whitehall Wharf. Before sailing Washington ventured the hope: "May the Ruins soon be repaired, Commerce flourish, Science be fostered, and all the civil and social Virtues be cherished in the same illustrious manner which formerly reflected so much credit on the Inhabitants of New York."

The Port of New York was not well prepared for this desired flourishing commerce. Its shipping was disorganized, its wharves rotted, and frosts had weakened the foundations of such empty warehouses as the British, in their foraging for firewood, had left standing.

Returning New Yorkers who marched up Broad Street with General Washington must have gasped at the canvas-covered ruins where prosperous commercial houses had stood when the patriots fled the city. As a result of two devastating fires one quarter of the buildings lay in ashes, the debris remaining as it fell. Troops and officers had occupied the better of the remaining buildings but had not improved them. Civilian Tories had hacked joists and girders to feed the ever-hungry open fireplaces. Thus great sections of valuable property had literally gone up chimneys. The desolation of the docks was even more pronounced. Under the ravages of storms and the fluctuating movements of tides, dock planks once soaked with rum and molasses and worn smooth by traffic now sagged into the rivers.

Although New York had lost perhaps half its buildings through incendiarism, collapse, and pillage, the city revived quickly. The population had been twenty thousand in 1776, dropped to half that by the end of the war, but returned to the first figure by 1787. During postwar rehabilitation there was great activity at the waterfront; the Common Council minutes for these years are filled with names of owners, locations of docks, petitions for repair, and generous grants of pounds, shillings, and pence to execute them. Another important city utility to appear at the time was the public market.

Fly Market

In the Dutch period an East River shore road was called De Smit's Valey (The Blacksmith's Valley), for a smith named Cornelius Clopper who had set up his forge at the point where the road crossed Maiden Lane. The word "Valey" was corrupted into "Vly" and finally became "Fly." Brooklyn farmers often landed there in rowboats or scows laden with country produce. Especially at high tide it was a quiet and safe landing place for small boats, and the characters of ferry landing and produce market continued to identify the locality, then known as Fly Market. It lay, when the surveys reached it, at the foot of Maiden Lane, that narrow crooked thoroughfare that earned its name much farther up its hill, where the housemaids gathered to do the domestic washing at a spring. The maids now had another reason for using the lane, for there were three meeting points of kitchen trade at its East River end: a meat market, a fish market, and a produce market. In the building surge following the Revolution the city erected its Exchange Market House at Fly Market, and other buildings followed from time to time, up to 1805, when other market centers began to supersede it.

Before the war broke the surface, it will be remembered that the merchants had striven for a commercial victory by organization, persuasion, and a boycott enforced with calm tenacity, until finally the opposite policy of the Sons of Liberty won them over to direct action. During this prewar era the merchant colony had organized two groups that survived the war itself and continued into our own times: the Chamber of Commerce of the City of New York in America, thus incorporated by the charter granted by George III in 1770, and the Marine Society of the City of New York, also dating from 1770. In this era of rebuilding the city and refitting the Port the merchant founders of the Chamber of Commerce first met at Fraunces' Tavern on April 5, 1768, although they did not petition for a charter until two years later.

Shipping at the Close of the Revolution

After 1783 American ships were "foreign" to the government of Great Britain. Britain could function as a unit, could harass American ships with duties and restrictions, whereas this country could not retaliate until it had developed national rather than local laws and had formulated a tariff policy. The ports of the West Indies were closed to American shipments of fish in 1783, and United States ships were barred from other ports by a prohibitive schedule of duties. Meantime the Empire was dumping its own products into American markets, chiefly through the Port of New York, and was on the way to gaining control of New York's trade. France and Spain, allies of the United States in war under the treaties of 1778, now closed their ports also. When Holland followed, Sweden was left as the only European power to welcome American goods and shipping, for the open nature of Mediterranean ports was so limited by the swarms of pirates as to make voyages there hazardous and unprofitable. In fact, almost every trade route known to the American merchant marine was closed. The Port's public utilities were being organized for city growth; its docks were rebuilt and extended; its expanding waterfront strengthened itself and reached out for a new world tie. In the period preceding the enactment of the first national maritime legislation—passed in New York by the Congress of 1789—there was need for such a tie, temporary though it might be.

As the Port had devised the expedient of bolting laws when lack of uniformity threatened its trade in grains, and as it had formed numerous trade combinations using molasses and alcohol, so now it had to improvise again. Ingenuity still lacked the tools of the nineteenth century—steam, electricity, steel—but it contrived an expedient equally important: the ginseng-fur-tea triangle of the first venture into the China trade.

CHAPTER V

China Trade and Protective Tariff—1784-1805

PIONEERS TO THE ORIENT

O N FEBRUARY 22, 1784, eleven weeks after the last British warships had cleared the harbor, the Port of New York made America's first venture into the China trade when the ship *Empress of China*, three hundred and sixty tons, sailed for Whampoa. Friends of the officers and owners were aboard for the run to Sandy Hook, and the guns of "this handsome, commodious and elegant ship" exchanged salutes with harbor batteries during her slow progress down the bay, giving flashes of color to a routine which lacked the maneuvering of tugs, the rattle of anchor chains, and the deep warnings of steam whistles that dramatize it for the observer today.

Behind the sailing of this copper-sheathed vessel— built in Baltimore, financed in Philadelphia, its affairs administered by a Bostonian, but managed and publicized in the Port of New York—lay a story of America's struggle for world trade between the time of the Revolution and the first national tariff act of 1789. Although in this period the China trade was never worth more than fifteen per cent of the total of America's world commerce, it gained the United States immediate recognition as an equal by all the nations represented at Canton, especially by the British, who now found the Americans their only allies when they quarreled with the Chinese.

Of the three men whose initiative and imagination put the new flag into Chinese ports after an earlier Boston attempt had ended with the sale of the ship's cargo at the Cape of Good Hope, Robert Morris was the leader, wrote the government's letter of authority, and raised the money; Major Samuel Shaw planned and executed the trading strategy, and Captain John Green chose the ship, equipped her, commanded her, and arranged for a friendly convoy through the last and most dangerous portion of the run.

Morris administered the financing of the Revolutionary War and was, at various times, called superintendent, dictator, or administrator in the raising of funds for the army. However, his true passion was the "venturesome pursuit of commerce," which, Morris said in a letter to John Jay, had captured his imagination. He had abandoned an earlier idea—to bring Pacific Northwest furs to the Atlantic coast—and had decided on a trading voyage to China.

Major Samuel Shaw, originally from Boston, had served as an officer in the Continental Army throughout the Revolution. He was General Knox's aide-de-camp, and it was perhaps his intense loyalty to all things American that made him favor ginseng, rather than the sea-otter pelts of the Pacific, as an item of export to Canton.

John Green, captain, was an American ship's officer during the struggle with Great Britain. Morris himself signed Green's release from active service, a document dated January 15, 1784, and still in existence. His standing—practically that of a navy officer on furlough—may have earned the cordial helpfulness of Captain d'Ordelin and his staff of the French man-of-war *Triton*, under whose pilotage and escort the *Empress* completed the outward voyage after meeting the French ship at the East Indian Islands.

Morris had a partner that shared equally with him in the investment of one hundred and twenty thousand dollars in cash—the firm of Daniel Parker and Company of Philadelphia. Shaw, who sailed as supercargo, and who did not, in his journal, count himself as part of the ship's complement, took along a friend, Thomas Randall, as assistant supercargo. These five men— Morris and Parker at home, Shaw,

Green, and Randall aboard ship—handled all the important details of this pioneering venture.

Flowery-Flag Kingdom

The new "Flowery-Flag Kingdom"—as the Chinese described the United States—which spoke the same language as the English but obeyed a different government, was about to engage with China in an interesting exchange of commodities, primarily the dried materials to make stimulating hot drinks and, secondarily, furs to warm the Orientals, and fans and silk garments to keep the Yankees cool. Tea, usually the black variety, was the import; and American ginseng, related closely to the Chinese ginseng, was the export. Ginseng, defined as an "alterative tonic, stimulant, carminative, and dimulcent," grew—at first plentifully—on the floors of those same East Coast forests that furnished timbers for the shipbuilders of New England, New York, and Baltimore.

In the outbound cargo of the *Empress*, not counting the private merchandise of Captain Green, were more than thirty tons of ginseng, about the same amount of pig lead, a ton of pepper, 1270 woolen garments then known as camlets, and 2600 fur skins. Since this did not entirely aggregate the value of $120,000, Shaw carried, for trading and probably for the necessary bribing of officials, the remainder of his capital in the form of specie. Besides Shaw and his assistant, the ship carried ten officers and thirty-four men before the mast and, in a voyage of nearly sixteen months, lost only one man, John Morgan, carpenter, who died at sea a month before the voyage ended.

Shaw's journal reports the *Empress* mileage as 18,248 miles outbound, New York to Whampoa, crossing the North Atlantic and joining the French convoy, and 14,210 miles returning, across the South Atlantic and running up the east coasts of the Americas. The entire voyage covered the period from February 22, 1784, to May 11, 1785; the ship was at anchorage at Whampoa for one month of this time.

So sure was this supercargo of his inventories and markets that he paid off his owners on an estimate without waiting for complete returns.

The profit, which he modestly called twenty per cent, was $30,727 on an investment of $120,000. But as other China traders bought ginseng more avidly and bid against each other for the Hyson and Bohea teas of the Canton Security Merchants, the margin on which Shaw's 25.605 per cent was based began to disappear.

Second China Voyage

The seventy-six-ton sloop *Experiment* undertook the second voyage from the Port of New York to Canton. Receiving the secondary interest of China trade historians, she has been variously reported as carrying ginseng worth five dollars a pound, as making no profit, modest profits, or great profits, as bearing the name *Enterprise* for the previous command of her captain, and as having a crew small, medium, or large. Actually her story is prosaic enough, except that she beat the other enthusiastic imitators of Shaw and Morris by sailing before Christmas instead of in February.

The *Experiment* was built in Albany for the Hudson River passenger service. She was possibly the same sloop *Experiment* that arrived in New York from Bermuda November 10, 1785. For on the eleventh a company was formed to operate her in the China trade, and on December 18 she had loaded dollar-a-pound ginseng, Madeira wine, silver dollars, and other merchandise, and was ready to sail. Under Stewart Dean, master, was John Whetten, first mate, and a crew of eight, two of whom were boys. The *Experiment* left Whampoa December 10, 1786, and arrived at New York April 22, 1787.

Northwest Trade

On September 30, 1787, two vessels, the two-hundred-and-twelve-ton ship *Columbia*, Captain Kendrick, and her ninety-ton tender, the sloop *Lady Washington*, Captain Robert Gray, left Boston for the Pacific Northwest. By April 1 they were near Cape Horn—the season in that latitude was late autumn—and the two ships separated for the long voyage up the Pacific coast. Almost a year out of Boston, they met in

Nootka Sound, a harbor well up on the oceanside of Vancouver Island. Here again it was autumn, the third autumn they had experienced in eleven months, and no furs came to Nootka's trading center until cold weather. Much like Block and his crew on Manhattan Island nearly two hundred years before them, Kendrick and Gray built log huts and wintered on Nootka Island.

The next summer they again parted. Their "trinkets and general merchandise" from Boston were more plentiful than the furs for which they traded. Provisions were low; both vessels could not remain. Kendrick, till then in command of the expedition, ordered Gray to take the *Columbia* and what furs they had. Gray sailed direct for Canton, where he took on tea and completed his circumnavigation under the new nation's flag by sailing into Boston Harbor in the summer of 1790. When he arrived, with some of his tea damaged, he found fourteen competing vessels selling tea to Boston. This circumnavigation—so circuitous is the Horn route—consumed 41,899 miles.

Despite poor profits, Gray made a second voyage, naming the Columbia River for his ship and trying his hand at smuggling into Spanish California by sufferance of the complaisant missionaries there. Kendrick, com-pelled to "live on the country" as an army sometimes does, never went back to Boston, but shuttled between North America and China. Perhaps his emergency rations were insufficient, for scurvy in his crew drove him to land on the Sandwich (now Hawaiian) Islands, where he found and harvested san-dalwood, readily salable in Canton. Being out of touch with Boston via Cape Horn, he nevertheless had procured Boston "trinkets and general merchandise" for trade purposes from Boston traders at Mauritius Island (Ile de France), which became an exchange center for international traders.

The voyages of Captain Gray and Captain Kendrick had important repercussions on New York Port. Gray's first loss showed that the nation needed a port whose market would not go to pieces in the presence of fourteen simultaneous cargoes. The export of "trinkets and general merchandise" was becoming more and more to mean the export of miscellaneous goods from the warehouses of South and Pearl streets.

So long as New York goods moved into the Indian Ocean and passed by open bidding into the hands of a Pacific trader like Kendrick and so to the Indians of North America, it mattered less that Kendrick and Gray were Bostonians than that the routing and management of most of the great body of such trade was passing into New York control.

End of the First China Trade

As the China trade, toward the end of the eighteenth century, withered away into that vestige which so tenuously connects the surges of 1785 and 1850, the function of the Port of New York was clarified. The traffic became distinguished from the haul, the flow from the container. Vessels returning to Baltimore, Boston, Providence, or Philadelphia, while earning a freight revenue for owners who might or might not be in New York, sold out their cargo at America's "main entrance," downtown Manhattan, where prices were always steadier and usually higher than elsewhere in the United States.

The tariff weapon, that delicate balance of nuisance and advantage with which nations hold one another at a profitable arm's length, was not America's till July 1789. But meantime her traders had entered Canton on an equal footing with those of other powers, had accepted valuable friendship from one major power (France), and had extended valuable friendship, intelligently and bravely, to another—a late enemy. These were the acts, the traits, the behavior of an adult nation. American sailors returning to New York showed a new pride of nationality in their swagger. A man—officer or seaman—gained stature after a China voyage, his sea chest full of lacquer or porcelain tea caddies, silk handkerchiefs, hair ribbons, carved ivory, and painted fans, his fund of anecdotes likewise enriched, and the devotion of his feminine admirers dramatized by a fast return crossing and a profitable South Street debarkation.

By 1789 this sharp focus of drama, adventure, and profits had begun a slow diffusion that was to continue to the almost complete fog of 1815-50. Though the trade was New York's largely, the fleet was only fractionally so. As an important palliative, the China trade had helped to bridge the gap, and now a new and solid weapon was to replace it permanently.

The Road to Protective Tariff

John Adams, representing the United States at the Court of St. James's, described the precarious condition of American commerce in 1784 when he wrote in a letter: "This being the state of things you may depend upon it the commerce of America will have no relief at present, nor in my opinion ever, until the United States shall have generally passed navigation acts; and if this measure is not adopted, we shall be derided; and the more we suffer the more will our calamities be laughed at."

Adams' use of the word "generally" implies two things which clarify the problem—that the states would be acting independently in any tariff legislation, but that the several states following the same general combative tariff line would, in a strong sense, be acting as a legislative unit. His letter was an initial force, the beginning of a progression of thought and action that led to the first Federal tariff act, passed on July 4 by the Congress of 1789, meeting in the City of New York.

This act set a few duties, cut ten per cent off them for ships owned and built by Americans, cut half or more from the rate on tea when imported directly from China, and adjusted other schedules so as to give Americans anything from small favors in the London haul to monopoly in the coastwise traffic. But this was only a beginning. Every tariff has a "nuisance" or combative value. The first tariff act served notice on the powers of the world that the states were uniting, were learning the power of their tariff weapon, and would use it. For the first time the question, "What will America do?" was a valid parliamentary query during tariff debates in Europe.

Washington favored the general tariff program Jefferson had initiated and Madison and others had introduced in Congress. In the July 4 act and those which inevitably followed, not only America's goods and ports gained protection, but also her registry, her bottoms, and the potential future of her shipyards. Ships built, owned, and manned by foreigners paid a tax of fifty cents a ton; if American-built but foreign owned and manned, the tax was thirty cents a ton; if American-built, owned and manned, the tax fell to six cents.

An act in the same series, passed in 1790, guarded the rights of American seamen, many of its provisions still remaining in force. The act allowing only American-built vessels to register under the United States flag remained in effect until 1912.

The maritime enterprise of the Atlantic seaboard responded magnificently to legislative encouragement, its trade penetrating to Europe, the Baltic, the Mediterranean, California, and the islands of the Pacific. The Port of New York made its final stride to first place during this commercial upsurge. Besides exporting such staples as wheat, flour, hides, and lumber, it distributed wines, spirits, tea, coffee, cocoa, chocolate, sugar, molasses, nuts, fruits, raisins, spices, indigo, and cotton to New Jersey, Pennsylvania, the New England States, and the interior.

Available statistics indicate the striking results of this important early legislation. Between 1789 and 1799 American deep-water shipping tonnage rose from 123,893 to 576,733, while the tonnage figures for British shipping engaged in United States commerce fell from 94,110 to 19,669 in the years between 1789 and 1796.

In 1789 American bottoms carried 17.5 per cent of the nation's exports and 30 per cent of its imports; in 1794 the percentage had risen to 91 of exports and 86 of imports. The Port of New York's registered tonnage in 1790 was 37,712; in 1794 it was 71,693, and by 1812 it had risen to 265,548.

The Port's exports were valued at $2,505,465 in 1790-91 and at $5,442,483 in 1783-84; by the year 1800 the figure was $19,851,136. The figure for imports—$1,169,809 in 1792—had risen to $2,000,689 by 1795.

Besides the novel, colorful, and spectacular ventures into strange seas, there was also the solid bulk of United States trade, which was with the first-class powers of Europe. This trade was soon threatened by the reopening of war between France and Britain. The President's proclamation of neutrality offended both belligerents, but France found it expedient to swallow her indignation and commission American ships in her fight against the British blockade.

In an attempt to mitigate the conditions that carried the threat of a possible new war, Washington sent John Jay to England in 1794. The resulting treaty did not take effect till 1797, and most of the "reciprocal and perfect liberty of commerce and navigation" was in its preamble rather than its provisions. However, the profits that Americans gathered under this benevolent overlordship of England offended France, and, without actually declaring war, she began to imitate the British search-and-seizure practices by turning upon our West Indies shipping the attacks of her fleet in those waters. Earlier, French privateers and the French navy had harassed American shipping with a little color of legality, but increased attacks in 1798, openly lawless, led the United States government in July to abrogate all treaties with France and to commence attacking and seizing French vessels on sight. This unde-clared war came to a climax when the U.S.S. *Constitution* whipped but failed to capture the larger French *Vengeance*, a frigate of forty guns. France lost twenty-four armed vessels and then signed a treaty February 2, 1801, ending a war never formally begun.

This war served to cement again the friendship and cooperation between the merchant marine and the American navy. The peace diverted attention from France, and once more Great Britain loomed up as the world power whose commercial interests were most directly and actively opposed to those of the United States.

CHAPTER VI

For Public Good and Private Gain—1806-16

"OUT CUTLASSES AND BOARD!"

Toward evening of April 25, 1806, the American coasting schooner *Richard* was making for New York. Suddenly, when she was about two miles from Sandy Hook and no more than a quarter mile offshore, the air was split by the roar of cannon aboard His Majesty's sixty-gun frigate *Leander*, one of three British warships bringing to and overhauling every passing vessel. Two shots from the *Leander* sped toward the *Richard*. One cut across her bow; the other flew overhead. She hove to immediately and waited for the Britisher to send out the customary boarding party. But no boat put off from the *Leander*. Instead a third and deliberately aimed shot struck the *Richard's* taffrail and cut off the helmsman's head. At the wheel was John Pierce, brother of the captain, and his death lit emotional fires that all the King's ships and all the King's men could not extinguish.

Next morning the *Richard* anchored in the East River. The news of her tragedy raced along the waterfront. Volunteers chartered a pilot boat and sailed after two ships that had been seized by the *Leander* and were on their way to Halifax. Others raided two boats which had anchored at the wharf and were loaded with food for the *Leander*, while still others, in fast-sailing vessels, went in pursuit of three more supply boats, overtaking them at Sandy Hook and bringing them back to the Port, where the provisions were unloaded, put into ten carts, and delivered to the poorhouses. Pierce's headless body was carried to shore and exposed to view at the Tontine Coffee House.

Fury Grips New York

The two major political parties—Federalist and Republican—were quick to exploit the anger aroused by Pierce's death. The Federalists believed that the government, by not taking a firmer stand against impressment and all the other actions by which Great Britain sought to interfere with the nation's foreign trade, had in effect encouraged these outrages. To the Republicans, then in power, the government was innocent; they claimed that the two previous Federalist administrations were to blame. In New York the Federalists tried to capitalize on the anger of the sailors, who naturally were most affected by the Pierce incident, and after rounding up a number of them at Hardy's Tavern—a waterfront hangout—had them pass resolutions condemning the government for its weakness in the face of British provocation.

The Common Council resolved that Pierce be buried at public expense and that the members attend in a body. Flags were half-masted on American ships, as thousands turned out to pay their respects to the Yankee seaman whose slaying had brought to a head the smoldering resentment of the American people against the many ways in which Great Britain had sought to exclude their commerce from the sea.

However, the popular wrath occasioned by the Pierce incident was not mobilized for war. It is possible that a war declared then, when Napoleon was powerful, would have quickly brought Great Britain to terms. The United States could have exchanged hazardous blockade running for open privateering, and American seamen could have profited, while at the same time effecting retaliation for the impressment of their fellows. Against this advantage Britain's exchange would have been of search and seizure for forthright blockade, a gain on paper only and nullified by the probability of intensive privateering activity.

On the other side, historians point to America's lack of national cohesion. The decapitation of John Pierce was a port, not an inland, episode, and an 1806 war would have aided, against the tyranny of Great Britain, another nation—France—equally contemptuous of American sea rights and American democracy.

Within seven months of the third *Leander* cannon ball Napoleon's Berlin Decree, November 21, 1806, barred American ships from Europe if they came from England or carried British goods. Great Britain replied by Orders in Council of January 7 and November 11, 1807. American ships had to pay duty at and clear from a British port before touching Europe. In other words, American ships must—and must not—stop at Britain on the way to France. They were in the middle!

Nevertheless, 1807 was a good year for New York shipping. John Lambert, an English traveler who visited the United States in 1807, described the Port thus: ". . . the port was filled with shipping, and the wharfs were crowded with commodities of every description. Bales of cotton, wool, and merchandise; barrels of pot-ash, rice, flour, and salt provisions; hogsheads of sugar, chests of tea, puncheons of rum, and pipes of wine; boxes, cases, packs and packages of all sizes and denominations, were strewed upon the wharfs and landing-places, or upon the decks of the shipping. All was noise and bustle. The carters were driving in every direction; and the sailors and labourers upon the wharfs, and on board the vessels, were moving their ponderous burthens from place to place. The merchants and their clerks were busily engaged in their counting-houses, or upon the piers. The Tontine coffee-house was filled with underwriters, brokers, merchants, traders, and politicians; selling, purchasing, trafficking, or insuring; some reading, others eagerly inquiring the news. . . . The coffee-house slip, and the corners of Wall and Pearl-streets, were jammed up with carts, drays, and wheelbarrows; horses and men were huddled promiscuously together, leaving little or no room for passengers to pass. . . . The people were scampering in all directions to trade with each other, and to ship off their purchases for the European, Asian, African, and West Indian markets. Every thought, word, look, and action of the multitude seemed to be absorbed by commerce; the welkin rang with its busy hum, and all were eager in the pursuit of its riches."

The Long Embargo

On December 22, 1807, the Jefferson administration initiated the long embargo, prohibiting all American vessels from leaving the United States for foreign ports and all foreign vessels from taking cargoes out of the United States.

The effect upon New York was devastating. By the following February five hundred ships were decommissioned in the Port. There were ninety-three crossings from New York or Boston to Liverpool in 1807, but not one in 1808. The East River and the short stretch of the Hudson were truly forests of spars, while an army of unemployed trod the waterfront, but the forests were decaying and the seamen were becoming restive. New York lined up these men before soup kitchens four times a week; many of them were driven to seek employment in British service. By September every port in the country had felt the paralyzing effects of embargo. Discipline had averted riots but could not prevent one hundred and twenty bankruptcies in the ensuing fifteen months.

Jefferson, long-range nationalist, disliked the carrying trade; the farmer, not the merchant, was his man; the interior, not the coast, was his first concern. Once more the New York merchant found that his was not the same viewpoint as the country's. To him the embargo was futile against a competitor so rich and an enemy so strong; smugglers and embargo jumpers were now moving through New York State or Vermont into Canada and promoting the shipping of Quebec and Halifax on their new route to Britain. The owners of New York's idle ships were angry.

In widespread resistance to the long embargo, merchants, their clerks, and unemployed seamen paraded openly. None could deny that America was damaging her economic position without bringing England to terms on a single fundamental issue. By repealing the embargo March 1, 1809, the government was merely correcting a mistake. The Port of New York celebrated repeal—with lights, bells, and the firing of salutes—on April 24.

The Short Embargo

Although 1810 was a boom year in deep-sea tonnage, the belligerents tightened their restrictions, Britain especially treating the United States more and more like a colonial vassal. As the provocative incidents piled up it became apparent early in 1811 that war was inevitable. Having for ten years neglected naval armament, the Federal government now needed time to reconsider and prepare, and this time was set by law at ninety days. The Madison administration declared the short embargo for that period early in April 1812. At the beginning Madison had opposed the initiation of this embargo because it meant severing commercial relations with France as well as protecting American ships from capture by the British. But it soon became known that French squadrons were capturing and burning American ships on the high seas. American indignation rose, and the Federalists in particular petitioned the administration to call a halt to these aggressive tactics of the French by imposing an embargo that would keep American ships at home.

New York, Boston, and Philadelphia were quite successful in evading this embargo. Congressman Emott of New York released the details of the proposed law three days before its passage. Leading merchants in the three cities were the secret beneficiaries of this action. The news reached New York on April 2, and in a few hours flour went up a dollar a barrel, and freight had a rise of twenty per cent. Ships were loaded frantically during the interval, and, from New York alone, forty-eight vessels were cleared before the dead line of April 4.

Rear Admiral Mahan has called this "a conspicuous instance of mercantile avidity wholly disregardful of patriotic considerations such as is found in all times and all countries; strictly analogous to the constant smuggling between France and Great Britain at this very time.

Its significance in the present case, however, is as marking the wide-spread lack of a national patriotism, as distinct from purely local advantage and personal interests, which unhappily characterized Americans at this period." Great Britain welcomed the supplies and extended special considerations to their carriers. But she retained her old contempt for our naval and military forces.

"Yet," our minister to Britain reported, May 9, 1812, "they will endeavor to avoid the calamity of war with the United States by every means which can save their pride and their consistency. The scarcity of bread in this country, the distress of the manufacturing towns, and the absolute dependence of the allied troops in the Peninsula on our supplies, form a check on their conduct which they can scarcely have the hardihood to disregard."

The British public, moreover, was tiring of the Orders in Council and agitating for their revocation. Our own public was tiring also—of diplomacy and compromise, of impressment and seizure. President Madison sent Congress a war-or-peace message on June 1, and—against thirty-eight per cent of the House and forty per cent of the Senate—Congress declared war on June 18, 1812, just one day before Britain's revocation! The privateer had become our first line of defense.

War—1812

The news reached New York on June 20, after overland messengers had relayed it from Washington in the then remarkable time of forty-two and one half hours. Here it met the same division of opinion as in Congress. This was a defensive war if ever there was one, yet a strong minority of merchant princes opposed it, even proclaiming their admiration for the enemy. Whereas during the long embargo such opposition had often been sincere and high-minded, now much of it was based on a desire for excessive profits.

These merchants pointed to their loss of nine hundred and seventeen ships as evidence of their desire for peace. But these seizures constituted a comparatively small loss, since inflated profits based on high rates covered them when marine insurance—also based on high rates—did not. Fully compensated for all war risks and never in personal jeopardy, their plight was quite different from that of their employees, the merchant seamen. Impressment was an occupational hazard against which there was no insurance. Pay was not increased to compensate for the risks of violating the Orders and running Napoleon's blockade. It was not surprising, therefore, to find South Street's seamen pleased with the declaration, eager to get even with the jailers of six thousand of their fellows, happy at the discomfiture of their employers, and at the prospect of early privateering dividends.

The merchants, the seamen, and the general public were meantime the objects of persistent political propaganda. A contributor to *The War*, a New York weekly, thus described the publicity methods of the 1800s:

"The magnanimity, piety and justice of England, forms the character which she claims as exclusively her own; the contrary vices are charged to [the] account of her adversary. The war with America had been preceded by arguments grounded on these principles. Spies, agents, and money, were employed to promote this opinion, and the loyalty of the citizens was attempted to be shaken by the comparison. It was insinuated that every 'republican' was a friend to Bonaparte and influenced by him and that every 'federalist' was attached in an equal degree to England; thus dividing the citizens of the United States into French and English, and leaving no portion of the people to be distinguished as Americans, whereby could be established, the monstrous and inconsistent doctrine, that the democratic republicans must rank themselves under the banners of a monarch whose interest it is to destroy all popular government, and that federal republicans should rally round the standard of a king who feels himself conscientiously bound to deny to a large portion of his subjects the most obvious rights of freemen . . . the distinctions of federalist and democrat must cease, and those of WHIG and TORY must mark us as friends of America or adherents of England ..."

Thus a fully developed national patriotism met the shock of a war in 1812, as it might have done in 1806. On New York's waterfront the economic extremes met for the purpose of engaging in privateering, that opportune combination of vengeance, warfare, and quick enrichment which disappeared with sail.

Privateers and Prizes

The British blockade of the Port of New York was not made effective until the summer of 1813, and it was not until November of that year that the New England coast was blockaded, finally cutting off escape from the Port by way of the Sound.

In the meantime the Federal government was active, forthright, and bold in sending a swarm of privateers against the enemy. The imperfect regulations were later made more explicit by Congress, but from the start—when New York was most alert—they produced great activity. Privateers roamed the seas and, in conjunction with the official navy, took thirty thousand prisoners; the damage to British shipping has been estimated at $49,600,000.

New York's 102 privateers were manned by 5852 men, mounted 698 guns, and in seven months made seven hundred captures. The nation's land forces, meanwhile, were taking six thousand prisoners, and the navy was bringing in six million dollars' worth of prizes.

New York privateers known to have taken ten or more prizes each were: *Scourge*, first with twenty-seven; *General Armstrong*, second with twenty-four; *Saratoga*, twenty-two; *Governor Tompkins*, twenty; *Prince de Neufchatel*, eighteen; *Divided We Fall*, sixteen; *Paul Jones*, fifteen; and *Teazer*, fourteen. (As poetic running mate, if not sister ship, of *Divided We Fall* there was, of course, the *United We Stand*.)

The *General Armstrong* was owned principally by Thomas Jenkins, Rensselaer Havens, and Thomas Farmar, besides whom there were numerous small stockholders who held shares in her privateering career. She was a little less than two hundred and fifty tons' burden and armed with six long nines, one long torn, and one forty-two-pounder. In September the owners gave command of the ship to a veteran merchant master, Samuel C. Reid. The officers and crew of the ship numbered ninety men.

On September 3, 1812, Captain Reid, in the dignity of burnsides, tall hat, and tail coat, met his officers: First Lieutenant Fred A. Worth, Second Lieutenant Alex O. Williams, Third Lieutenant Robert Johnson, Sailing Master Benjamin Starks, Quarter-master Bazilla Hammond, and Captain of Marines Robert E. Allen. Also in the crew, to sail home such prizes as Reid might capture, were four prize masters: Thomas Parsons, John Davis, Eliphalet Sheffield, and Peter Tyson. In his coat pocket Captain Reid had his instructions from the ship's agents. Dated the same day, and typical of similar instructions to many a privateer master, they read:

> The private armed brig-of-war, *General Armstrong*, under your command, being now ready for a cruise, it becomes necessary for us to furnish instructions thereto. In doing this, we do not mean to debar you the privilege of exercising your discretion in the choice of a station, but we recommend, as in our opinion being the most likely of offering objects for enterprize and profit, that you stretch off to Madeira, where you will be more likely to intercept the Brazil convoys, and should you be successful in falling in with vessels, finish your cruise there.
>
> If on the contrary, you cannot succeed in capturing vessels enough, and of sufficient value to man, we would recommend you to go through the Cape Verde Islands and fill up your water, and from there on to the coast of Brazil.
>
> The prizes you may order for the United States, we think will be best to be ordered direct from New York or Wilmington, and in the event of their safe arrival at any port in the United States, you will direct them to write to us immediately on arrival, that we may send on a confidential person to take charge of the property, in preference to appointing agents at different places.
>
> On your return to the United States, should you have any prisoners aboard, take care to secure them until they are delivered to the proper officer in order to obtain the bounty.

Hoping that your cruise terminates successfully and honorably to yourself, officers, and crew, and your country, we are

Your assured friends,
Jenkins & Havens, Agents

P.S. Be very particular in strictly prohibiting any plunder or depredations on neutrals or other vessels.

This "P.S." meant, in layman's language, that the privateer must not forget himself and become a pirate.

Six days later Reid left the shelter of the Port. A British ship of the line and a frigate chased him all night and half the next day before giving up. On September 12, three days out, the *General Armstrong* exchanged a few shots with another British man-of-war and proceeded on her way. Then nothing happened for a fortnight, when she reached, a supposedly neutral port in the Azores under the domination of Portugal, and put in to take on supplies.

Just before sunset three British warships—the sloop *Carnation*, eighteen guns; the frigate *Rota*, thirty-eight guns; and the ship of the line *Plantagenet*, seventy-four guns—entered the roadstead. Reid, suspecting they might intend doing more than merely provision and depart, as would have been legal, hastily moved into the shelter of the castle, whose guns dominated the harbor, and there demanded the protection due him under international law. The Portuguese refused, and the British then sent four hundred men in eleven heavily armed boats against the *General Armstrong*. Counting the master, the *Armstrong* had exactly eleven officers, one to each small boat of the enemy. Divided equally, her seamen would number eight or nine for each attacking party. The ensuing battle, in full moonlit view of the entire town, was probably the bloodiest in which privateers ever engaged. Each gang of eight or nine resenters of impressment had some thirty-six Englishmen to wound or kill. This made for action of the bloodiest kind.

An eyewitness said, "The Americans fought with great firmness but more like bloodthirsty savages than anything else. They rushed into the boats sword in hand and put every soul to death as far as came within their power. Some of the boats were left without a single man to row them, others with three or four . . . Several boats floated ashore full of dead bodies . . . For three days after the battle we were employed in burying the dead that had washed ashore in the surf."

British casualties numbered one hundred and twenty killed and one hundred and thirty wounded; the *Armstrong*, two killed and seven wounded. The next morning one of the British warships commenced a heavy cannonade of the privateer. Unable to reply effectively to a ship of the line, especially as she had two or more others in her support, and knowing that to stay aboard was a futile gesture, Captain Reid stripped his ship and took his crew ashore, where all found sanctuary in an old Gothic convent building. Later he protested against the British commander and the Portuguese government; these protests were followed by lawsuits that dragged on for years. As late as March 1880 the *Armstrong* claims were before the United States Senate.

Off Nantucket quite a different type of privateer master combined bravery, bravado, and guile to win a victory and to preserve a part of it. Captain John Odronaux of the *Prince de Neufchatel* (out of New York: her bag for the duration of the war was eighteen prizes) was "a Jew by persuasion, a Frenchman by birth, and American for convenience." "So diminutive in stature as to make him appear ridiculous," he commanded the seventeen-gun privateer so gainfully that on October 11, 1814, he had thirty prisoners aboard and a prize in tow when H.M.S. *Endymion* gave chase. Late in the afternoon Odronaux cut the prize's hawser and ran for Nantucket Shoals. The breeze failed him at sundown, when both vessels were close inshore. The reasonable solution was to abandon ship, especially as the crew had been reduced to thirty-three through repeated manning of prizes, and there were thirty potential enemies locked in the hold. But the captain prevented any capitulation by shouting, "I'll blow up the ship and every man aboard before I'll strike my colors."

The *Endymion* attack came late the same evening—five barges bearing one hundred and fifty men. Faced with the threat of their own mass burial at sea, Odronaux's thirty seamen beat off a first and second wave, but when the third attempt to board was successful, the master of the *Prince de Neufchatel* disconcerted both his own crew and that of the *Endymion* by waving a lighted match over the hatch above the powder magazine and threatening death to all—master, friend, and foe—if his men gave back another inch. Fighting with knives, bare fists, cutlasses, pistols, and even teeth, the Americans slashed, hacked, and drove the British overboard. This left Odronaux, who was wounded, the task of escaping from the watchful *Endymion* and landing his prisoners where a United States marshal would guarantee a bounty for every one of them. Being so close inshore suggested that, for all the British knew, the *Prince de Neufchatel* might be taking on reserves. The master, therefore, had a sail hung up, abaft the main hatches, to serve as a screen behind which he could conceal his activities. While two boys tramped heavily around the deck, one drumming and the other fifing, Odronaux shouted commands to an imaginary force. The stratagem fooled the British completely, and the *Endymion* held off long enough for Odronaux, who had only eight fit men remaining, to use five of them for landing his thirty prisoners across the surf and shoals of the Massachusetts shore. These—his assets—once secured for bounty, it was simple for the captain to lie quiet until dark and then slip off to Boston.

The blockade of Long Island Sound, beginning November 16, 1813, had kept many privateers at the Port, but there were always a few who were able to evade the blockade and escape to sea. Once the ships left the shelter of the Port, they were free to "order their prizes" into any quiet waters on the coast, to replenish water and supplies in any neutral port, and might, with luck, continue activity and profits. Thus on March 15, 1814, New Yorker George Coggeshall was master of the letter of marque schooner *David Porter*, afloat, free, and operating, though his port was closed. He expanded his log entry of that date as follows:

> Saw a large ship on our weather quarter. I soon made her out to be a frigate, distant about two miles ... I held a short consultation with my officers on the subject of attempting to get to windward (which would involve our receiving a broadside), or of running off to leeward . . .
>
> I gave orders to get the square-sail and studding-sails all ready to run at the same moment, and thus when everything was prepared, the helm was put up, and every square-sail set in a moment. The frigate not dreaming of my running to leeward, was unprepared to chase off the wind, and I should think it was at least five minutes before she had a studding-sail set, so that I gained about a mile at the commencement of the chase.

That head start turned the trick, and Captain Coggeshall sailed on to other captures and more prize money.

Seventh on the Port's list was the *Paul Jones*, whose log for December 28, 1812, read: "Captured the British ship *St. Martin's Planter*, of twelve guns, from London to Malta, with sugar, spices, etc., valued 150,000 dollars. Same day, captured by boarding the ship *Quebec*, 12 guns, from London for Gibraltar, with 750 packages of dry goods, including 100 bales of India prize-goods, etc., estimated at 300,000 dollars."

Here was an apparent total of $450,000 in prize money for one day's work. However, the customs duties were so great and there were so many men sharing in the division of the money that the profits from privateering were disappointing. Aroused by this discovery, New York owners of twenty-four privately armed vessels, together with their agents and some of the best-known merchants in the city, sent a signed petition to Congress. In June 1813 the Navy Department issued an order granting pensions equal to navy pensions to disabled privateersmen or to widows or orphans of privateersmen who had been killed in performance of duty. In August Congress guaranteed a bounty of twenty-five dollars for each enemy taken prisoner or killed as a result of action by privateers. There was also to be a one-third cut in the customs duties on prize goods. The last, of course, was the most important.

Before bequeathing these substantial reforms to the exceptional New York privateers that dodged through or stayed outside of the blockade, the Port of New York at the start of the war showed the rest of the country a privateer production line. Given a war starting on June 18, New York had by September 1 outfitted and manned 19 privateers, 11 of which had put to sea. By the fifteenth of October 2233 men had rolled aboard 26 such craft, whose armament included 194 guns.

Blockade Breakers

The vicious system of fighting with the right hand and feeding with the left, as it operated in certain South Street countinghouses throughout the long and short embargoes, and as it reached its worst among the Long Island food speculators during the war, was perpetuated and strengthened by the licensing machinery of the British, a peacetime euphemism carried over into a stratagem of war. A typical document under this licensing system was issued "By Herbert Sawyer, esq. vice-admiral of the Blue, and commander in chief of his majesty's ships and vessels of war employed, in the river St. Lawrence, along the coast of Nova Scotia, in the islands of Anticoste, Madelieine, and St. John, and cape Breton, and the bay of Fundy, and at and about the islands of Bermuda or Somers Islands, &c. &c."

The licenses, as they came from the hand of Admiral Sawyer, read in part as follows:

> Whereas, _____, his majesty's consul at _____ has recommended to me Mr. _____, a merchant of that place, *and well inclined towards the British, interest,* who is desirous of sending provisions to Spain and Portugal, for the use of the allied armies in the Peninsula . . ." Admiral Sawyer therefore directed that "all captains and commanders of his majesty's ships and vessels of war, which may fall in with any American, or other vessels bearing a neutral flag, . . . laden with flour, bread, corn, and pease, or any other species of dry provisions, on board, ... to suffer her to proceed without unnecessary obstruction or detention in her voyage.

Ships thus protected could not enter blockaded ports, being shunted to those still open; but between February and June 1813, New York enjoyed much of this sort of trade, diverted from Chesapeake Bay and the Delaware River, which were closed.

There was also a great volume of neutral trade as long as ships managed to slip through the blockade. This drained the city of foodstuffs, and the resultant hardships are described in a letter written by a New Yorker to her sister in 1813:

"The times are very hard. Money almost an impossibility. The necessaries of life are very high. Brown sugar $25 per cwt., Hyson tea 17 shillings per lb. . . . We are obliged to use beans steeped in hot molasses. Many are living on black butter-pears, apples and quinces stewed together—the poverty in the city is very great."

Yet a gentleman living in these conditions wrote to his father that he could see "no change in the manner of living, nor more attention than usual to economy.

"People," he continued, "seem to be now living on their capital and to calculate that before it is exhausted the return of peace will more than repair any inroads they will make on it in the interim." This correspondence was between William Jay and his father, John Jay, first Chief Justice of the United States.

In 1813, however, the British armies entered Paris, opened the continent of Europe as a source of supply, and eliminated any necessity for leniency toward New York. As the Sound blockade tightened, only an occasional swift-sailing privateer slipped past the blockading squadrons.

An incident of the period that followed was the capture of the *Eagle*, a tender of H.M.S. *Poictiers*, off Sandy Hook, by the fishing smack *Yankee*. With tempting provisions displayed on deck, the *Yankee* set sail as if bound for the fishing grounds. In her cabin and forepeak were secreted thirty armed men. When the *Eagle*, bustling up and down the roadstead under the seventy-four guns of her mother ship *Poictiers*, hailed her, the *Yankee* promptly put up her helm and came alongside.

New York from Brooklyn Heights, 1802 by William Birch (Engraving)

The Launching of the U.S.S. *Fulton*, the First War Steamer in the World

As the British officer in charge prepared to question Sailing Master Percival of the *Yankee*, the smack's hidden men poured a volley of musketry into the *Eagle* and let go a rousing "Out cutlasses and board!" That afternoon the *Yankee* and her prize arrived off the Battery amidst the shouts and plaudits of thousands of spectators.

East River to Lake Erie

The Port's participation in the war centered around shipbuilding as well as privateering. At Corlear's Hook, Henry Eckford and Noah Brown, technological heirs of Adriaen Block, were to establish New York's shipbuilding internationally, to make the Port pre-eminent as long as wood and canvas were pre-eminent.

A stroll through the East River shipyards in 1812 would have revealed the forest products of the New World. Masts and spars from New England, elbows and ribs from Southern states, timbers, planking, and sheathing from many points in North and South America. Even without such diversity of supply these craftsmen were able to migrate to the shores of the Great Lakes and there build greater ships than ever of such timbers as grew near by.

The first stage in the construction of the Great Lakes fleets began on the afternoon of September 4, 1812, in the third month of the war. Eckford and forty ship carpenters boarded the steamer *Paragon* at the foot of Cortlandt Street on the first stage of their journey to Sackets Harbor on Lake Ontario. The *Paragon*, one of the eight steamers plying the Hudson, moved out into the river and turned her nose upstream, as Captain Wiswall signaled for full speed ahead. Suddenly a sloop, riding the tide to smarten her speed, bore down on the *Paragon* in the hope of smashing a paddle wheel. Sail hated steam in those days, and the sloop's passengers crowded to the rail to enjoy the smash. But Captain Wiswall skillfully bore away amid the cheers of Eckford and his men. The sloop's crew burst into North River profanity, which met its match once more as forty ship carpenters hurled back the compliments of Corlear's Hook.

On September 6 Eckford was in Albany, and on the eighth he started through wilderness roads and tedious water stretches to the lake. There he and his men, reinforced by skilled mechanics sent on from New York by Christian Bergh, built the fleet with which Commodore Chauncey kept Sir James Yeo and the British fleet at bay until the end of the war.

Five months later Noah Brown set out with another band of ship-building craftsmen for "the then almost unknown forest fastnesses surrounding the shores of Lake Erie." After great hardships they launched the fleet with which Commodore Oliver Hazard Perry won the strategically important Battle of Lake Erie. Thus were smashed all possibilities of an invasion of the United States by way of Canada. To Brown's party, also, Bergh contributed skilled mechanics.

Brown was especially beloved along the waterfront, crew members manning the shrouds whenever he came aboard ships. Many a sailor knew from his own experience the importance of Brown's work. The Lakes had known only fore-and-aft rigged cockleshells before Eckford floated frigates on Lake Ontario as powerful as any on the ocean and before Brown turned out such vessels as the *Niagara*, mightiest of all warships on Lake Erie.

Merchants and Money

Private capital hired Eckford and Brown and Bergh to build privateers and later the packets of Corlear's Hook shipyards. But the paymaster for navies, whether salt-water or fresh, was of course the government. In the War of 1812, as always, the ability of the government to borrow money was indispensable to its conduct.

Although the shipowners, brokers, underwriters, wholesalers, jobbers, and retailers of the Port—generically called the "merchants"—detested many administration measures, they gave substantial support to Washington in a number of small ways and in the one big way of war-loan subscriptions. One of the most active of these men was Jacob Barker, a financial power of the generation and closely identified with politics.

Although referred to in many documents of the time as "Jacob Barker of New Orleans," most of his interests were in New York, and his fleet of ships in the Port had a total tonnage more than double that of the Black Ball packets. He belonged to the Democratic party and was a figure in the anti-Federalist Tammany Society. His Washington political connections were important, and although on occasion he may have helped influence the nation's fiscal policies to serve his own ends, he nevertheless worked feverishly to raise millions for the government.

An even more important financial figure was John Jacob Astor. He also loaned money to the government and manipulated the markets on many issues for his own profit. Owing to the war blockade, Astor was able to increase tremendously the fortune he had built up through his fur-trading operations. He loaned money to distressed merchants, refusing all collateral but mortgages, and wound up in 1815 on the way to becoming, through foreclosures, the "landlord of New York."

Against Barker's unconventional and quixotic shrewdness and Astor's intelligent ambition was a background of the merchant colony, gentlemen traders into New York Bay, whose kid-gloved contests (East River versus North River; tea versus coffee; auction versus normal billing; steam versus sail) mildly enlivened the social atmosphere in which they transacted a business quite "genteel."

"N" stood for "Noah" in the firm of N. & D. Talcott, tea merchants at 64 South Street. A Talcott ship in the sugar trade brought in coffee so steadily that its price fell to compete with the price of tea. Coffee, thanks to Talcott, the giant of 1810, began to appear on the tables of New Yorkers generally.

"T" stood for "Tea" and "Thomas" in the firm of T. H. Smith and Sons, greatest in their trade from 1803 to 1827. Thomas Junior was famous in the firm during its war years, when its enormous store in South Street, near India Wharf, was the show place of the strand. The Smith tea business grew so vast that one check, for duty alone, was drawn in the sum of $526,000.

The auctions of New York in the period have furnished material for a number of historians. Starting as legitimate outlets for distress goods—the residue of bankruptcies, wrecks, customs seizures, the cargoes of prizes, fires, floods, and collisions—auctions eventually so encroached on the normal processes of legitimate commerce that the state passed law after law to curb them. Popular whim made them the giants they became, and popular whim later pushed them back into their own grooves. In the early 1800s auctions were almost the only sources for daily bid and asked quotations, the sources from which regular merchants replenished their stocks of staples, and the basis for retail prices.

In the feverish procedure of the auctions a cargo was unloaded as soon as it arrived and piled on the ship's wharf for examination by bidders. Then urbane Philip Hone, perhaps, or his brother John, or one of their contemporaries would start the proceedings. Philip Hone, whose diaries are still read for their flavor and minutiae, was a well-to-do merchant and the leading auctioneer. There was no shouting, no tumult, as Hone's cultured voice called off the lots or items. Punch from a big bowl was passed around to all bidders, who drank each other's health while competing for goods. Ladies hovered on the fringe of the throng in which shipowners, wholesalers, underwriters, brokers, retailers, and politicians rubbed elbows. Here was the commercial cream of New York, with men whose personal property assessment alone was more than one hundred thousand dollars (a high figure at the time)—Jacob Barker, John Jacob Astor, Thomas H. Smith, Jr., John Clendenning, William Edgar, Jr., Robert Lenox, John G. Coster, Francis and James Thompson, John I. Clover, Stephen Whitney, the two John Taylors, Richard Varick, John Kane, and the auctioneer himself.

The waterfront along which these genteel merchants operated grew enormously during the thirty years before 1812. Ocean shipping tied up along the East River the Hudson craft and New Jersey ferries in the five principal "basins" or docks that extended from Cedar to Bank streets

and constituted the only North River development. The rocky shores—
or their tradition—that made the Hudson a scene of churchyards and
cemeteries in Dutch colonial times persisted even into the war years,
for in 1813 the Common Council resolved that it was "much more
hazardous to Vessels to lie at Wharves in the winter at the North, than
the East Side," and that Hudson property would never approach East
River property in value.

South Street was the waterfront from the Battery to James Slip, a
little more than a mile. Then for half a mile to Jefferson Street, Front
Street was the strand. After that South Street resumed for three quarters
of a mile, to East Street, just north of Corlear's Hook.

There were fifty numbered piers in that stretch. The thirteen princi-
pal slips were Whitehall, Exchange, Coenties, Old, Coffee House, Fly
Market, Burling, Peck, James, Catharine, George, Charlotte, and
Rutgers. The principal streets leading back from them, often named
identically, were: Wall, Pine, John, Ferry, Roosevelt, Catharine, George,
Charlotte, Rutgers, Jefferson, Clinton, Montgomery, Gouverneur, Bar,
Walnut, and Corlears.

Aftermath

The paralyzing effect of the blockade really hit the Port when the
peace news came. Sugar fell from twenty-six dollars a hundredweight
to twelve dollars and fifty cents, the premium on specie from twenty-
two to two per cent, and a "box" of tin from eighty dollars to twenty-
five dollars. Bank stocks rose five to ten points, other stocks six to ten
points. The cheap merchandise astute English merchants had been
amassing for the carnival of peace poured in, lowering the solvency of
the Port's merchants, who had to fall back on the resiliency of the interior demand to save themselves.

The peace treaty was a modern thing; no longer were abrupt price
changes to enrich speculators and bankrupt merchants, or distant
captains to be punished for violating a peace of which they had not yet

heard. Ships might leave for the West Indies, Great Britain, France, Spain, and Portugal on and after March 19, 1815, for the North Sea, the Baltic, and the Mediterranean on and after March 24. For South America the date was April 18, for subequatorial points May 18, and for total trade June 17.

In 1815 New York-owned ships totaled 278,000 tons; in 1816, 299,000; in 1817, 306,000. The military difficulties had disappeared; growth was steady, and new problems—sail versus steam, for example—had not yet risen to plague South Street.

To New York and every other world port the War of 1812 had been primarily significant as the dividing line between the two great eras of commerce and navigation. Before the war merchantmen of all nations had sailed seas infested with pirates and privateers and imperiled by the doctrine that the great trade routes of the world belonged to whatever power could show the most cannon afloat. After the war freebooters were reduced to impotence, and the purely idealistic proposition that the high seas were open equally to all nations became an established and accepted fact.

Freedom of the seas had been won. America had wrenched herself completely loose from British domination, but the nation was still young, comparatively poor, and not yet a great power. To win her share of the world's carrying trade under the new conditions called for something new, something startling. In this the Port of New York, having already contributed her considerable share to the winning of the war, was about to lead the way.

CHAPTER VII

River Steamers and Ocean Packets—1817-45

INLAND WATERWAYS & TRANSATLANTIC TIMETABLES

IN THE EARLY DAYS of the nineteenth century New York's European trade was greatly impeded by the restrictions attendant upon the Napoleonic Wars and by the War of 1812. During the same period settlers in ever-increasing numbers were passing over the Appalachians to Ohio, Michigan, and Illinois. As a result, the chief commercial development for the first two decades of the century was toward the interior of the country. Since overland traffic was slow and arduous, internal waterways became the leading trade routes. Commerce multiplied enormously on river, sound, and bay; canals were planned that would make the Great Lakes and Lake Champlain readily accessible to the Port of New York.

Sail versus Steam

The growth of inland navigation was greatly stimulated by the advent of the steamboat. Previously Connecticut farmers and merchants had sent their wares to New York via Long Island Sound in sailing skiffs and shallops. Such commerce was bound to be irregular; a vessel might lie becalmed for days while its cargo rotted and the consignee waited. By sail the voyage from New York to Albany required from three to nine days.

The recognized American pioneer in applying steam power to navigation was John Fitch (1743-98). At the age of eleven, according to his diary, he was "nearly crazy with learning." At thirteen he was the "best geographer that Connecticut could produce." In early manhood he came under the influence of Henry Voight, a "mechanical genius" who made watches and clocks.

Fitch's chief contribution to steam navigation was his invention of the revolving chain and paddle wheels. In 1787 Fitch and Voight launched a steam skiff on the Delaware, which, after one failure, worked—upstream!—though Fitch admitted that it made a "very disagreeable noise." In high elation Fitch wrote to Benjamin Franklin, to Congress, and to several state legislatures in an effort to obtain financial backing. No one seemed interested. But in 1796 Chancellor Robert R. Livingston and several of his friends crossed the Collect Pond in lower Manhattan Island in a steamboat built by Fitch. Fitch died two years later, discouraged by lack of recognition.

It was not until 1807 that Robert Fulton's *Clermont*, based on Fitch's ideas, moved slowly but triumphantly up the Hudson, belching smoke and sparks like "the devil going up the river in a sawmill." With Fulton on board was the chancellor who had acquired Fitch's patents. The travel time from New York to Albany had been reduced to thirty-two hours. Within a few years this record was cut in half. In 1808, when the *Clermont* was rebuilt and lengthened, the paddle wheels were inclosed in great clumsy boxes to protect the mechanism.

By 1809 a steam route to Philadelphia was opened; up the Raritan River from New York Bay to New Brunswick, eighteen miles by overland stage to Trenton, and down the Delaware by steam for the remainder of the journey.

Owners of sailing packets soon realized that steam was a potential menace to their livelihood. They rammed and battered the early steamboats, whenever opportunity offer-ed, to such an extent that special legislation was passed in Albany to protect steamers from attack by sailing vessels.

On Long Island Sound the sailing vessels put up a stronger fight. They offered to carry passengers for little or no fees if they did not beat the time of the steamships on the same run. The *Firefly*, which in 1817 opened a steam service between Newport and Providence, often sailed without a single passenger and within four months was driven from the run.

Yet the chief obstacle to the development of steam navigation was not the competition of sail but the Fulton-Livingston monopoly, which prevented outsiders from operating the steam vessels they optimistically called *Hope* and *Perseverance*, Fulton cried that "pirates" were out to destroy his livelihood, and in the following year the two "pirate" ships were destroyed by court order.

At Fulton's death in 1815 only eight steamboats were operating on the Hudson. Most of the space on these craft was taken up by machinery. Passenger accommodations were very limited, and there was almost no room for freight. The monopoly's only other contribution to river navigation was a steam ferry between Manhattan and Jersey City, competing with the venerable Hoboken ferry propelled by horses harnessed to drive shafts.

In 1815 the Fulton-Livingston monopoly started the *Fulton* on the Sound run to New Haven, and soon other steamers were added to the line. But in 1822 Connecticut shipowners caused the legislature at Hartford to pass a law denying the use of Connecticut ports to New York shipping as long as the monopoly should remain in force. Thereupon Providence, Rhode Island, was chosen as the terminus of the Sound run, despite the headshaking of skeptics who maintained that a steamer could never withstand the heavy seas off Point Judith. On June 6, 1822, Captain Elihu Bunker brought the *Connecticut* into Providence without mishap. From then until 1837 this remained the favored route for travelers, and freight between Providence and Boston was transported overland.

Commodore, Comedy, and Monopoly

The *Mouse of the Mountain* was the first steamboat to challenge the Fulton-Livingston monopoly successfully on its home ground. Owner of the vessel was Thomas Gibbons, a Southerner who maintained a summer home at Elizabeth, New Jersey, outside the jurisdiction of the New York courts. Business was so good that a second steamboat, the *Bellona*, was built and put in operation in 1818. Cornelius Vanderbilt, who had earned the unofficial title of Commodore by his operation of a ferry between Staten Island and the Battery during the War of 1812, was the *Bellona's* captain on its run between New York and Elizabeth. The *Bellona* was also run up the Raritan from Elizabeth.

The New York authorities hesitated to seize the *Bellona*, for fear that the New Jersey authorities would retaliate by attaching a monopoly steamboat on the west bank of the river. They decided instead to arrest the captain and spent two months vainly searching for him. Vanderbilt had constructed a secret panel in the wall of the steamboat's cabin and hid behind it whenever the vessel docked in New York.

One Sunday Vanderbilt was arrested while lounging about the Battery and haled before Chancellor Kent, but he was able to prove that for this particular Sunday he had hired his services to D. D. Tompkins, who held a monopoly license. The chancellor was forced to release the prisoner.

Gibbons then persuaded the New Jersey legislature to pass a law to the effect that any New York officer arresting a citizen of New Jersey for monopoly violation was liable to arrest on crossing the state line. Vanderbilt, always eager for a prank, kidnaped a New York deputy and threatened to transport him to New Jersey.

The controversy progressed from mere horseplay to the legislative stage. Gibbons prevailed on the New Jersey legislature to invoke the right to regulate steam navigation on the west side of the lower Hudson. This brought the issue into the sphere of interstate commerce and therefore under the jurisdiction of the United States Supreme Court, which heard the case in 1824. Daniel Webster and Attorney General William Wirt argued the case for Gibbons, and Chief Justice Marshall read a decision ruling navigation monopolies in foreign or interstate commerce forever void. After the historic decision Vanderbilt secured control of the *Bellona* and continued for a time to run his vessel up the Raritan from New York and Elizabeth, while his wife added to the family income by operating the Bellona Tavern at the New Brunswick terminus.

A few weeks after Chief Justice Marshall's decision the *Olive Branch* began to compete with the monopoly line on the Hudson. Aaron Ogden, who had inherited the Fulton-Livingston scepter, obtained an injunction on the ground that the ship was not engaged in interstate commerce, whereupon its owners established their terminus at Jersey City. In 1825 the New York Court of Errors ended the monopoly in state waters.

Life on the Hudson

Travel on the Hudson in the monopoly era has been described as "pleasant and socially charming." The fare between Albany and New York never fell below seven dollars. The Van Rensselaers, Roosevelts, Ten Eycks, Brevoorts, and other Hudson River families had private docks on their estates, where the boats stopped when signaled.

With the close of the monopoly era the scene rapidly changed. New lines sprang up as fast as boats could be built. Vanderbilt's People's Line was followed by Daniel Drew's Citizens' Line, the Union Line, the North River Line, and many others. In the course of various rate wars the fare fell to three dollars, to one dollar, and occasionally to ten cents or nothing. The better-financed lines were able to survive these wars, compensating to some extent for the low fares by charging high prices for staterooms and meals. But one by one the smaller companies were driven from the river. Despite rate wars, Vanderbilt's company was able to make as much as thirty thousand dollars a year.

Only a few years after the end of the monopoly New York's Mayor Philip Hone wrote: "Our boat had three or four hundred passengers and such a set of ragtag and bobtail I never saw on board a North River steamboat." Ministers denounced the ships as places of assembly for "women of low and venal character" and inveighed against the Sunday excursions up the Hudson which emptied their churches.

By 1840 more than one hundred boats were plying the river. At the main terminals "runners" touted the advantages of the various competing vessels. Fanny Kemble, the British actress, was impressed by their eloquence. "Speechifying," she wrote, "is a favorite species of exhibition with the men here. The gift of gab appears to me to be more widely disseminated amongst American men than any other people in the world."

The lines sought to excel in comfort and elegance. Decorations and furnishings became progressively more elaborate. In that period crystal chandeliers, rococo ceilings, and Corinthian columns were the symbols of luxury. Orchestras were provided for the passengers' entertainment. Only the sleeping quarters were generally out of keeping with the sumptuousness of these floating palaces. Captain Marryat, an English traveler, described the whimsical sight of five hundred people sleeping in five long rows of triple-tier beds, "lying in every state of posture and exhibiting every state and degree of repose." "As for privacy," wrote Fanny Kemble in this connection, "at any time or under any circumstances, 'tis a thing that enters not into the imagination of America."

Most of the lines sought to attract passengers by speed, and for more than two decades steamship races were a conspicuous feature of river competition. In 1826 the *Olive Branch* raced with the *Chancellor Livingston*. For a space the two vessels chugged along side by side; then the captain of the *Olive Branch*, fired with the old anti-monopoly fervor, decided to ram the *Chancellor Livingston*. "Damn her," he cried, "put your helm aport and we're plump into the ladies' cabin." The helmsman, his not to reason why, obeyed. A terrible crash ensued. But when the wreckage was examined it became clear that the *Olive Branch* had suffered greater damage than her rival.

Speed records became an obsession with shipowners. Engineers tied down safety valves and raised steam pressures to three times the safe mark. In the forties anthracite coal replaced wood as fuel, and still greater steam pressures became possible. Boiler explosions occurred aboard the *Aetna* and the *General Jackson* with appalling loss of life. In 1845 the *Swallow*, while racing with the *Express* and the *Rochester*, ran into an island in the river, with a resulting loss of twelve lives. "The traveler walks and sits and sleeps," wrote a thoughtful editor, "in contact with a volcano that in an instant may blow him to atoms." Disasters were frequent, but it was not until 1852 that an accident of major proportions led to legislative action intended to curb steamboat racing.

Some lines introduced "safety barges" towed at a distance behind the steamer. But Americans preferred speed to safety; the barges were not a success.

Repair Shops, Towboats, and Shipping News

In the early steamboat days there were no repair shops. In 1818 the *Paragon's* engine broke down near Albany, and ship and cargo were obliged to wait while the engine was sent overland to Canaan, Connecticut, for repairs. Two years later the *Olive Branch* broke the strap of her air pump off Perth Amboy. The captain was obliged to "travel three or four miles in search of a blacksmith."

New York, however, soon developed its own mechanics and machine builders, then known as "artists" or "machinerists." A leader among these was James P. Allaire, who established a brass foundry in 1815. Shortly after Fulton's death Allaire took over the Fulton-Livingston yards at Jersey City but soon transferred them to Corlear's Hook on Manhattan. By 1829 he had two hundred "machinerists" in his employ. A sign in the plant read: "Any person that brings or drinks spirituous liquors on my premises will be discharged without any pay for the week."

For some time towing remained a part-time job for harbor steamers and ferries. The first instance of those recorded took place in 1818, when the bay steamer *Nautilus* "towed the ship *Corsair* from one mile below the Narrows to the Quarantine Dock in three quarters of an hour." Brooklyn commuters were responsible for the passage of a law forbidding ferryboats to leave their runs to engage in towing. It was not until 1832 that the *Hercules* was constructed expressly for this purpose. After the opening of the Erie Canal strings of barges were towed on the Hudson between New York and Troy. Formerly this operation had been conducted by steamers.

The first shipping news association in the Port of New York was organized in the late 1820s, when it occurred to the editors of the *Courier* and *Journal of Commerce* that merchants, bankers, and the general public would be attracted to their papers by early reports of news and travelers from foreign parts.

The *Courier* and the *Journal of Commerce* first shared in the upkeep of a rowboat for this purpose at a cost of about twenty-five hundred dollars a year. Later the *Courier* acquired the *Eclipse*, a schooner able to equal the speed of any New York pilot boat. In 1828 the *Journal of Commerce* operated a schooner of its own, named for the publication.

This vessel often sailed out a hundred miles from shore to obtain the latest foreign papers and tidings. These were rushed to Fort Lafayette and delivered to a waiting horseman, who carried them overland to the paper's offices. Before long the *Journal of Commerce* acquired a second schooner, the *Evening Edition*.

By 1837 there were three associations engaged in gathering shipping news. One served the *Journal of Commerce* and the *Courier* and *Enquirer*, another the *Mercantile Advertiser* and the *Gazette*, while the third served the *Commercial Advertiser*, *Evening Star*, and *American*. In 1840 the *Herald* won leadership in the field with its speedy *Fanny Elssler*.

The Harbor News Association was reorganized in 1849 when a telegraph service was established between New York and Sandy Hook.

News was sent from the ships to the Hook by carrier pigeon, though the various pickup boats continued to bring in the foreign papers and reports too bulky for the birds.

Clinton's Big Ditch

There is some disagreement among historians as to who first put forward the idea of the Erie Canal. In any case it is certain that the project was much discussed by visionaries and men of affairs in the last quarter of the eighteenth century. In 1773 Christopher Colles, an Irish-American, gave a series of lectures in New York on the possibilities of such a canal. Gouverneur Morris is said to have brought the matter up in 1777. Thomas Jefferson opposed the plan on the ground that his near-by Potomac provided a more suitable route to the West. George Washington, however, favored the scheme, despite his personal interest in the projected Chesapeake and Ohio Canal.

From 1779 to 1784 Elkanah Watson made a careful study of the canals of France, Holland, and England and, in 1791, submitted a report to General Schuyler. But it was not until 1810 that the canal enthusiasts were joined by De Witt Clinton, then Mayor of New York City, who was to carry the project through to its completion while Governor of New York State.

By this time the Midwestern pioneers, after the preliminary hardships of homesteading, were beginning to call for the machinery and luxury articles of Europe and the Eastern seaboard. These could be obtained only by exchanging the products of the settlers' own industry. The first exports consisted of furs, and pot, or pearl, ashes. Soon it was found that the level land of the new territories grew better wheat than could be obtained from the soil of the East. Cattle and hay were later articles of export.

These products were all too bulky to be transported profitably by land. The cost of shipping wheat from Buffalo to Albany was one hundred dollars a ton. It was routed up the Oswego River in flat barges from Lake Ontario to the vicinity of Rome by way of Lake Oneida and Oneida Creek. From this point a portage of seventeen miles led to Utica; thence the Mohawk River provided easy sailing to Schenectady except for a one-mile portage around Little Falls. Here the travelers had to pay the Dutch farmers of the region to transport them and their freight. Sometimes the whole boat was mounted on a great broad-wheeled cart.

The voyage from Oswego to New York required at least three weeks. By the close of the War of 1812 the farmers around the Great Lakes were paying three million dollars annually in freight charges on their wheat alone. Transportation from the Lakes to Montreal cost less than a third of the charge to New York. The Canadian city threatened to replace New York as the gateway to the West. The crying need was for a waterway connecting the Hudson River with the Great Lakes.

With uncommon foresight De Witt Clinton staked his political career on the canal. When the legislature at Albany killed the canal project by talk of the high taxation it would involve, he appealed directly to the "people"—that is to say, the merchants of South Street. He convinced them that only the canal could keep New York on the map as a port. More than one hundred thousand New Yorkers signed a petition for the canal. Mass meetings of merchants and shopkeepers were held throughout the state. It was on this issue that in 1816 Clinton was elected Governor of New York. On April 15, 1817, the authorizing act for the Erie and the Champlain canals was passed by the legislature, and on July 4 of the same year the first shovelful of earth was turned near Rome. Thus began eight years of prodigious labor. Two thousand men cut through marshes and forests, across hills and rivers, for a distance of three hundred and sixty-two miles. There were no trained engineers to direct the work, so the canal had to develop its own engineers. One of these was Canvass White, who had made a detailed study of English canals. One of the greatest difficulties encountered in the Erie construction was the high cost of cement, which had to be imported from England. Some suggested building the locks of wood, but this material was judged too perishable. It was decided to use great stone blocks, with cement only in the seams. Fortunately White discovered near Chittenango, traversed by the canal route, a deposit of stone from which the best hydraulic cement could be made. At Lockport and Little Falls locks were blasted out of solid rock with black powder. Feeders were constructed to supply the higher levels of the canal with water.

In the swamps of Montezuma, near Syracuse, half the workmen were stricken with ague, malaria, or typhus. Transportation of materials was slow and difficult. Some of the lock machinery had to be brought from Europe. And yet, as a journalist of the day reported, it was "the longest canal in the world, built in the least time, with the least experience, for the least money, and to the greatest public benefit." On its completion the "ditch" was four feet deep, forty feet wide at the surface, and twenty-eight at the bottom. Eighty-two locks overcame a difference of five hundred and seventy-one feet between the level of the Hudson at Troy and that of Lake Erie. The cost of the undertaking was approximately eight million dollars. The canal was opened to traffic on October 26, 1825.

When the Governor's barge entered the canal at Buffalo, a signal cannon was fired. Down the waterway, just within earshot, a second cannon relayed the report, and so from cannon to cannon the news was carried to Troy and down the Hudson, reaching New York one hour and twenty minutes later. Bells rang; whistles blew; the whole state went wild with excitement. When Governor Clinton arrived he poured a keg of Lake Erie water into New York Harbor.

Canal-Borne Commerce

An endless procession of flatboats began to pass through the canal, bringing wheat, cattle, spirits, lumber, and passengers to the sea. A great part of this merchandise was diverted from the Mississippi and St. Lawrence routes. The challenge of Montreal and New Orleans to the hegemony of New York was ended for all time.

Freight rates from Buffalo to New York fell from one hundred dollars to six dollars a ton. New York real-estate values skyrocketed. The western part of the state saw the mushroom growth of great commercial centers. Buffalo, a little village which had been left with but one house standing after a fire in 1814, grew like magic until in 1837 it attained a population of 25,000. In the first year an average of forty-two boats a day passed through the canal at Utica. Eastbound cargoes totaled 185,000 tons, including 221,000 pounds of flour, 562,000 bushels of wheat, 435,000 gallons of domestic spirits, and 32,000,000 board feet of lumber. Westbound cargoes amounted to only 35,000 tons of foreign and manufactured goods. Served by the canal, Rochester, Rome, Schenectady, and Troy became thriving cities. The journey from Buffalo to New York was reduced from three weeks to ten days. With this short and easy road to market, the farmers of western New York prospered. In 1836 a gross tonnage of 420,000 reached tidewater by way of the canal, 87 per cent originating within the borders of New York State.

On the return journey the barges brought machines, manufactured goods, and men. Families of immigrants, with their cooking utensils and household goods, were transported to the western part of the state or to the edge of the great Western plains, whence they continued by covered wagon. All through the 1830s and 1840s this human stream continued; sometimes as many as two thousand passengers a week traversed the canal. Men and women from many lands rubbed elbows on the slow-moving barges, singing songs to pass the weary hours. One of these Erie Canal chanteys ran:

Drop a tear for big-foot Sal
The best damn cook on the Erie Canal
She aimed to heaven but she went to hell—
Fifteen years on the Erie Canal.
The missioner said she died in sin;
Hennery said it was too much gin;
There warn't no bar where she hadn't been
From Albany to Buffalo.

The canal was a major influence in the growth of Cleveland, Chicago, and the cities of Michigan, furnishing them first with men and then with goods. In 1833 a merchant in Middleburg, O., advertised that he had received a shipment of merchandise straight from New York via the canal for $1.371/2 a hundred-weight. By means of an overland haul to the headwaters of the Ohio, the Erie Canal served regions as far distant as Arkansas Territory. Some persons even traveled to New Orleans by the overland route.

The revenue in tolls surpassed all expectation. In 1825 receipts were $521,000, or more than 6 per cent of the total investment. By 1830 they had passed the one-million-dollar mark.

Bargemen and Barleycorn

Soon the "canawl" developed a colorful life of its own. Many of the workers, Irish for the most part, who had built the ditch stayed on to tend locks and man towropes. Some who were able to resist the canal's multifarious temptations and save a little money invested in barges of their own. The barge crew consisted at most of the owner-captain, a cook, two drivers, and two steersmen. The drivers walked the entire length of the canal, along the towpaths, waving long snake whips over the flanks of their mules. Their pay up to the period of the Civil War was ten dollars or twelve dollars a month, depending upon whether they were boys or grown men. Nearly ten thousand boys were employed on the canal as drivers in its boom days. Steersmen received twenty dollars a month.

The canalmen were a lusty, brawling, hard-drinking, and hard-cursing lot. Every major lock was graced with wide-open taverns. When the barge tied up for the night, even the boys repaired to the bar, where blackstrap, a mixture of rum and molasses, could be had for three cents a drink. Such a reputation for debauchery did the canal people build up that one missionary felt called upon to write: "Many seem to think, and do actually assert, that religion and boating are incompatible—that a boatman cannot be a consistent Christian. The assertion, of course, has no foundation in fact." Yet M. Eaton, the first missionary to attempt to bring the canal folk to God, sometimes found life hard. "Occasionally," he wrote in 1845, "I come across a set of blacklegs who are traveling for no other purpose than to steal or gamble, and I will relate an instance of the kind . . . Just before we started six new passengers came on board, whose appearance and actions I did not much like. I saw by their appearance they were a set of vile fellows. ... As I returned over the deck, I remarked to those ruffians that we were going to have prayer in the bow cabin, and I should be pleased to have them go in. One of them said: 'Pray and be d—d. I shan't go to hear you.' I made no reply, went in and commenced talking, but they made such a noise overhead that it was impossible to be heard." The divine also complained that the canal was "infested with Universalists and Roman Catholics, a sorry state of affairs."

There was lively competition among the bargemen. Speeding along at the inordinate rate of four miles an hour, they turned the placid towns into bedlams with their whistles. When two barges raced to be first at a lock, a brawl between the rival crews nearly always occurred at the gate. Drivers were picked as much for their fighting prowess as for their driving ability. It was as an Erie bargeman that James A. Garfield, at the age of sixteen, began the long career which was to end at the White House.

The dingy square-bowed canalboats atoned for their ugliness by the beauty of their names. *Humility, Ado, Cleopatra,* and *Young Lion of the West* were among the proudest. To the clumsy freight barges soon were added the gay passenger packets. These were ornate houseboats, fully equipped with ladies' cabins, bars, cooks' galleys, and saloons which served at night as men's dormitories. The windows usually were adorned with bright red curtains and green shutters. The cabin roof, known as the promenade deck, offered a fine vantage point for viewing the scenery. "The women passengers in fair weather," wrote Henry Collins Brown, "carried little sunshades, wore poke bonnets and daintily colored cotton frocks, distended like a balloon with hoop skirts." Fanny Kemble spoke well of the canal journey, but Mrs. Trollope wrote: "I can hardly imagine any motive of convenience powerful enough to induce me again to imprison myself on a canalboat under ordinary circumstances." Charles Dickens likened the night sounds on the canal to "a million of fairy teams with bells," but complained that it was "impossible for a man to walk around the cabin without making bald places on his head by scraping it on the roof."

Ocean Commerce

Soon after the War of 1812 New York's seagoing trade began to boom, though at first the balance was heavily on the import side. The country's westward growth created an increasing demand for manufactured goods our own infant industries were powerless to provide. At the same time the British pursued a policy of deliberate dumping, for the very purpose of stifling the new American industries. Henry Brougham, a British merchant and member of Parliament, outlined this policy in Parliament thus: "It is worth while to incur a loss upon the first exportations in order, by a glut, to stifle in the cradle those rising manufactures in the United States which the war has forced into existence contrary to the natural course of things."

Yet the European market for American foodstuffs and raw materials was reviving. If our export trade had languished it was largely because of the chaotic conditions prevailing in the shipping industry. Ships sailed only when they were good and ready—that is, when they had a full cargo. Cargoes moved only when a ship happened to be available. Under such conditions costs mounted and it was impossible to fulfill contracts or guarantee deliveries.

Cotton from New Orleans, tea and silks from China, barrels of flour and apples from the Hudson Valley were piled high on dock or quayside or in warehouses along South Street. Impatient passengers, who could not well be piled on top of them, cooled their heels and wet their palates in waterfront taverns. Merchants fumed; there was much writing of letters, but ships could not be hurried. It was considered bad business to set out without a full hold; moreover, a ship was rarely dispatched to Liverpool, Havana, or other foreign ports without assurance that a cargo would be available for the return voyage. The propitious combination of cargo, passengers, and ship all destined for the same place at the same time was not easy to attain.

"Regular Traders" and "Coffin Brigs"

"Regular traders" had plied the seas since 1700, when the *Britannia* was launched for the London trade, but, despite their designations, these vessels did not operate on regular schedules. They were as likely as not to turn off from their direct route to pick up or discharge cargo. Traders they were, but scarcely regular. The merchants who used them could guarantee neither shipment nor delivery.

Before 1817 the nearest approach to scheduled sailings was achieved by the packet brigs of the British government mail service, operating between Falmouth and New York on what approximated a monthly schedule. These little ships had a high record of achievement in the colonial service but carried few passengers and no cargo other than mail. In their design, stability had been sacrificed to speed; as a result they were difficult to handle and dangerous. Losses at sea were so frequent that the vessels were nicknamed "coffin brigs," and high bonuses were required to induce seamen to sail in them. The chroniclers do not state how the few passengers were persuaded to take the chance.

The Black Ball Line

The remedy for this state of affairs rested in the establishment of a line providing regular sailings between New York and foreign ports. On October 24, 1817, five New York shipowners published the following statement in the *Commercial Advertiser*: "In order to furnish frequent and regular conveyance of GOODS AND PASSENGERS the subscribers have undertaken to establish a line of vessels between NEW YORK and LIVERPOOL, to sail from each place on a certain day in every month of the year."

The advertisement was signed by Isaac Wright and Son and Francis Thompson. Later the names of Benjamin Marshall and Jeremiah Thompson were added. Four vessels were chosen for the venture; one was to sail from New York on the fifth, and one from Liverpool on the first of every month.

On the morning of January 5, 1818, the packet *James Monroe* lay at her berth alongside Pier 23 on South Street, her three lofty masts towering above the warehouses, ship chandlers' shops, and mercantile establishments across the street. The first American packet liner was about to set sail for Liverpool on schedule, whether she had a full complement of passengers and freight or not. From her main truck fluttered a new house flag, a red pennon with a black ball in the center. Another black ball, much larger, was sewn on her fore-topsail, high up where it would be visible even when the sail was partly furled. This symbol was later to give the line its name.

The term "packet," later used to designate the famous "line" ships, had from the first been loosely applied and has caused much confusion among students. Strictly speaking, there is no such thing as a packet design; before 1817 "packet" meant any vessel, whether brig, sloop, or square-rigger, that functioned as a carrier of freight. The Black Ball Line called its ships packets to distinguish them from the irregular "regular traders." The name clung to scheduled vessels through the evolution of naval architecture from the bulbous prow and broad beam of the Black Ballers to the sharper-bowed, more graceful ships of the clipper era.

Sailing on Schedule

The sailing of the *James Monroe* occasioned much headshaking among the coffeehouse skeptics, and plentiful were the predictions of failure. Only eight passengers ventured aboard, though there were accommodations for twenty-eight. The cargo, well below the ship's capacity, consisted of seventy-one cotton bales, eight hundred and sixty barrels of flour, two hundred barrels of apples, fourteen bales of wool, and small quantities of cranberries and turpentine.

"That wily old Quaker," Jeremiah Thompson, is generally believed to have originated the idea of regular sailings. Prior to 1818 he had established himself as an international shipper, exporting more cotton to England and importing more British cloth than any other New York merchant. He maintained agents in Boston, Philadelphia, and other shipping centers and owned ships in both the Atlantic and the coastwise trades.

The first packet line was largely a family affair. Isaac Wright and Son, with countinghouses on South Street, was an important shipping firm interested in English imports. Isaac Wright, who was Francis Thompson's father-in-law, was also president of the City Bank. In 1807 Wright and Thompson bought the new *Pacific*, three hundred and eighty-four tons, and placed her in the New York-Liverpool run. Jeremiah Thompson and his partner, Benjamin Marshall, soon bought an interest in the *Pacific*, and the five became partners. In 1816 they acquired the *Amity*. The *James Monroe* and the *Courier* were added the following year.

The new line did not immediately prosper. Turpentine, cotton, and naval stores, shipped coastwise from the South to New York, were loaded for Liverpool. Return cargoes included salt, coal, and cloth. These items were shipped in half cargoes in the face of certain loss. Passengers, accustomed to the old procedure of waiting for a ship and bargaining with a chance skipper for passage, were amazingly slow to change their habits. But the partners persevered. Merchants and travelers were forced to recognize the advantages of the line principle, and by 1820 the success of the venture was assured. Quality freight, hitherto insured only at exorbitant rates, soon became virtually a Black Ball monopoly. Rates on the Black Ball Line rose, and the owners found that they could choose their cargo and passengers. Jeremiah Thompson is said to have run his line with Quaker righteousness. He paid good wages; food and working conditions were superior for the times, and he picked his crews carefully from cabin boy to captain. As a result the line became a standard of excellence in every respect. Among masters and seamen, Black Ballers stood at the top of their vocation.

In waterfront grogshops the world over seafaring men talked of the Black Ball Line and boasted of their service in this or that liner. It was easy to recognize a Black Ball cabin boy along South Street by the smugness of his strut. To be a Black Ball captain was the highest ambition of every seaman who chanted with his shipmates:

> " 'Twas on a Black Baller that I first served my time
> Ho Ho, blow the man down!
> And in that Black Baller I wasted my prime
> Oh, give me some time to blow the man down!"

Barnyards Afloat

The ships, though essentially no different from any of the individually owned "regular traders," were new and excellently equipped. A. H. Clark, in his *Clipper Ship Era,* writes: "These ships were all flush deck, with a caboose or galley and the housed-over long-boat between the fore- and main-masts. The long-boat, which was, of course, securely lashed, carried the live stock,—pens for sheep and pigs in the bottom, ducks and geese on a deck laid across the gunwales, and on top of all, hens and chickens. The cow-house was lashed over the main hatch, and there were also other small hatch-houses and a companion aft leading to the comfortable, well-appointed cabins . . . The steerage passengers lived in the between-decks amidships, and the crew's forecastle was in the fore-peak. . . "* Freshly killed ducks, geese, and chickens were available for first-class passengers, while fresh milk became a feature of the daily fare.

---

* From *The Clipper Ship Era* by Arthur H. Clark.

Danger and Disaster

The Black Ballers were broad of beam and blunt of bow; sturdy sailers built for cargo and safety rather than for speed. They had fine straight lines and were heavily sparred to carry a vast spread of canvas. By crowding on sail they could increase their speed considerably, but it was dangerous going. Many a packet was lost in a storm, before her great array of sails could be furled.

One of the early packet disasters that horrified two continents was the sinking of the Black Ball Liner *Albion*, off the Irish coast, near Kinsale, in 1822. The *Albion* was a typical liner of the period. She had been built just before poop cabins came into style, and her twenty-three cabin and six steerage passengers were housed between decks. The chief cargo was cotton. She was under command of Captain John Williams, who had been master of the *Pacific*.

The vessel left New York on schedule and nearly completed the Atlantic crossing in the excellent time of eighteen days. But approaching Ireland, she encountered a terrific gale. Captain Williams furled sail and did his best to heave to, but the storm increased in fury, and all his efforts to keep away from the rocky coast were in vain. Virtually under bare sticks, her decks swept clean by the raging seas, the *Albion* could only run before the storm. The captain summoned all the passengers on deck and told them the ship could not be saved.

The *Albion* swept on and was battered to pieces on the rocks. Captain Williams went down with his ship. All but two of the passengers were lost; these two men, with the mate and five members of the crew, clung to projecting rocks until a rescue party reached them.

Yet, despite danger and disaster, the packets kept to their schedules with remarkable accuracy. The speed with which their hardy masters and mates drove their ships over the Atlantic is still the marvel of seafaring men. Jeremiah Thompson's packets established an average time schedule of twenty-two days from New York to Liverpool and forty days for the more difficult return voyage. This schedule seldom was departed from by more than a day or two.

Success Brings Competition

Such was the success of the Black Ball Line that prospective passengers were willing to pay bonuses in addition to the $175 passage money. Under such circumstances Thompson and his associates could not long enjoy their monopoly. On January 3, 1822, the firm of Byrnes, Trimble and Company, engaged in the flour trade, announced their inauguration of a new line, the Red Star, with monthly sailing of four ships —*Panther, Meteor, Hercules,* and *Manhattan*—all new packets of four-hundred-ton burden and fitted with the latest luxuries. Thompson met this challenge by adding four more ships to his fleet. A Black Baller now sailed every two weeks between New York and Liverpool.

The Red Star Line was followed by the Swallowtail Line, founded by Thaddeus Phelps and Company. One of the Swallowtail's ships was the famous packet *Leeds*, reputedly never defeated in a transatlantic race. The short-lived Havre Packets were inaugurated in the same year by Francis Depau, a merchant interested in the wine and luxury-goods trade.

Cargoes piled up faster than the humming shipyards of the East River could build hulls to carry them. In 1823 another line was established, this time to trade directly with London. John Griswold was its founder, and the line's insignia, a black X, flew from the trucks of four new ships, the *Hudson, Sovereign, Cambria*, and *President*. To command the Hudson, Griswold chose E. E. Morgan, who had made a name for himself with the Black Ball Line.

Captain Morgan was typical of the bearded giants who commanded the early packets. Reared in the backwoods of Connecticut, he had little formal education; yet at the height of his career he became a social lion, host to Queen Victoria, and the friend of such distinguished authors as Thackeray and Dickens.

Other great skippers were Samuel Samuels, John Collins, Asa Eldridge, and Robert H. Waterman. Some of New York's foremost citizens began their careers as officers or masters of packets.

Samuels has been called the greatest of all packet commanders. He captained the fourteen-hundred-ton sailing palace *Dreadnaught*, known to seamen as the "wild boat of the Atlantic," and was still in his heyday when steamers entered the transatlantic competition. Adventurer, diplomat, and businessman all in one, he recorded his life and adventures in a book of memoirs entitled *From the Forecastle to the Cabin.* "I never rejected a crew, or a part of one, on account of their bad character," he remarks. "I generally found among these men the toughest and best sailors. I frequently had a number of the 'Bloody Forties,' as they styled themselves, among the crew. These rascals could never be brought to subjection by moral suasion."

The old seadog goes on to describe his own sort of suasion, in which pistol, cutlass, and belaying pin mainly figured. There were no spoiled children in his crew.

The Cotton Triangle

An important factor contributing to the success of the regular lines was the development in the 1820s of the "cotton triangle," which insured a regular volume of exports. Enterprising New York merchants had observed that the Southern cotton planters had little taste for the commercial end of their business. New York agents invaded the cotton centers and garnered a large share of the trade for New York shippers, in spite of the fact that producers would have found it more economical to ship their cotton directly to England from Charleston, Savannah, or New Orleans. Thus Southern cotton was shipped to New York, loaded for England, the proceeds returned in part to the planters—completing the triangle.

The opening of the Erie Canal in 1825 gave additional impetus to New York shipping. In that year New York handled thirty-five per cent of the nation's export trade. The canal alone, with its Western grain and farm produce, provided an increase of six million dollars in the city's gross business. Five hundred new mercantile establishments opened their doors in the first few months of 1825, and the April *Gazette* carried 1115 new advertisements. Twelve banks and thirteen marine insurance

Landing of General Lafayette At Castle Garden, New York, 16th August 1824

Brooklyn Navy Yard, view from New York, 1831,
from an original engraving, published in the Fay-Peabody views.

companies, representing an aggregate investment of twenty-three million dollars, were established the same year.

The demand for more and larger ships became so great that every yard in the city was flooded with more orders than it could fill. The overflow passed to Boston, Philadelphia, New Bedford, and Gloucester. Not until the depression of 1833-34 was there a temporary lull.

Races and Ruins

In the summer of 1835 a historic race was held between a dozen packets in the Liverpool-New York trade. Official entrants were Black Ball's *Columbus*, Red Star's *Sheffield*, and Blue Swallowtail's *George Washington*, owned by Preserved Fish.* Added starters were the "regular traders" *Star, Congress,* and *Josephine*. After seventeen days of hard sailing the *George Washington* drove up the Mersey and anchored off the great stone docks of Liverpool, a winner by several hours. The *Sheffield* came in next, but the generally favored *Columbus* did not appear until the following morning.

The winter of 1835-36 was one of the most severe in New York's history. On the night of December 16 a fire broke out in the vicinity of Wall Street. The volunteer fire department found the water supply nine tenths frozen and otherwise inadequate. A high wind spread the flames through the shipping, wholesale, dry-goods, and other commercial establishments until a detachment of marines from the Brooklyn Navy Yard checked it by blasting a firebreak. Nearly seven hundred buildings, including the Merchants Exchange, lay in ruins. The damage amounted to twenty million dollars, and numerous mercantile establishments and insurance companies were bankrupted. The harbor froze over so that one could walk between Manhattan, Brooklyn, and New Jersey. Shipping was at a standstill. The northern lights illumined the city on three successive nights. Superstitious citizens believed the end of the world to be at hand. Yet, despite the unpropitious season, in January E. K. Collins founded the new Dramatic Line, whose *Sheridan*

---

* Preserved Fish was the improbable name of the senior partner of packet company Fish, Grinnell Co., in operation from 1822 to 1880.

challenged the Black Baller *Columbus* to a race the following year. Each ship had a picked crew spurred on by promises of a big bonus. The *Columbus* achieved a new record by crossing in sixteen days under adverse weather conditions. This is the more remarkable in view of the cumbersome design of these ships. It was necessary to pile on every square foot of canvas to make twelve knots in a fair breeze. Unlike the later clippers that could keel over and cut through the waves, the packets had to shoulder the full force of the seas on their broad bows.

The Peak of the Packets

It was in the years 1835-40 that the packets reached their peak. Some of the ships built in this period exceeded one thousand tons. A shortage of seamen now began to develop. Formerly every boy had wanted to go to sea. Now, with the rise of industry and the opening of the interior, other occupations offered opportunity. English, Scottish, Irish, Scandinavian, and West Indian sailors filled the breach; only the officers were still preponderantly of Yankee stock. These were the days of "packet rats," often shanghaied from saloons and waterfront dives, the boys who made it tough for tough skippers. These were also the days of beans and salt horse, brutal mates, backbreaking toil, and unreported sea burials.

American products—chiefly wheat, cotton, and lumber—were finding their way into the markets of the world, and New York packets were carrying a major portion of this trade. "They served as the 'passenger train' on the great highway between the old world and the new," wrote the *Southern Literary Messenger* in 1839. "New York now carries on a trade in her foreign packets alone, of twenty-four cargoes a month, equal to seventeen thousand tons, and sufficient to give constant employment to one hundred and forty ships."

The flood of immigration following the opening of the Erie Canal offered a new source of revenue to the packet lines. The majority of immigrants entered the country through the Port of New York. From twelve thousand in 1825, their number increased to twenty-one thousand in 1827 and to seventy-five thousand in 1836. This trade constitutes a sordid page in the history of New York packets. Though an occasional skipper might treat the bewildered strangers with some degree of humanity, most of those engaged in the trade were utterly indifferent to their human cargo. Immigrants were crowded into ships. Disease and death haunted the forecastle and between decks of the packet ships; many a poor immigrant who had paid his passage in advance was buried at sea. In league with the unscrupulous packet owners were the emigration agencies set up in many foreign ports to lure the unsuspecting to the land of milk and honey. These agents issued misleading advertisements and handbills shamelessly exaggerating the prosperity prevalent in America. They persuaded many European communities to ship paupers and other public charges to America, where they became indentured servants and spent years in virtual slavery, working out their passage. It was not until 1847, when these conditions received official attention, that the Board of Commissioners of Immigration of New York was organized.

In 1840, at the height of the packet era, New York, with 414,000 tons, had more than one fifth of all the United States tonnage registered. Though only one third of this total was engaged in the packet service, this third carried the cream of the freight and passenger trade. New York's total tonnage was greater than that of any city in the world except London. Five to seven hundred sailing vessels and some fifty steamboats docked in the Port. The value of merchandise loaded and unloaded on South Street had risen from $84,000,000 in 1825 to $146,000,000 in 1836.

Port facilities for handling this increased trade were totally inadequate. Port organization had not kept pace with the growth of shipping. The wooden piers which then lined lower Manhattan for three miles were rotting away. Sand and silt sifted into the slips between docks, while graft and political patronage sifted in heavily behind them. Legislators and mayors made campaign speeches but did nothing to remedy the situation. In 1836 Mayor Lawrence pointed an admonishing finger at the "decaying timbers around our wharves and bulkheads that cause spread of disease." The shipowners declared that "our business is being curtailed and hampered by such neglect." In 1840 there were sixty-three wharves on the East River and fifty on the Hudson. Docking facilities were beginning to be developed in Brooklyn and Jersey City. It was not until the 1870s, however, that a serious attempt was made to keep these wharves in good condition.

The Challenge of Steam

Coincident with the rise of the packet lines, steam began to compete on the transatlantic crossing, though it was not until after 1850 that this competition began to be seriously felt.

The first steam vessel to cross the Atlantic was Captain Moses Rogers' *Savannah*, financed in Savannah but built in New York. She was full-rigged and had detachable paddle wheels which could be folded up and stowed away whenever it seemed advisable—which was most of the time. On May 24, 1819, she left Savannah for Liverpool, where she arrived on June 20 of the same year. However, she used steam for only eighty hours of the trip.

For the next two decades there were no ocean crossings by steam vessels out of New York, but progress was made in the coastal traffic. For several years in the 1820s David Dunham's *Robert Fulton* plied between New York and New Orleans. Between 1834 and 1838 five steamers were put on the Charleston run, which they accomplished in three days while the sailing packets averaged six. In 1837, however, the *Home*, owned by James P. Allaire, went to pieces off Cape Hatteras with a loss of one hundred lives, and soon afterward the steamer *Pulaski,* running between Baltimore and Savannah, suffered a boiler explosion. These two disasters discouraged coasting steamships for some years to come.

In the late thirties interest in transatlantic steam service was revived. In 1830 the Dutch steamer *Curacao* crossed between Holland and Curacao, and in 1833 the *Royal William* crossed from Nova Scotia to Liverpool. This showed that it could be done, but American backing of the project was thwarted by the panic of 1837.

English interests were more successful. On April 4, 1838, the seven-hundred-ton *Sirius,* a London-Cork packet chartered by Junius Smith, an American residing in England, left Cork for New York. Four days later she was followed by the 1340-ton *Great Western*, owned by the British Great Western Railway. The *Sirius* arrived off Sandy Hook on April 22 but required another twelve hours to reach the harbor, either because she ran aground or because her coal supply had been exhausted. The same day at three o'clock the swifter *Great Western* steamed into the harbor amid "a dense black cloud of smoke." The *Great Western* had made the crossing in fourteen and one half days. She continued to ply back and forth between New York and Liverpool until 1846, carrying passengers but little freight.

In 1839 Smith put the *British Queen* in operation and in 1840 the sumptuous two-thousand-ton *President*, offering monthly service in both directions. But in the following year the *President* disappeared without trace in a storm off Nantucket, and Smith soon gave up his venture.

Samuel Cunard, who was to offer the first serious competition to the sailing packets, ran his subsidized steam packets to Boston until 1846, later transferring his American terminus to New York.

CHAPTER VIII

Clippers—1846-60

'CARRYING SAIL NEW YORK FASHION'

ONE OF THE most spectacular acts in the drama of American shipping was staged in New York in the two decades preceding the Civil War. On the verge of being superseded, sailing vessels achieved new heights in speed and design, while American sailing masters established amazing new records. New York builders and designers created hulls that are copied in the finest of today's ocean liners. The sailing masters remained obstinate and defiant to the end, refusing to recognize the dirty, noisy steamship as a rival.

In 1843 Captain Nathaniel B. Palmer was on his way home from China in the *Paul Jones*, carrying as passenger William Low, brother of Abbot Low, whose firm owned Palmer's ship. The opium war between England and China had just opened up four additional treaty ports besides Canton to foreign commerce. Palmer was aware of the new possibilities for trade and was especially impressed with the opportunities presented by the opium trade between India and China. During the course of the voyage home he had several discussions with Low on the type of vessel best suited for the China trade. Palmer made a model of a ship embodying speed, rather than cargo space, as the primary requisite. When William Low reached New York he introduced Captain Palmer to his brother, and as a result Palmer was given authority to have a ship built for the firm of A. A. Low and Brother, which would follow the lines and general design of his model.

The First Clippers

By the end of that year Palmer's model was serving as a pattern in Brown and Bell's shipyard in New York. On May 3, 1844, the ship was launched and christened *Houqua* in honor of a Chinese merchant. Steam-driven river and Sound boats made way for her as she glided down the river. Steam winches helped to load her cargo. For five years the *Great Western* had been crossing regularly between New York and Liverpool, yet neither Palmer nor his associates heeded the challenge of steam.

Though the *Houqua* is not always classified as one, she had the chief characteristics of the clipper. The sharper lines of her hull gave her greater speed and less cargo space than a packet, and she carried a greater spread of sail than a packet of her tonnage. Her lines were not quite so sharp as those of the later clippers. She had man-of-war bulwarks, pierced on each side for eight guns.

The New York *Herald* greeted the launching of Palmer's model ship with characteristic exaggeration. "One of the prettiest and most rakish-looking packet ships ever built in the civilized world is now to be seen at the foot of Jones Lane on the East River—we never saw a vessel so perfect in all her parts as this new celestial packet. She is about six hundred tons in size—as sharp as a cutter—as symmetrical as a yacht —as rakish in her rig as a pirate—and as neat in her deck and cabin arrangements as a lady's boudoir. Her figurehead is a bust of Houqua, and her bow is as sharp as the toes of a pair of Chinese shoes."

In defiance of shipbuilding tradition the *Houqua* was launched on a Friday. Her hold was soon full, though other China-bound ships were riding high. Four weeks after the launching Captain Palmer cleared for Canton, where the *Houqua* dropped anchor eighty-four days later—far less than the average time then required.

Impressed by the speed of this voyage, New York merchants began to figure the additional profits to be made in the China trade through savings in transportation time. Backing was now available for the completion of a new ship designed by John Willis Griffiths. Modern authorities generally regard his ship, the *Rainbow*, as the first of the extreme clippers.

Son of a carpenter skilled in shipbuilding, Griffiths had attracted considerable attention among merchants in the late 1830s by his articles on ship design, though builders had ridiculed his idea of prefabricating the parts. Griffiths finally found a financial backer in W. H. Aspinwall of the firm of Howland and Aspinwall.

Griffiths had encountered plenty of trouble in building his dream ship. Aspinwall blew hot and cold on the proposition. Old seadogs shook their heads at the plans for a sharp concave bow and at the projected height of the masts. A ship so top heavy, they said, could never survive the winds and seas of the China course. Mechanics balked at Griffiths' insistence that everything should be cut to specifications; hitherto planking and other parts had been fitted into place as the building proceeded.

The Natchez

His troubles were ended abruptly by an event that threw the whole Port into a high pitch of excitement. On April 3, 1845, news raced from office to office that a ship was romping up the Narrows, having crossed from China in seventy-eight days, little more than half the average time. The vessel, which was wide and high-rigged, much like the *Houqua*, was the fourteen-year-old *Natchez*. That explained everything, for the *Natchez* was captained by Robert H. Waterman.

"Sea riggin'," changing sail while on a voyage, was a confirmed habit with Captain Waterman. It was said that he could "take a coal barge to sea and bring her home in creditable time looking, aloft at least, like a clipper . . . given a few spare spars, plenty of stuns'l poles, and an extra bolt or two of canvas." He was never satisfied until he had every stitch of sail aloft that his ship would carry.

Waterman was outstanding among the colorful characters of the clipper-ship era. A veteran of the sea at thirty-five, he had seen service in many parts of the world. While driving packets he met Palmer. They transferred to the China trade at about the same time.

"In an age and service famous for supermen," writes Carl Cutler, in *Greyhounds of the Sea*, "these two men would have made a very creditable clipper ship era by themselves. . . . Waterman and Palmer in some respects best represent the two leading but essentially different types developed in the hard school of the American merchant marine. Both were absolutely fearless 'drivers,' but where Waterman was wholly reckless of life and limb, Palmer felt his way carefully to the extreme edge of safety and stayed there. Waterman was all sailor. Palmer was that and a shrewd businessman besides, and something more than an average good ship designer."

When Waterman brought the *Natchez* into New York after her record-breaking run the ship carried the masts and spars to spread a full clipper rig of sail. In less expert hands such an expanse of canvas might have torn the bottom out of a ship of the *Natchez'* design.

W. H. Aspinwall, owner of the *Natchez* was fired with enthusiasm. He vowed he would build Waterman the "fastest and trimmest" ship afloat and ordered Griffiths' ship rushed to completion.

The *Rainbow,* as the new ship was christened, was launched in the latter part of January 1845, sixty-one years after the sailing of the *Empress of China*, America's pioneer in the China crossing. A great crowd had assembled for the occasion. The traditional bottle of wine was broken on the ship's prow; the chocks were knocked clear, and the ship began to move. Gathering momentum, she thrust her graceful stern into the East River. The ship careened badly but righted herself and on a steady keel yielded gracefully to the restraining hawsers. She was described as the most beautiful thing that ever floated.

Records of the China Voyage

But Waterman did not sail the *Rainbow.* Aspinwall held that she was not large enough for his "champion master," and command of the ship was given to Captain John Land. Four days out Land drove the top-gallant masts out of her. Once he drove her under head seas and nearly lost her, but destiny appeared to be watching over the *Rainbow*, for she made an out-of-season run to China in one hundred and two days and established a new round-trip record of seven months and seventeen days. Captain Land took her out again and made the return voyage from China in seventy-nine days. So stirred was Captain Land by his record that he "spoke up for the papers" for the first time in his life. "The *Rainbow*," he insisted, "is the fastest ship ever to sail the seas, and what's more, the ship can't be built to beat her."

Griffiths' fame did not end with the *Rainbow*. Aspinwall was true to his promise to give Waterman the finest and fastest ship afloat. Soon after the *Rainbow* had been launched the shipyard of Smith and Dimon, where Griffiths was still chief designer, was commissioned by Howland and Aspinwall to design and build a world-beater. Griffiths' answer was the *Sea Witch*, launched on December 7, 1846. The New York *Herald*, in reporting the event, stated, "The *Sea Witch* is, for a vessel of her size, the prettiest vessel we have ever seen, and much resembles the model of the steamer *Great Britain*, only on a smaller scale.

"She is built of the very best material, and although presenting such a light appearance, is most strongly constructed . . .

"Her length is 192 feet over all, 34 feet beam, 19 hold, and 900 tons burthen, making as fine a specimen of New York shipbuilding as we have seen in a long time."

Captain Waterman, with the *Sea Witch*, set the tempo for the clipper era—and more than once established records which still stand for sail in the various courses of the China route. He sailed for Canton on December 23, 1846, and on the return voyage brought the *Sea Witch* back in eighty-one days against the monsoon—a record at the time. Outward bound, the *Sea Witch* sailed 8894 miles in forty-two days, at an average speed of about 212 miles daily for six consecutive weeks. On the return voyage Waterman sailed from Anjier, Java, to the Cape of

Castle Garden

The Clipper Ship, *Flying Cloud*

Good Hope in twenty-six days and Anjier to the pilot boat off New York in sixty-two days.

Steam Subsidized

In 1843 the Cunard Line of steamships received a subsidy from the British government. Two years later President Polk, aroused by this challenge, sent a subsidy message to Congress, stating that a "national policy by which rapid communication with the distant points of the world is established, by means of American-built steamships, would find an ample award in the increase of our commerce. ... A just national pride, no less than our commercial interests, would seem to favor the policy of augmenting the number of this description of vessels."

Though the proposal was supported in Congress, the only subsidy granted (to a new American steamship line to Le Havre and Bremen) amounted to two hundred thousand dollars—less than half the sum received by the Cunard Line.

Edward K. Collins, head of the Dramatic Line of sail packets, did his best to convince New York that the future of ocean navigation was in steam. In 1845 he announced that all his sail packets were for sale and declared his intention of going into steam exclusively.

Collins' move did not impress New Yorkers. He was known as the man who had applied to President Van Buren in 1838 for a government subsidy to help launch a line of transatlantic steamships. Among the benefits that would accrue to the country from this project, he had emphasized a ready-made navy. Van Buren had scornfully turned him down, declaring that America needed no navy. Early in 1847 Collins placed a contract with the Brown shipyards in New York for the construction of four steamships—roomier, more comfortable, and higher powered than anything then afloat. Jointly with James and Stewart Brown, Collins received a contract from the Postmaster General, granting $385,000 for twenty annual round trips between New York and Liverpool.

Collins' transfer to steam might have attracted more attention had it not been for the records being made by the clipper ships. The Cunard steamers were achieving no spectacular speeds. They carried only a few wealthy passengers, leaving the steerage trade to the clippers. In 1847 the potato crop in Ireland was a complete failure, and scanty crops were harvested elsewhere in Europe. The demand for supplies from "the granary of the world" busied every ship in New York Harbor. Before the grain rush was over gold had been found in California. This created a new demand for speed, which only the clippers could satisfy.

The Gold Rush

In the fall of 1848 one Midshipman Beale arrived in Washington after a dashing trip from the Pacific, bringing news of the discovery of gold in California. Respectable businessmen now lost all sense of caution and decency. Ships barely fitted to cross the harbor took on a number of passengers that pushed them below their safety draught. Gold-hungry multitudes were crowded into unbelievably dirty and cramped quarters. Weeks were required to beat around the Horn; none of the ships carried sufficient supplies for the feeding or comfort of the passengers. Half-starved adventurers were landed in San Francisco months after the advertised or promised one hundred days.

The wreckage of ships and men strewed the seventeen-thousand-mile course to the "gold coast." By March 1849 more than one hundred and forty ships—many of them pitifully inadequate for the journey—had left on the long, grueling voyage to California. Thirty-seven more had cleared for Chagres, a port on the eastern coast of the Isthmus of Panama. These ships carried out of New York eleven thousand passengers, who were dumped at Chagres and had to make their way across the Isthmus as best they could. More than half succumbed to hunger or tropical fevers.

Yet nothing could stop the rush save the end of the gold itself. New York's shipyards could not meet the demand for ships for the California run. Places close to the lumber supply offered quicker deliveries. Maine, with shipyards on the edge of the forests, soon wrenched the leadership away from New York, which, with 44,104 tons, was second to Maine's 82,256 tons in production.

By 1850 the human wave rolling to California had become tidal in its proportions. A total of seven hundred and seventy-five vessels cleared from New York before the close of 1849. Rio de Janeiro was full of stranded passengers from crippled ships.

To this reckless traffic the *Sea Witch* contributed the first record. Waterman, who had returned from Canton in the record-breaking time of seventy-four days and fourteen hours, turned the vessel over to his first mate when she was put into the San Francisco run; George Fraser was a driver of whom even Waterman could be proud. On April 13, 1850, Captain Fraser took the *Sea Witch* out of New York Harbor and on July 24 arrived in San Francisco in ninety-seven sailing days.

The Collins Line

Collins had spent three years and considerable money in building the four ships that were to take up the schedules of his United States Mail Steamship Company to Europe.

Contracts for the construction of the ships were divided between the shipyards of William H. Brown, where the *Atlantic* and the *Arctic* were built, and Brown and Bell, who were commissioned to build the *Pacific* and the *Baltic*. Service was inaugurated between New York and Liverpool on April 27, 1850, by the *Atlantic*. In the same year the *Pacific* was put on the same run, followed a little later by the *Arctic* and the *Baltic*. They were the first steamers with straight stems instead of clipper bows. A patented device called the annunciator provided the staterooms with bell service.

These New York-built steamers soon established their supremacy on the seas. They were not the first to operate a regular European schedule out of New York, for the Ocean Line had put the *Hermann* and the *Washington* into operation on a New York-Southampton-Bremen route in 1847, but the Collins steamers proved unbeatable in luxury and speed from the day they were launched. When the *Baltic* made a run from Liverpool in nine days and thirteen hours the commercial supremacy of the line was established. From that time on the Collins ships carried forty per cent more passengers than the Cunarders.

The speed contest between the Collins and Cunard steamers attracted international attention. Newspapers and magazines published reports of individual races. The Collins ships, however, were not built to withstand the speed at which they were driven. After virtually every trip they were subjected to secret repairs. This was an expensive method of gaining supremacy, yet in 1853 Collins' subsidy was increased to $33,000 a round trip, making an annual total of $858,000, a figure slightly above the subsidy allotted to the Cunard Line by the British government.

Despite the fury of these contests, both sides displayed unusual fairness. One magnanimous act of the Collins Line was given considerable play in the English press. A Cunarder had been detained in the Port of New York for customs irregularities on the part of its crew. The ship was required to post a bond for one hundred and fifty thousand dollars before it could clear the Port. The Collins Line put up the bond in order that the rival line should not miss a scheduled sailing.

In 1849 the Cunard Line commissioned construction of the *Asia* and *Africa,* to replace the *Britannia* and *Acadia.* These two ships, with their indicated horsepower of twenty-four hundred, were expected to offer a serious threat, but when launched they failed to equal the Collins speed and regularly arrived twelve to fourteen hours behind their rivals.

Faster and Finer Clippers

Yet it was the clippers that had caught the popular imagination. The profits of the California and China runs had turned the heads of American shipowners. Some vessels had more than paid for themselves on their first voyage. The *Samuel Russell* earned well over seventy thousand dollars in freight charges on a single voyage.

The argument that such conditions could not last went unheeded. No one could expect the once conservative firm of A. A. Low and Brother to worry about the future when the firm's *Surprise* made a fifty-thousand-dollar profit, net, from a two-hundred-thousand-dollar cargo because it was docked in San Francisco in quicker time than other ships. In the early 1850s the fantastic profits to be made from speed alone changed the pattern of New York ship construction. Cargo space was definitely sacrificed to speed lines.

The *Celestial*, launched early in June of 1850 by the William H. Webb yards for Bucklin and Crane, and the *Mandarin*, launched a week later by Smith and Dimon for Goodhue and Company, exemplified this development. The *Mandarin* "was as nearly flat-floored as it was possible to build a ship, while her sides were almost perpendicular." The *Celestial*, compared with the sharply built *Samuel Russell*, was relatively flat-bottomed and was very similar to the later packets, although much sharper in line. Both the *Mandarin* and the *Celestial* are classified as extreme clippers by most authorities. The *Mandarin* has been described as the sharpest ship built up to that time. Here were three ships, built within three years, differing considerably in appearance, yet all three built for speed.

The early part of this decade saw a burst of ship-building such as New York had never before witnessed. In Brooklyn's Williamsburg, Jabez Williams was putting the finishing touches to the *Eclipse*. Smith and Dimon were busy on two clippers in addition to the *Mandarin*. William H. Webb announced that he had received a commission for the building of the largest merchantman ever projected. This ship, the *Challenge*, proved to be the most extreme clipper constructed thus far. She was the first three-decker turned out by an American shipyard.

The *Challenge* registered two thousand and six tons. Her mainmast measured two hundred ten and a half feet from heel to truck. The lower studding of the *Challenge* was one hundred and sixty feet from leech to leech. Even in those days of supermasters not many could be found who would sail this giant in the rig supplied by the designers. There was one man, however, who had no hesitation, and that was Robert H. Waterman. After Waterman left the *Challenge* her spar plan had to be reduced several times before other captains could be induced to take her out of port.

The Webb yards started work on three other clippers, the *Gazelle, Comet,* and *Invincible.* Westervelt and Mackay turned out the *N. B. Palmer* and the *Eureka,* while Perine, Patterson, and Stack were building the beautiful *Ino.* Before these were completed the keels of other ships had been laid, and before these reached the launching stage commissions for still more ships had been awarded the various yards.

On June 2, 1851, the *Flying Cloud,* Captain Josiah P. Cressy, cleared from New York for San Francisco. The log of her first voyage discloses that "two auger holes had been boared in the Deck close to the after sill of the fore Castle" which was "done by some one of the sailors." The culprit was "seen coming out of the fore Castle with an auger in his hand" and clapped in irons; the "main mast was badly sprung four feet below the hounds" when the ship was but twelve days out of New York and had to be "releaved" later in "Gales and Harder Squalls"; the wind carried away the "Main Topsail tie & Truss band round the mast"; and "light, baffling and squally airs" caused frequent tacking. There was "Much & very severe thunder and Lightening" as the ship wester-ed around the Horn. Yet Cressy brought his beauty into San Francisco on August 31, just eighty-nine days and twenty-one hours from anchor to anchor.

Waterman's Last Voyage

The *Challenge* was ready to sail before the *Flying Cloud* had hung up her San Francisco record. The crew shipped for the maiden voyage were sailors only in the sense that they had been supplied by crimps under that classification. Few of the fifty-six men and eight boys who had made their mark on the ship's roster could by any stretch of the imagination be classified as seamen. The rest were the dregs and sweepings of many world ports. Waterman's mates were not to blame for having accepted such a crew, as New York was scoured clean of sailors. It is doubtful that any one except Waterman could have made the voyage. Even he considered "taking the ship back into New York for another crew," but this would have involved a heavy expense to the owners, and Waterman was not the kind who invited responsibility for piling up costs.

Having made his decision to reach San Francisco or go under in the attempt, Waterman called all men aft as the *Challenge* was still in sight of Sandy Hook. There he gave a twenty-minute sample of his oratorical power, although he did not expect to convince his audience of anything. His motive was to hold their attention until his officers could search the crew's dunnage. The officers combed the forecastle thoroughly. They broke open chests, emptied sea bags, and found an amazing assortment of rum, knuckle-dusters, slingshots, bowie knives, and pistols. The mates dumped this collection over the side with the exception of the knives, which were needed for work aboard the ship. These were rendered less effective as weapons by breaking off their points.

After a physical examination of the crew seventeen men were immediately ordered into sick bay. Five had died, and eight were still in the sick bay when the voyage ended. Of the forty-seven men and boys who passed the physical test, only six were found who had sufficient knowledge of the ways of the sea to act as steersmen. "For some time after sailing from New York," writes Captain Arthur H. Clark in *The Clipper Ship Era*, "Captain Waterman and his officers were always armed when they came on deck, but after a while the crew appeared to be in such good shape that this precaution gradually became neglected, until, one morning off Rio Janeiro, while Captain Waterman was taking his sights, he heard shouts for help from the main deck. He at once laid down his sextant and hurried forward to find the mate, Mr. Douglas, with his back to the port bulwark just abaft the main rigging, defending himself with bare fists from four of the crew armed with knives, who were attacking him. As Captain Waterman ran along the main deck he pulled a heavy iron belaying pin out of the rail, and using this with both hands as a club, he dealt a terrific blow on the skull of each of the would-be assassins, which laid them out on deck—two of them dead. Mr. Douglas had received no less than twelve wounds, some of them of a serious nature; indeed, he barely escaped with his life. From that time the officers always carried arms, and there was no further trouble with the crew."*

Captain Waterman made what was considered very good time in reaching San Francisco. The ship was one hundred and eight days out of New York when she came through the Golden Gate, but it was an out-of-season sailing. His crew left the ship immediately after dropping anchor, as was the custom then, and spread hair-raising stories of brutality and hardship on the voyage; one paper declared that such a captain "should be burned alive." A mob went searching for Waterman, but when the vigilantes turned out the mob dispersed. Waterman offered to appear as a witness before any legal body, and when no complaint was filed with any of the constituted authorities he insisted upon an inquiry. The inquiry was held and, largely through the testimony of crew members, Waterman was exonerated. Several days after Waterman's trial and exoneration a San Francisco newspaper carried the following: "A gentleman of this city informs us that nine of the seamen who have just arrived in her (the *Challenge*) have waited on the consignees of this ship and informed them that they are willing to make a voyage to China, in the *Challenge*, with Captain Waterman as master. Five of these seamen are Americans and four are foreigners. The same gentleman states that the passengers are unanimous in justifying the course pursued by the Captain on the way out." Waterman, however, retired after this voyage and, with Captain A. A. Ritchie, founded the town of Fairfield, California. In 1852 he was appointed Port Warden and Inspector of Hulls for San Francisco, a position he held for twenty-eight years, when he retired to a farm on which he remained until his death at seventy-six.

* From *The Clipper Ship Era* by Arthur H. Clark

The scarcity of men that plagued Waterman was also felt in the ship-yards of New York. Ship carpenters and calkers were paid two dollars a day during the decade 1840-50. In 1853 the wage rate for these skilled workers rose from two to three dollars a day, but even with this increase the city's shipbuilding firms experienced great difficulty in engaging a sufficient number of men to fulfill their contracts. In this year clipper construction should have declined. The California-rush demand had subsided. Freight rates were still high, but cargoes were fewer. Yet New York shipowners, intoxicated by the ease of past profits, continued to order clippers. The demand for speed was as great as ever, since a one- or two-day lead over a rival might result in the sale of a cargo. Non-shipping capital had also come into the market. Clipper building attained its peak in 1853.

Up to 1850, since most of the clippers having New York as a home port were built in local shipyards, it was possible to measure New York clipper tonnage by the number of locally built ships. In 1853 New York owners increased their shipping tonnage by the addition of thirty-eight new vessels, of which thirty-five were clippers and three barks. However, only twelve of the clippers and two of the barks were New York-built.

The McKay Clippers

The supremacy of New York-built ships had been maintained up to 1853, but early in May of that year a Boston-built ship, owned by Andrew F. Meinke of New York, came inbound past Sandy Hook only eighty-two days out from Honolulu. In establishing this world's record Captain Lauchlan McKay had driven the *Sovereign of the Seas* to new records between all points on the Hawaiian route. Then, having demon-strated his ship's ability in the Pacific, the same captain drove her to an Atlantic record by sailing from New York to Liverpool in thirteen days, twenty-two hours, and fifty minutes.

These two performances turned the eyes of the shipping world to the designer of the *Sovereign of the Seas*, Donald McKay of Boston, who turned out more clipper-ship tonnage and more "uniformly successful" clippers than any other builder.

Meanwhile William H. Webb was preparing to launch the *Young America,* his last extreme clipper. She was towed to Pier 28, East River, where she hoisted the familiar "Up for California" pennant. Webb challenged the owner of the *Sovereign of the Seas* to a race to San Francisco for a purse of ten thousand dollars, but the challenge was turned down because of the depressed condition of the California market.

In the same year, however, a New York-built clipper was to have its chance against a McKay design. This contest developed into the closest race ever run by clippers. Involved were the *Flying Cloud*, designed and built by McKay, and the *Hornet*, built in New York. Both were New York-owned. The *Hornet* closely followed the design pioneered by Griffiths in the *Rainbow,* while the *Flying Cloud*, most famous of the McKay clippers, was a perfect example of the Boston designer's art as a builder of ships. The *Hornet* left New York several hours ahead of the *Flying Cloud,* but so closely was the course contested that Captain William Knapp brought the *Hornet* into the San Francisco anchorage but forty minutes ahead of the *Flying Cloud.* Two thirds of an hour advantage for the winner of a race over a sixteen-thousand-mile course! Before the year ended several records had been set by New Yorkers. The *Comet,* an extraordinary performer which appears to have received less than her share of laurels, was built by Webb in New York and launched in 1851. In her brief career of about five years she established three world's records. Her 1853 record of thirty-five days and seven hours from San Francisco to Cape Horn still stands for sailing ships, and her twelve days from San Francisco to the equator established a record which "is believed to have been beaten only twice up to the present time and then by some twelve hours only."

New York ships continued to establish new records in 1854. The *Flying Cloud,* under Captain Cressy, went to China from her home port, via San Francisco, in one hundred and twenty-seven days, and Captain

Gardner drove the *Comet* to New York from San Francisco in an even seventy-six days.

This year ended the era of speed records. Although clipper tonnage reached an all-time high in 1856, both the California and China markets had begun to decline. The year also witnessed dramatic episodes in sailing history. In the late spring of 1856 the ship *Rapid*, Captain Phineas Winsor, left the Port of New York bound for San Francisco. Several weeks later Captain Joshua Patten, accompanied by his young wife Mary, sailed from New York for the same port in the *Neptune's Car.* Another ship, the *Intrepid*, captained by E. C. Gardner, weighed anchor at the same time, also bound for the Golden Gate. The three ships ran into violent storms in approaching the Horn. The *Rapid* received such a battering that two of her crew were killed, and four remaining members of the crew and the officers turned tail to the storm and ran back to Rio de Janeiro. Captain Winsor of the *Rapid* later reported that the *Intrepid* had been close by and had paid no attention to his distress signal, but Captain Gardner's log showed that the *Intrepid* had been more than a thousand miles from the *Rapid* at the time.

The *Neptune's Car* encountered bad luck almost from the moment she left New York. Captain Patten became ill but stayed on duty until his ship was approaching the Horn. There his first mate was put in irons "for incompetence and neglect of duty." Under the strain of his double duties the young captain broke down and at the worst of the storm was confined to his bunk, delirious. His wife took command and brought the ship into San Francisco, arriving almost ten days ahead of the much larger *Intrepid*. In that day of superseamanship there were few who could have matched her navigation, yet she was apparently so modest about it that her name was nearly lost to history.

Decline of the Clippers

The gold rush had been chiefly responsible for the great mass of clipper-ship building. When California began to produce her own food supply and land travel to the Pacific coast became a routine instead of a dangerous adventure, the need for speed was ended. The roomier, bulkier freighters became profitable once more.

Furthermore, the maintenance cost of clippers was found to be excessive. The wide spread of rigging put a strain on the hulls that very few of them could stand. After two years of driving nearly all required dry docking and expensive repairs. Ships in dry dock earn no money. Rigging was reset and cut down until the wave-battered and wind-strained hulls could withstand the pull of the canvas. This reduced the clippers to a speed not far superior to that of the roomier cargo ships.

A third factor which entered into the decline of the clipper was, of course, the advance of steam. Where the paddle-wheelers had required so much space for machinery that there was no room for steerage passengers, the application of the screw propeller to transatlantic ships removed the inequality between sail and steam. The sail-driven ships held this form of passenger trade for years. With the enlarged space released upon installation of the screw propeller, steerage passengers took to the steamers.

Gradually one trade route after another went to the steamers. The California and Australia trades were the last to go. Steamers had not yet reached the point where they could compete on distances which required recoaling. Ultimately the opening of the Suez Canal threw the China trade to the steamers, and the completion of transcontinental railroads lessened the demands on coast-to-coast navigation. Meanwhile economic factors were working against American shipping. America was becoming self-sufficient. Public attention was turning to land frontiers. The financial panic of 1857 virtually signed the death sentence of the sailing ships.

Thousands of firms failed, among them numerous shipping concerns. New York shipyards languished for want of new accounts. When general business recovered in 1858 and 1859 an attempt was made to revive the clipper traffic. But of ninety clippers which cleared for San Francisco during 1859, eleven were turned out at Mystic, Connecticut, while New York supplied nothing which even resembled the clipper mold.

Collins had kept the United States supreme in steam as long as he received government subsidies equaling those of his competitors. Then in the mid-fifties the Collins boats ran into a series of disasters. On September 27, 1854, the *Arctic* collided in the fog with a small French steamer, the *Vesta*, off Cape Race and sank with nearly all on board. Collins' wife, son, and daughter were among the victims. Despite this personal tragedy, Collins replaced the *Arctic* with a larger boat, the *Adriatic,* in 1855. But still disaster pursued him. The *Pacific* sailed from Liverpool in January 1856 and disappeared without trace. Seven months later Congress withdrew its subsidy from Collins. This was a blow from which he could not recover, and in 1858 the last three ships of his line were sold at auction to satisfy creditors.

At this time those clippers still in use were functioning as tramps, many of them carrying guano fertilizer from South American ports, a dismal finish for the former queens of the sea.

CHAPTER IX
Steamers—1861-1900
THE TWILIGHT OF SAIL

SAIL had called for iron men, men trained to drive a ship around the Horn, through a China Sea monsoon, down the long Atlantic slant to the Cape of Good Hope, and up the Indian Ocean. "Iron men and wooden ships" had been more than a phrase.

Now the scene was changing. Steam was no longer a novelty. Speed could be developed without superseamanship, and machinery was fast replacing the hard-bitten officers and crews of the packets and clippers. New York's shipowners and operators could no longer win cargoes from foreign competition merely because they had captains like Waterman, Land, and Palmer. Paddle wheels and screw propellers were about to move vessels faster than even a genius like Waterman could ever hope to drive a sailing ship.

The merchant gamblers were being supplanted by calculating bankers. The days of long chances were over—for one thing, steamships cost too much.

The First Superliner Arrives

Early in the morning of June 28, 1860, the news was relayed from Sandy Hook to New York's waterfront that the *Great Eastern* had anchored off the lightship. With high water she would cross Sandy

Hook bar and proceed through the harbor to her North River berth. High water was at 2 P.M. By that time thousands were jammed in Battery Park, and other spectators used downtown roofs, trees, and windows. Many business houses closed for the day. New York was turning out to greet the world's greatest steamship on her maiden voyage.

While waiting at Sandy Hook for high tide the *Great Eastern's* crew was shifting and reshifting her cargo. She drew twenty-seven feet aft, and there would be little more than thirty over the bar. Sweating seamen trimmed her to an even keel under the direction of New York Pilot Murphy, who had gone to Europe and come back aboard the *Great Eastern*. Murphy turned to the chief engineer and gave the command to go ahead, and the huge paddle wheels began to turn. She neared Sandy Hook bar. Speed was slackened as Murphy waved his orders to the helmsman. The *Great Eastern* obeyed her helm readily, and the perilous sand bar was soon astern.

Fort Lafayette fired a salute. The *Great Eastern's* four guns returned it. Other cannons boomed their welcome. The liner's six hundred and eighty feet of riveted iron moved toward the Battery, as steam whistles called their greetings to the new queen. Her ten boilers and one hundred and eighteen furnaces were almost shut down, for she needed only a part of her twenty-six-hundred horsepower in New York's calm harbor. Flags were dipped. The ninety-ton paddle wheels, each fifty-six feet in diameter, propelled her with majestic steadiness. Deep within, her one-hundred-sixty-foot shaft was revolving just enough to keep the twenty-four-foot propeller from "dragging." As the *Great Eastern* neared the Battery scores of small craft shot out to ride her wake. Only a few of her twenty anchors were visible. She was fitted to carry eight hundred first-class, two thousand second-class, and twelve hundred third-class passengers. Her crew of three hundred and fifty stood at their stations.

The *Great Eastern* proceeded up the North River. In her double bottom she carried the skeleton of a riveter who had been trapped there while she was building. He had been unable to make himself heard above the din of fellow workmen busy driving three million rivets. Nobody knew of this until 1888, when the ship was broken up. To this circumstance seafaring men attributed the many mishaps that befell her before, during, and after launching.

Pilot Murphy warped the superliner into the North River dock without the aid of a single tug. For this very skillful feat some of the credit must be given to designer I. K. Brunel's steam-steering gear, an innovation introduced on the *Great Eastern*.

Down the gangplank came forty-five passengers, greatest number that could be found to risk a North Atlantic gale on the new British ship.

Foreign Flags Fill the Waterfront

The beginning of the decline of the American merchant marine had set in five years before 1860. When New York's recently supreme clipper ships were not idle they were shopping for cargoes like "irregular traders" or transporting guano. Passengers and fast freight to Europe were shifting from the beautiful clippers of the fifties to the ugly but increasingly efficient steamships of the sixties. More immigrants than ever were arriving in New York on steamers. These vessels were predominantly foreign-flagged. In 1860 Britain's Cunard Line carried nearly sixty per cent of American mails to Europe; American steamers carried less than one third.

The Civil War dealt the final blow to America's position on the high seas. During the four years of that conflict British-armed Confederate raiders destroyed 110,000 tons of American shipping, much of it from New York. In addition, more than 750,000 tons sought safety under foreign colors. Congress refused to let this foreign-flagged tonnage return to American registry after peace had been restored. The resultant total loss was 861,595 tons of shipping out of the prewar total of 2,496,894 tons. About sixty-five per cent of America's imports and exports had been carried in American bottoms. War cut this percentage almost in half. America had lost control of the carrying trade for even her own commerce, and the American flag was disappearing from world ports.

More and more foreign ships entered New York. For the next forty years the commerce of the Port was dominated by them. South Street became an international shipping settlement, in which New York's shipowners and operators were being pushed out of the picture. The Port was developing, but New Yorkers were no longer doing the job.

British Lines

Cunard was planning to regain its old supremacy in speed temporarily lost to Collins, now bankrupt. Cunard's first iron-screw mail steamer was by no means a satisfactory vessel, but she demonstrated that line's active interest in new developments. The Inman Line, also British, extended its transatlantic sailings to one a week in 1860. Three years later, while New York was preoccupied with the Civil War, Inman again increased its sailings. By 1866 Inman ships ran twice a week during the busy spring and summer months and three times fortnightly in the winter.

Speed was rewarded with long passenger lists. A fast vessel was patronized about four times as much as a ship grown old in service, and possession of the mythical Blue Riband, symbol of the North Atlantic speed record, had great publicity value. Size and power increased steadily as a result. Propellers largely replaced paddle wheels during the 1860s, although screwships had the disadvantage of rolling considerably.

Inland Waterways

No foreign competition troubles inland-water steamboating. The Hudson River—birthplace of the American steamboat—retained its pre-eminence. The *Alida, Chauncey Vibbard, Jenny Lind,* and many others plied the Hudson. These were all pushed into the background with the appearance of the *Mary Powell,* which held first place in the hearts of rivermen and the public for sixty-two years—from the time of her first run in 1861 until 1923, when she was broken up.

The *Mary Powell* was remarkable, not only for her long service, but also because during all these years there never appeared to be any deterioration in the boat, owing to expert maintenance service. After each summer the steamboat underwent a complete overhauling as she lay in Rondout Creek (near Kingston), so that by the opening of the next season she was in perfect condition.

The *Mary Powell* was built by Michael Allinson from plans by Absalom Anderson. Anderson was the boat's captain for many years; his son carried on after his death. She was never beaten by another steamboat, never lost a passenger, maintained perfect schedules, and to the last remained one of the most graceful craft in the river.

Important development in Long Island Sound steamboating marked the year 1866. The Merchants Steamship Company, resulting from the consolidation of the old Neptune and Stonington Lines, planned a service to Bristol, Rhode Island, with rail connections to Boston. Contracts had been signed for two huge side-wheelers which later became known as the *Bristol* and the *Providence*. However, one of this line's steamers burned at the wharf and two others were wrecked. The Merchants Steamship Company went bankrupt, stockholders receiving but three cents on the dollar.

Three new Long Island Sound lines appeared after the bankruptcy. One was the Narragansett Steamship Company controlled by James Fisk who announced that he was about to start a new steamboat line to Bristol.

Fisk's Bristol Line had two major competitors—the Fall River Line and the revived Stonington Line. Competition became so bitter that the New York-Boston fare was slashed to one dollar. Fisk finally grew tired of such profitless tactics, consolidated his property with the Fall River Line, and had himself elected president of the new company. He often traveled on the *Bristol* and the *Providence*, his prize steamboats. New York contributed their engines and 333-foot hulls. The engines were the largest of their type ever installed in any steamboat. Each of these

vessels had two hundred and twenty staterooms with a total passenger capacity of eight hundred and forty, as well as considerable
space for freight.

Anchor Line

In 1861 the Anchor Line decided to concentrate on the New York—
Glasgow run. Ignoring the disorganized state of the American market,
the line built ships especially for that trade. The first was the *Caledonia*,
which was wrecked soon after launching. Undismayed, the Anchor
Line produced two more ships in 1862—the second *Caledonia* and the
Britannia. Neither their size nor speed was unusual, but the foresight of
the line's owners was shown by the steerage accommodations. Each
ship carried five hundred and fifty third-class as against only sixty first-
cabin passengers. The Anchor Line was depending on resumption of
emigration to the United States after the Civil War and prospered when
these calculations proved to be right.

German as well as British steamship operators were out to capture
the profitable emigrant trade. The North German Lloyd built the *Hansa*
in 1860 and the *America* in 1861. Like the Scots who controlled the
Anchor Line, the Germans were looking forward to the day when the
Civil War's end would mean a financial harvest for those lines ready to
pick up renewed emigration.

Paddle Wheels versus Propellers

Inman, Anchor, and North German Lloyd activities finally convinced
the conservative Cunard directors that they had been wrong about two
things. One was the paddle ship, to which Cunard had clung until the
Inman Line in the 1860s demonstrated the advantages of the screw
propeller. Cunard compromised by turning out its first screwship, the
China, and the last and greatest of the paddlers, the *Scotia*. The *China*'s
superiority over the *Scotia* was evident in two important features: she
needed only 2250 horsepower to get up normal sea speed, whereas the

paddler required 4900; and her daily coal consumption was 82 tons against *Scotia*'s 164. Another point on which Cunard's directors reversed themselves concerned steerage accommodations. Before the *Scotia*, Cunard's mail steamers had no third class. The *Scotia* had quarters for 771 steerage passengers. It was about this time that Cunard issued another of its "Instructions to Captains," which revealed the line's emphasis on safety above all else:

"You are to understand that you have peremptory order, that, in fog or snow storm, or in such state of the weather as appears attendant with risk, you are on no account whatever to move the vessel under your command out of the port or wherever she may be lying in safety, if there exists in your mind a doubt as to the propriety of the proceeding . . . You are not to be actuated by any desire to complete your voyage, your sole consideration being the safety of your ship and those under your charge."

Another section of Cunard's instructions pertained to spirits: "We beg your special care of the drawing-off of spirits. The spirit-room should, if possible, be entered during the day only . . ."

Competition in the Port of New York increased during the Civil War. The National Steam Navigation Company, organized to run cargo and steerage passenger ships between the Mersey, in England, and the Southern states, shifted its three steamers to the New York-Liverpool run. Sailing packets no longer served as steerage carriers. In 1863 the owners of the famous Black Ball Line of packets entered into an agreement with Cunard and the National Line to supply them with emigrants, and Black Ball packets were withdrawn.

The French Line

In 1864 the Compagnie General Transatlantique, better known here as the French Line, inaugurated a New York service. The organization of this company was due in great measure to the desire of Napoleon III to improve French shipping. Various services to ports other than New York had been started in 1862. Two years later the new iron paddler Washington sailed for New York, arriving June 28, 1864. She was the first French Line steamer to carry passengers and mail across the North Atlantic.

The Sunday schedules of French Line ships did not meet with the approval of Henry Fry, Lloyd's representative in Quebec. He admitted that French Line vessels were "beautifully decorated and fitted with every luxury. But," he added, "they do not suit the British taste inasmuch as no notice is taken of the Sabbath Day, while on board British ships Divine service is always held at 10:30 A.M., and it is often impressive."

The Inman Line made quick headway in the postwar emigrant trade with its *City of Boston*. She had several new safety devices, including a hull divided into six watertight compartments. Other steamship operators avoided taking such precautions on the ground that liners so expensively built could not be made to pay their way. The *City of Boston's* many safety features did not save her from disaster, for within a few years she disappeared in the North Atlantic. The Anchor Line put its Glasgow-New York service on a weekly basis, added a new ship, commissioned two more in 1866, and put the *Europa* in the northern Ireland emigrant trade in 1867. The French Line brought out the *Pereire*, about fifteen hundred tons larger than the *Washington*.

New Transatlantic Lines Serve New York

Revival of the North Atlantic trade after the Civil War was brief. After the peak year of 1866 a decline set in. Yet two new companies serving New York were organized in 1867—the Guion Line and the North American Lloyd.

The first was the Liverpool & Great Western Steamship Company, a British firm in which nearly all the stockholders were Americans. This new organization, called the Guion Line, was the result of the previously cited agreement between Black Ball interests (Williams & Guion) and Cunard and National Lines. Williams & Guion had supplied immigrants instead of transporting them in Black Ball sailing packets. Within three years Williams & Guion concluded that they should go after all of the profits instead of sharing them with Cunard and National. The result was their own line headed by Stephen Barker Guion.

Although American-born, Guion had built up a highly efficient emigrant organization in Europe. He next sought this business for his own steamships. The Guion Line's first ship, the *Manhattan*, was soon followed by six others. They grossed but thirty-five hundred tons each and had comparatively little speed. However, all had one supremely important characteristic—ample steerage space. Below decks each of the Guion ships could stow one thousand emigrants.

The second line, the North American Lloyd, was founded by the Ruger Brothers of New York in 1867. The Rugers bought two old Collins liners and a smaller ship or two, planning to run a regular service to Bremen by way of Southampton. They failed within a few months, revived the venture in 1868, and in 1869 again failed.

Existing lines met the challenge of these new companies by building new ships. The Inman Line built the first *City of Paris* in 1866. Cunard produced the *Russia*. Meanwhile the North German Lloyd monopolized the postwar emigrant trade by extending its fortnightly schedule to a weekly one, putting eight ships on the Atlantic crossing and obtaining an England-America mail contract from the United States government. In the late sixties the Inman Line commissioned the *City of Brussels*, which reduced the eastward record from eight days and four hours to seven days and twenty-two hours, averaging 14.66 knots. She was typical of the third major type of steamship to hold the Blue Riband. This was the iron-or steel-hulled screw steamer, which dominated the field from the mid-sixties to the late eighties.

At this period the larger European powers discouraged emigration because their conscript armies needed man power. The Anchor Line added three ships and went after the emigration trade from Scandinavia, where this impediment did not exist.

One of the interesting experiments in developing man power for New York's merchant ships and the United States navy was the nautical school ship *Mercury*. Bought by the city in 1869, it took young first offenders committed to Harts Island Reformatory and trained them "in seamanship and gunnery to fit them for a useful occupation." Other youths between fourteen and twenty-one, whose parents wished to pay for their training as seamen, also were accepted. The regular ship's company consisted of the captain, three mates, and twenty-two petty officers and seamen; two instructors taught English and elementary mathematics.

The last of the sailing packets especially built for North Atlantic trade was launched in 1869. She was the Black Baller *Charles H. Marshall.*

Port Improvements

Piers and wharves had been built, according to the Harbor Board, both by the municipality and by private owners, but never with thought of any comprehensive plan. As a consequence the Port developed along a hit-or-miss policy—here a well-built structure and there a makeshift.

The condition of piers and wharves was noted in a resolution adopted at the September 1, 1870, meeting of the Board of Docks, which had been created that year in an attempt to remedy the situation. The busiest part of the Port of New York was in the district lying between Pier 1, North River, and the foot of West Twelfth Street. Yet "no part of the waterfront of the city is more encumbered with permanent obstructions to commerce, fixed and floating, including lumberyards, coalyard, firewood yards, counting-houses, a dwelling house, fruit warehouses, oyster warehouses, grain warehouses, with large elevators attach-ed, floating smithy, floating boiler yards, brickyards, manure yards, hay barges permanently anchored; and, in fact, almost every other sort of obstruction to commerce which ought not to be there."

The board decided that the private owners of these various obstructions should have "some colorable pretext for their occupancy." To get at this pretext, the board resolved that "the Superintendents of the Dock Districts from Pier #1, North River, to the foot of West 12th Street, North River, report to this Board forthwith the names of the occupants of all permanent obstruction, fixed or floating, on the west side of West Street . . . and the amount of rent paid and to whom, for the premises held by the said occupants, together with the date and term of their occupation." At this same meeting of the Board of Docks it was resolved that "Whereas, nothing destroys the surface of a pier more rapidly than the sharpened shoes of horses employed in the loading and unloading of vessels . . . all parties employing horses on piers belonging wholly or in part to the city . . . provide themselves with temporary platforms to be laid down on the pier for the horses to walk upon. . . ." In addition, the board resolved "that the parties employing horses for the purpose specified, be requested to fill up all auger holes made in the piers by them, to the satisfaction of the district Superintendent of Docks."

Behind all this had been an almost unbelievable administrative confusion: "The Commissioners of the Sinking Fund issued grants of land under water and leased wharf property; the Board of Aldermen authorized the construction of piers, bulkheads and filling in; Dock-masters collected wharfage; the Comptroller collected rent; the Street Commissioners took charge of repairs and dredging of waterfront property; Harbor Masters appointed by the Governor regulated and stationed vessels at their wharves." This chaos began to straighten out after the creation of the Board of Docks.

The towing industry, which had been rapidly developing throughout the 1860s, assumed major proportions in the 1870s. South Street was crowded with towing-company offices. Each maintained a street broker or "scalper," the forerunner of today's telephones. The business was highly personalized, a tug owner usually commanding his own vessel and being personally acquainted with most of the ship captains. He seemed to have a sixth sense that told him when a ship was due, and he would slip out to Sandy Hook to pick her up. Other tug captains invariably got the same idea at the same time, and Sandy Hook waters took on a regatta air whenever a profitable tow was expected. On such occasions business often went to the tug whose crew had the handiest fists.

Cargoes and Carriers

In the 1870s New York handled slightly more than fifty per cent of the nation's sugar-and-molasses imports, about fifty-two per cent of the coffee, approximately eighty per cent of the wool and manufactures, and more than ninety-two per cent of silk and manufactures. In exports only twenty per cent of the nation's cotton and manufactures then cleared through New York. About fifty-eight per cent of breadstuffs and eighty per cent of provisions were exported here. With the exception of cotton and manufactures, the Port of New York was handling fifty per cent or more of the nation's leading imports and exports.

The North German Lloyd increased its New York sailings to two a week. Owing, however, to the French blockade during the Franco-Prussian War of 1870-71, North German Lloyd's increased sailings netted the line very little as their ships were stopped on the high seas. The war also disorganized the French Line, which shifted its base from Le Havre to Bordeaux and began to use its large mail steamers to carry war supplies and reservists from America to France. Virtually all of these ships cleared from the Port of New York. After the war all of the French Line ships were taken from their regular runs and sent to Germany to bring back prisoners of war.

Meanwhile the Anchor Line was inaugurating bi-monthly sailings from Mediterranean ports—the first service of its kind. As man power for the enormous internal expansion of the United States, Italian laborers soon began to stream through New York.

American-Flag Lines

Among the American-flag coastwise steamship lines at the beginning of the 1870s were the Santo Domingo, Merchants, Pacific Mail, and

Texas lines. The Santo Domingo Line had a regular mail steamer, *Tybee,* which went to Puerto Plata, Samana, and Santo Domingo. A cruise offered by this line cost only "$160, gold." The line's announcements appealed to "persons wishing to visit a mild climate during the winter and spring months." The Merchants Steamship Line had six "first-class steamships" carrying freight and passengers to the New Orleans district.

The Pacific Mail Steamship Company advertised through rates from New York to San Francisco at $140 to $180 first class, $86 steerage. One hundred pounds of luggage were allowed to each adult passenger without transportation cost. Medicine and "attention" were also free.

The Texas Line furnished steamship service to Galveston with free forwarding of goods to Houston or the interior.

White Star and Holland-America

The White Star Line was established in 1871. It started with the *Oceanic,* first of her name to be brought out by White Star. Three sister ships, *Atlantic, Baltic,* and *Republic,* followed. They demonstrated the improvements then being made in engines, for they required only fifty-eight tons of coal a day to maintain their top speed of fourteen knots. This represented a fuel consumption at least seventy per cent less than that of earlier steamships; power and speed were increasing.

The *Oceanic* tried for the Blue Riband but burned out her bearings on her maiden voyage. The White Star Line was somewhat compensated for this mishap when its *Baltic* beat Inman's fast *City of Paris* by five hours. At that time White Star built three fast cargo ships—*Tropic, Gaelic,* and *Asiatic.*

Another foreign line entered the New York field. This was Plate, Reuchlin & Company of Rotterdam, whose first two ships, *Rotterdam* and *Maas,* made their maiden voyages to New York in 1872. Using steam and sail, they crossed in sixteen days. They had steerage accommodations for three hundred and eighty-eight as compared with only eight in first class. About a year later Plate, Reuchlin & Company was reorganized as the Netherlands-American Steam Navigation Company, better known as the Holland-America Line.

Inventions and Innovations

Technical advances were rapidly appearing. The first was the expansion engine. Its forerunner, the simple engine, used steam in one cylinder. In the expansion engine steam was made to work twice by using it at a lower pressure in a second cylinder. This fuel saving device had resulted from the pioneer work of James P. Allaire, an American engineer prominent in New York. The steady increase in steam pressures made further innovations, such as the triple-expansion engine, possible. Water-tube boilers were the next major improvement. The earlier practice had been to pass an enclosed flame through the water. Now boilers were being constructed so that water in tubes passed through the flame. This water-tube boiler, which is in general use today, dates from about 1875.

The Anchor Line added a ship to its Glasgow-New York run in 1873 and introduced such passenger-comfort innovations as a better-lighted dining saloon, electric bells, and larger cabins. The National Line set a record when its *Egypt* landed 1767 steerage passengers. This record stood until 1900.

German competition was increased by the formation of the Adler (Eagle) Line which, in September 1873, started three ships in fortnightly service between Hamburg and New York. By mid-1874 it had seven ships in service.

Disaster and Decline

Several serious disasters occurred in 1873. The *Atlantic* was wrecked with a loss of five hundred and sixty-two lives out of the total of nine hundred aboard. The French liner *Ville du Havre* went down with a loss of two hundred and twenty-six lives after colliding with the sailing ship *Loch Earn*. Other ship disasters included Inman's *City of Washington*, wrecked with no loss of life; Guion's *Colorado,* six lives lost; and the

French liner *Europe*, no loss of life. As a result of these wrecks, Cunard again issued very strict instructions regarding safety. Oddly enough, they emphasized the danger of collision rather than the far greater peril—icebergs.

The sailing-packet business came to an end in 1873 when Grinnell & Minturn's London Line, a New York firm, quit the passenger-carrying field. Ten years later the freight-packet connection between England and America was broken forever.

A severe economic slump began in 1873. All the continental companies serving New York were hard hit. Freight and steerage rates dropped. The old companies weathered the storm; newcomers like Adler went under. Hamburg-American took Adler over, after the latter's *Schiller* had gone down with heavy loss of life.

Despite poor business conditions, harbor improvement went on. Congress authorized the New York and New Jersey Channels Project, providing for a fourteen-foot channel between Elizabethport, New Jersey, and the westerly end of Shooters Island off Staten Island.

Faster Steamers and Frozen Cargoes

The slump of 1873 did not deter various companies from adding new ships. White Star built the *Britannic* and *Germanic,* both modeled after the *Oceanic*. These two-funneled flyers held the Blue Riband at various times.

The *City of Berlin* was the Inman Line's answer to the challenge of the two White Star flyers. In September 1875 she won both the westward and the eastward records. The *City of Berlin* was the first ship to have electric lights. These were installed in her saloon in 1879.

The Allan liner *Caspian* sailed from New York in 1874, carrying a dozen tons of frozen beef. This marked the beginning of today's huge Atlantic meat trade. The Anchor Line promptly went into this traffic on a much larger scale. All weekly express ships to Glasgow were fitted with refrigerators having a capacity of about four hundred tons of frozen meat.

Hell Gate Freezes

Two new American lines were founded in 1875: the Red D Line, operating between New York and Venezuela, and the Ward Line, whose iron vessels began the New York-Cuba service.

The East River and Long Island Sound from Hell Gate to Sands Point froze during the winter of 1875. During the ten days of this ice blockade the Fall River and Stonington Lines sent their steamboats around Long Island by the outside route. It was the first time that Sound steamers had been forced to take to the ocean because of ice.

Hell Gate Channel was the nightmare of Long Island Sound navigator's until the middle 1870s. The name Hell Gate is a corruption of the Dutch *Hellegat*, meaning "entrance to hell." It was a fitting name to give a channel in which so many vessels were wrecked or seriously damaged. Losses in some years ran as high as $2,500,000. To do away with this navigational menace, attempts were made as early as 1851 to clear the channel. Losses continued chiefly because of Hallett's Point, a jagged rock seven hundred feet wide extending three hundred feet into the channel, which created a strong current tending to throw ships off their course. In 1869 Congress appropriated funds to begin the work of blasting the rocks out of the channel. Drilling and digging continued for seven years. September 24, 1876, the task was finished with fifty-two thousand pounds of explosive. Hallett's Point disappeared at a total cost of less than two million dollars.

Improvement of the Hudson River Channel was begun under authority of the Rivers and Harbors Act of March 3, 1875. Increasing size of steamships and the steady growth of the North River front necessitated the work, which began with the removal of sand bars off Jersey City.

The last year of the 1870s was marked by especially fine new ships. The Allan Line's *Buenos Ayrean* was the first important steel-hulled liner. Guion's *Arizona,* popularly known as the Atlantic Greyhound, lowered both eastbound and westbound records and took possession of the Blue Riband. On one of her earlier voyages she rammed an iceberg but escaped without any casualties. "If she can withstand an iceberg," people said, "she must be the safest thing on the Atlantic." She marked the first distinct differentiation between passenger and cargo steamers.

The Elegant Eighties

During the 1880s most of the steamship lines featured transatlantic rates approximating twenty dollars for steerage, ten dollars for children, three dollars for infants, and sixty dollars for saloon passengers. These lines included the Great Western, Cunard, Guion, Atlas, Red Star, and Inman. The Great Western offered "the cheapest and most direct route from the West of England to New York." Cunard's advertisements carried dignified reminders that the line had been established in 1840. The Guion Line promised service "To Europe in Seven Days," and described its steamships as the "fastest in the world." Red Star Line was going in for passenger comfort. It had ten ships operating between New York and Antwerp, with railroad connections to other cities on the Continent. Cabin passengers were carried "amidships, above the main deck (removed from the engines, screw, and all other objectionable points), where there is the least motion." Steerage accommodations were divided into rooms, "assuring an amount of privacy hitherto unknown to the third-class passenger."

Among coastwise and intercoastal lines were the Morgan Line, Pacific Mail, Ward, and Old Dominion. The "A-1 iron steamships" of the Morgan Line—Morgan Louisiana & Texas Railroad & Steamship Company—served New Orleans, Texas, and points west by rail. The Pacific Mail Line, running between New York and California, had offices at its pier, foot of Canal Street, North River. Steamship line service to Charleston, Savannah, and Florida catered to the growing leisure class by advertising vacations at Aiken "and other favorite resorts of the South." The Ward Line's advertising featured descriptions of "Life in the West Indies." The Old Dominion Steamship Company operated between New York and Norfolk, Virginia.

Long Island Sound Service

Long Island Sound steamboats were numerous. The Norwich Line vessels left daily from Pier 40 (new 32), North River, at the foot of Watts Street. This line advertised its *City of Worcester* as being "without any exception the fastest, most elegantly fitted steamboat on the Sound." The Fall River Line, at Pier 28 (new 18), foot of Murray Street, ran the *Pilgrim, Bristol, Providence, Newport,* and *Old Colony* exclusively for passengers; several others carried freight only. From Pier 33 (new 22), at the foot of Jay Street, the Providence and Stonington Steamship Company (the Stonington and Providence lines having consolidated) specialized in fast freight to Stonington, Conn. The Stonington Express Line offered rail connections to Boston and other New England points.

Despite an enormous increase in population, the city in the middle 1880s was still Little Old New York in many ways. The Brower House, at the corner of Broadway and Twenty-eighth Street, was "in the center of the uptown business part of New York and near all the principal hotels and restaurants." At Fulton, Water, and Pearl streets was the United States Hotel, a favorite with seafaring men. The comparative newness of the telegraph was shown by advertisements of various banking houses announcing "telegraphic exchanges of money" as a special service. Among such firms was Brown Bros. & Company, 58 Wall Street. William Wall's Sons specialized in cordage and oakum at 113 Wall Street. On Broome Street was Brewster & Company, makers of carriages "for the elite." Far uptown, at Ninety-first Street and Third Avenue, J. Ruppert's Brewery was turning out lager beer. Sweet Caporal cigarettes were advertised everywhere.

The American Express Company had nine city offices. Four other companies also functioned as carriers. Everett's Hotel, at 102 Vesey Street, boasted that it was open day and night and was illuminated by "the Edison System of Isolated Lighting." The Singer Manufacturing Company, 34 Union Square, was giving out a pamphlet entitled *Genius*

Rewarded: or The Story of the Sewing Machine. The Pennsylvania Railroad Company was the great trunk line of the United States; it said so itself. Its famous New York-Chicago express, "composed exclusively of Pullman, Hotel, Parlor, Dining and Sleeping Coaches," was an important connecting link between New York and the interior.

Steam ferries added to the Hudson River traffic, most of them running between New York and Jersey City or Hoboken. There was also service between New York and Staten Island and Long Island. The Hoboken and Brooklyn ferries left every five to ten minutes during the day and every fifteen to twenty minutes at night.

Steel Displaces Iron

It was in this decade that steel finally won out over iron on the high seas. This was made possible by the Bessemer-process patents. Cunard launched its *Servia* in 1881, and although she was not the first steel vessel, her commissioning marks the beginning of the widespread use of steel. *Servia*'s cost would have been considerably lower had she been built of iron, but steel's advantages compensated for the added outlay. It was about twenty-five per cent lighter than iron, more easily fashioned, and stronger.

Another technological advance was the twin screw. Practically all steamships had been using one propeller, but it was not until 1881 that the *Notting Hill* demonstrated the superiority of twin screws on the North Atlantic. Their advantage lay in smoother propulsion and less danger if a driving shaft were to break. Yet the twin screw did not become common equipment until long after the *Notting Hill* had been launched. Today the majority of big liners have at least two, and some three or four, propellers.

Improvement in engines is shown by comparing 1881 with 1872. In these ten years steam pressure rose about twenty pounds, while piston speed increased from three hundred and fifty to four hundred and sixty feet a minute. Coal consumption decreased.

Steamboat Landing, Pier No. 1, North (Hudson) River, looking north from Battery Park, 1845 by William Wade engraved by William H. Dougal published by Disturnell in *Views of New York, No. 2*

New York from the East River, John William Hill, 1852;
wash, gouache, graphite on paper, overall 26.5" x 48" (neg. #72392)

Courtesy of the New-York Historical Society (ID# 1906.9)

New Ships

Splendid new ships to serve New York were added in 1881. Among them was the *City of Rome*, considered by some authorities to be "the handsomest steamship ever built." She was of clipper mold. A shortage of steel developed while she was building, and iron was substituted in her hull. This made her too heavy to attain the speed originally specified, and the Inman Line refused to take her from the builders—one of the very rare cases of an express liner being refused by those who had ordered her. The Anchor Line took over the *City of Rome*, and she proved to be a favorite with the traveling public.

Cunard met the *City of Rome*'s challenge with the previously mentioned *Servia*. She more closely resembled the modern liner than contemporary ships, which were speedier and considerably more elaborate. Her protective devices, including a cellular double bottom, were in keeping with the growing trend toward safety at sea.

Possession of the Blue Riband—won in 1879 by the *Arizona*—was one of the Guion Line's greatest assets. To maintain its hold on this symbol of speed supremacy, the line brought out its *Alaska*, whose launching was marred when she stuck on the ways. As soon as she got to sea, however, the *Alaska* justified Guion's investment by winning the westward record and then making the eastward crossing in six days and twenty-two hours. The latter crossing marked the first time the Atlantic had been spanned in less than a week's time. Guion then brought out the *Oregon*, a single-screw seven-thousand-ton steamer with triple-compound engines. The *Oregon* sailed on her maiden voyage from Queenstown to New York in October 1883. She crossed in six days, ten hours, and ten minutes, smashing all records and securing Guion's prestige as operator of the fastest ships in the North Atlantic.

Foreign Shipping Increased in the Port

The extent to which foreign-flagged ships were in-creasing in the Port of New York is shown in the following table of foreign entries into the Port:

Year	Steamships	Ships (Sail)	Barks (Sail)	Brigs (Sail)	Schooners (Sail)
1821	0	260	4	315	331
1844	3	471	351	929	451
1859	268	713	872	1269	885
1865	455	625	1420	1184	1042
1877	1074	389	2234	1076	1451
1882	1945	407	1857	896	1371

The significance of the table lies in the enormous increase of foreign steamships within the twenty-four years from 1859 through 1882. For every foreign steamer entering in 1859 seven were admitted in 1882. Still another indication of how swiftly foreign lines turned to steam, while New York operators were caught fast in their stubborn adherence to sail, is the fact that New York-owned transatlantic tonnage in 1859 was almost exclusively in sail, whereas foreign entries showed about seven vessels out of every one hundred under steam. Foreign steamship competition thus won precedence over local shipping interests. Merely to maintain this lead would have been enough to assure steamship domination in the Port of New York. But the foreign lines were not satisfied merely to hold a lead; they increased it year after year. Thirty out of every one hundred vessels they brought into the Port in 1882 were steamships—about twenty-three more per hundred than in 1859. New York operators could not begin to match this enormous addition to steam tonnage. It was steam that counted in the carrying trade after 1860.

The real beginning of German transatlantic express service occurred on June 26, 1881, when North German Lloyd's *Elbe* sailed from Bremen to New York. This line had been operating since 1858, chiefly from Bremerhaven. In 1882 it commanded the fourth largest shipping fleet in the world, comprising ninety-eight ships with a registered tonnage of one hundred thousand.

"Queen of the Sound"

Keeping pace with advances on the Atlantic, Long Island Sound steamboats were demonstrating what American operators could do in the way of technological development. Prior to 1883, when the Brooklyn Bridge was opened, the Union Ferry Company had been carrying about forty million passengers a year between Manhattan and Brooklyn. On Long Island Sound the big attraction at this time was the *Pilgrim*. She was the first Sound steamer to have electric lights as the sole means of illumination. According to the line's announcement, Thomas A. Edison "exhausted his inventive faculties" in fitting up the *Pilgrim* with "one thousand incandescent electric lights, aggregating twelve thousand candles." Most Sound steamers had huge gas tanks, which were charged daily to supply the chandeliers in the saloons. Many staterooms had no light other than that filtering through the filigree work. A few were equipped with oil lamps, which, together with gas pipes that frequently broke in heavy weather, constituted a serious fire risk. Edison's one thousand incandescent lights on the *Pilgrim* did away with that hazard.

Electricity on the *Pilgrim* did not extend to such devices as call bells. Staterooms had none, and it was not unusual to see passengers roaming the corridors at night, looking for stewards. The *Pilgrim* was, however, the first steamboat in which fireproofing was attempted. Boilers, kitchens, and smokestacks were inclosed with iron. As an added precaution a watchman's clock system and automatic fire alarms were installed. They were the first on any steamboat. New York contributed hull, engines, and joiner work to the *Pilgrim*.

Transatlantic Competition Stiffens

Transatlantic competition was enlivened when Cunard met the challenge of the Guion Line's *Alaska* and *Oregon* in June 1884. Cunard produced the *Umbria,* and three months later it brought out the *Etruria.* They were the last giant single-screw Atlantic liners. Both did valiant service for Cunard, and years later the *Etruria*, by crossing from Queenstown to Sandy Hook in less than six days, demonstrated that the speed of express liners often increased with age. The National Line was also active in 1884. It brought out the *America*, one of the earliest steel liners. She had the first elliptical funnels. In June 1884 the *America* won the eastward speed record.

Some idea of foreign shipping dominance in the Port may be formed from a passing glance at Hamburg-American's fleet. In 1885 its twenty ocean steamships made one hundred and twenty-six round trips, carrying a total of fifty-eight thousand passengers and four hundred and twenty thousand tons of freight in and out of New York. Other foreign companies serving New York were taking their share of the Port's business on a similar scale.

Guion Dies

Stephen Barker Guion, directing head of the Guion Line, died in 1885. How essential he had been to his line's success was shown when the Guion Line was re-organized about a year later as a limited-liability company. The line continued weekly sailings for a few years, but the vessels did not pay expenses. In 1894 they were withdrawn from service and put up for sale. In a single decade of the line's operation under Guion (1875-85) its ships had brought 237,836 passengers to the Port of New York.

At about the time of Guion's death Cunard bought the famous *Oregon* from his line. She did not serve Cunard very long, for she was wrecked off Fire Island on March 14, 1886. Owing to the quick work of North German Lloyd's *Fulda*, there was no loss of life. When their New York agent cabled to ask what compensation to demand of Cunard for having effected the rescue, the directors of the German line replied: "Highly gratified having been instrumental in saving so many lives. No claim."

In this same year T. Hogan & Sons of New York organized the Manhasset Line. Its founders were Americans, residing in New York, yet their ships were under the British flag, because it was cheaper "to operate British."

The increasing use of steel made possible still bigger ships, thus necessitating further harbor improvements. The first contract for work on the Gedney Channel was awarded to Roy Stone of New York on February 7, 1885. He guaranteed to provide a channel two hundred feet wide and twenty-eight feet deep, extending from the sea to the Narrows. Before the initial dredging of Gedney Channel was completed recommendations had been made for a thirty-foot channel one thousand feet wide. The Rivers and Harbors Act of August 5, 1886, appropriated seven hundred and fifty thousand dollars for this purpose. The revised project included the Gedney and Main channels. The growth of commercial vessels kept pace with the channel improvement and, by 1895, the need for increased navigation facilities again became urgent. On June 3, 1896, Congress authorized a survey with a view to providing a thirty-five foot channel at mean low water from the Narrows to the sea. Recommendations were submitted and approved for the dredging of the East Channel to a forty-foot depth and a two-thousand-foot width. Funds were appropriated by the Rivers and Harbors Act of 1899 for the improvement of East Channel—the name of which was subsequently changed, by an act of Congress in 1900, to Ambrose Channel, in honor of John Wolf Ambrose, who had long advocated the improvement of New York Harbor.

The Twin Screw Wins Out

The twin screw came into general use in the 1880s. The *Notting Hill* of 1881 was one of the first transatlantic steamers so fitted. She belonged to the Hill Line, often referred to as the Twin-Screw Line, which eventually went into the business of transporting live cattle between New York and London. After the success of the *Notting Hill* the disadvantages of the single screw became more apparent, especially since two magnificent single-screw ships, Cunard's *Umbria* and *Etruria*, had both been towed home after breakdowns. In 1888 the desire for twin-screw propulsion resulted in Inman's *City of New York*, a 10,400-ton ship often regarded as the Atlantic's first important twin-screw express liner. The *City of New York* and her sister ship, the *City of Paris*, marked the last great effort of the Inman Line, which had been battling Cunard and White Star since the 1850s. These were the first Atlantic liners of more than ten thousand tons gross. They had raked funnels and clipper stems and were the first ships of their size to have bulkheads and double bottoms. Each had twenty watertight compartments separated by solid transverse bulkheads. These extended from the keel to the saloon deck, about fifteen feet above the water line, and had no doors or other openings.

Inman's new beauties later went under American registry and served in the Spanish-American War. After the war they again entered the transatlantic service under their former names. They ran between New York and Southampton, and it has been claimed that they helped to make Southampton the express service port it is today. Years later, after both ships had undergone several changes of name, they were sent to Italy to be broken up. Their sea lives had covered nearly half a century.

The *City of New York* and the *City of Paris* were the first of their type to hold the Blue Riband. This type was the steel-hulled twin-screw ship driven by triple-expansion engines. The last of this fourth major type of steamship to hold the Blue Riband was the *Kaiser Wilhelm II*, launched 1903.

The success of Inman's twin-screwers led to Hamburg-American's entry into the growing twin-screw field. In 1889 it launched the *Columbia* and the *Augusta Victoria*, said to be the first passenger vessels with bulkhead openings that could be closed automatically from the bridge.

Stars and Stripes Rare at Sea

The end of the American Steamship Company in 1884 emphasized how scarce the American flag had been on the North Atlantic since the days of New York's E. K. Collins. Except for a short-lived Boston firm, which operated two wooden-screw steamers on the Liverpool run in 1866, there was no other American line until 1872-73, when the American Steamship Company put four iron-screw steamers on the Philadelphia-Liverpool run. Each of the line's ships cost six hundred thousand dollars. This proved too great a handicap in competition with lower European shipbuilding costs and subsidies. In 1884 the ships were sold to another Philadelphia firm, which converted them into freighters and immigrant carriers. When the original American Steamship Company withdrew its ships it published a statement in which the scarcity of American shipping was emphasized:

> For more than two decades they [American's four ships] have had the melancholy distinction of being the only merchant steamships to show the Stars and Stripes regularly in the ports of western Europe . . . They succumbed at length to their subsidized rivals.

The measure of control exercised by foreign lines over the business of the Port of New York becomes apparent when the forty-eight companies operating out of the Port during 1865-90 are analyzed. They operated a total of one hundred and eighty-two ships. Of the forty-eight lines, nine owned fifty-four per cent of the total number of ships. Not one of these was an American-flag liner.

The growing wealth of the United States, and especially of its greatest port, was reflected in the increasing number of cabin passengers arriving at New York. About eighty per cent of these were Americans returning from business or pleasure trips abroad. In 1881 there were 51,299 cabin passengers; in 1886, 68,742; in 1890, 99,189.

The Last Decade

In 1889 Long Island Sound steamboats finally began to lose their prestige as the foremost passenger carriers between the Port of New York and New England points. From 1815, when Sound service had been inaugurated, until 1889 there had been no through rail service to Boston except via Hartford and Springfield. Completion of the Thames River drawbridge at New London in that year changed the picture, providing a more direct route by land.

The beginning of the last decade of the nineteenth century showed more clearly than ever the rise of American ports other than New York. In virtually every export and import commodity New York dropped below its 1880 share of the national total. Ships and tonnage entered and cleared were lower than in 1880. Of the nation's total exports, New York handled 40.57 per cent in 1890, as compared with 46.98 in 1880 and 41.71 in 1870. In imports the Port accounted for 65.43 per cent of the national total, as against 68.86 for 1880 and 64.47 for 1870. Within the Port itself, however, total tonnage handled was increasing. This was especially true of imports. Gains were shown in sugar and molasses, coffee, wool and manufactures, and silk and manufactures. Coffee increased nearly 413 per cent over 1880. New York had won the undisputed world leadership in coffee imports which it holds to this day.

The effects of foreign competition for world markets was strikingly reflected in the percentage of foreign trade carried in American ships. In 1860 about 66 per cent of this trade had been American-bottomed; in 1870 the percentage was less than 36. An even better indication of the decline was furnished by averages for American-bottomed foreign trade: 23.9 per cent for 1876-80 and 14.1 per cent for 1886-90. The United States had lost control of the carrying trade for her own foreign commerce.

Courtesy of the New-York Historical Society (ID#2088a)

South Street, Looking North from Coenties Slip, *circa* 1884 (Photograph)

New York Harbor, 1941

Shipbuilding Supremacy Ends

In New York shipbuilding figures for the Port further emphasized the decline. During clipper days the city's shipyards, from the Battery to Corlear's Hook, had been busy day and night. Thousands of tons of shipping had slid down the ways as proof of New York's dominant position in shipbuilding. The year 1855 had seen the beginning of the end. But not until 1860 was the full importance of steam made manifest in a community stubbornly committed to outmoded sailing ships. From 1860 to 1890 the story unfolds in disheartening statistics. During these years the Port of New York produced an average of 187 ships a year, totaling 62,470 tons. Only seven out of these thirty-one years were above the average, and three of these unusual periods were war boom years. In 1886 only 75 vessels, totaling 7293 tons, were built. New York had lost her shipbuilding supremacy, in addition to her control of ships and navigation.

An incident in 1892, little noticed at the time, was later to effect great changes at sea. Dr. Rudolf Diesel patented an engine in which crude oil was used as fuel. In the third decade of the twentieth century this engine began to demonstrate its importance as an efficient and economical means for power on land and on sea.

Cholera Frightens the Port

Another event of 1892 was the cholera scare precipi-tated when the immigrant ship *Moravia* arrived in port from Hamburg. Twenty-two people died while the ship was at sea, and she was quarantined in the Lower Bay. Numerous European steamers were soon being held at the quarantine station near Fort Wadsworth. The excitement was intensi-fied when the *Scandia* reported thirty-two deaths. Passengers were subjected to great inconvenience as a result of the frantic attempts to keep out the plague. Cabin passengers on the crack liner *Normannia*, on which no sign of cholera had been reported, were put to such discomfort that J. P. Morgan purchased the abandoned steamer *Ston-*

ington and arranged with health authorities to transfer the *Normannia's* passengers to her. Meanwhile the authorities purchased the western end of Fire Island for $210,000, including a summer hotel having accommodations for one thousand persons. During that period armed citizens of Islip and Bay Shore prevented the landing of the *Normannia*'s passengers. For two days the passengers were subjected to great hardships on the vessels being used to disembark them. They had very little room, no sleeping accommodations, and no food. Finally Governor Flower ordered National Guardsmen and naval reserves to the scene. Under their protection passengers were landed and transported to their homes.

Cholera continued to be a deterrent factor in immigrant transportation in 1893, when the epidemic in Hamburg stopped emigration from that port to the United States. This seriously affected the earnings of the Hamburg-American Line. Yet the sound financial judgment of foreign operators was demonstrated in this poor year when Hamburg-American charged off every cent of net earnings (about one million dollars) to depreciation of its vessels.

The great naval review on April 26, 1893, was one of the memorable harbor events of the 1890s. Thirteen American naval vessels, four British, four Russian, three Italian, three Spanish, two German, two French, and several South American cruisers participated. The guns of Forts Hamilton and Wadsworth and the Naval Review Fleet greeted the vessels upon their arrival in the Port, and vast crowds watched the procession as it steamed up the Hudson River.

One of the most important technical developments of the 1890s was the turbine engine. In 1897 Charles Parsons of England applied this invention to the *Turbinia*. She was a small vessel of only one hundred tons' displacement, but she was the test tube in which Parsons developed the turbine until he was able to achieve a speed of thirty-four and one half knots.

In 1894 four steamers were constructed by W. R. Grace & Company, an outstanding pioneer in the development of South American trade since the late 1840s. The line had previously chartered its vessels.

An unusual corporation was organized in 1899. It was the United Fruit Company, which now dominates the banana business. The big business potentialities of this food had been visualized by United Fruit, and since its formation the company has expanded enormously. It owns or leases nearly two million acres in Central and South America and the West Indies; has an average of about sixty-eight thousand people on its pay roll in season; operates hospitals, hotels, and factories; has radio, telephone, and telegraph stations. The company operates fifteen hundred miles of railways and seven hundred miles of tramways. In addition to bananas, this commercial empire is based on the production, transportation, and marketing of other tropical foods such as sugar, cacao, and coconuts. Its eighty-odd ships compose what is known as the Great White Fleet. It is another of the few lines out of the Port of New York that operate vessels under American registry.

Another portent of the late 1890s was the establishment of Marconi wireless over a short sea distance. The *Ponce* and *Grand Duchess* observed the America's Cup yacht races in 1899 and reported results by wireless to the cable ship *Mackay Bennett*, which immediately relayed bulletins to London via the submarine cable. The *Ponce*'s set was so feeble that when she herself was disabled the following winter it gave her no help, and she drifted five days with a broken shaft before United States naval vessels found her. In 1898 wireless was applied to communication between lightships and shore.

American-Built Liners at Long Last

The success of two of the twin-screw steamships of the late 1880s led to the building of the first big Atlantic liners constructed in the United States since 1860. They were the American Line's *St. Louis* and *St. Paul*, each of 11,630 tons and with a speed of twenty-one knots. They were laid down in American yards in the mid-1890s because Congress stipulated in 1893 that the *City of New York* and *City of Paris* could go under American registry only if ships of at least equal tonnage were built in the United States. After the *New York* and the *Paris* had been transferred to the American flag White Star challenged their twenty-one-knot speed with its *Teutonic* and *Majestic*. The struggle was a short one, for Cunard soon dominated the scene with its *Campania* and *Lucania,* each of which turned up twenty-two knots. The power plants of these two ships were the last word in the 1890s. Thirteen boilers furnished steam at a pressure of one hundred and sixty-five pounds to the square inch; one hundred and two furnaces supplied the energy. In 1893 the *Campania* made her maiden voyage; in 1895 she smashed the eastward record with a passage of five days and ten hours. Her last trip was in April 1914, when she was taken off the North Atlantic to make way for the *Aquitania*. During the World War she served as a seaplane carrier with the British navy.

The dominance of the North Atlantic by foreign lines was again demonstrated in 1897. Germany's North German Lloyd captured the coveted speed record with its *Kaiser Wilhelm der Grosse*. To this challenger the other German company, Hamburg-American, made no reply. Instead, it settled on a policy of comfort plus cargo capacity.

The year 1899 saw the first transatlantic steamer larger than the *Great Eastern*. Nothing had been built to exceed *Great Eastern* in size in all the years since 1860. Now White Star brought out its second *Oceanic*. She was 685 feet and 7 inches long, slightly more than 68 feet wide, 44 feet deep, and of 17,274 gross tons. The *Oceanic* had electric lights, wireless, refrigerating machinery, sumptuous staterooms, and many other improvements. Her cost of $3,695,000 was the highest for any ship up to that time. To maintain her speed of 20 knots, she required 400 tons of coal a day. The *Oceanic* was a fitting introduction to the race for speed and size which the twentieth century was to see intensified.

Much of the American-flag shipping at this time was under sail. Among the large operators of such vessels were L. Luckenbach, 129 Broad Street, with 24 ships; Swan & Son, 66 South Street, 17 ships; W. P. Clyde & Company, 5 Bowling Green, 15 ships; Miller, Bull &

Knowlton, 130 Pearl Street, 3 ships; Flint & Company, 68 Broad Street, 12 ships; C. H. Mallory & Company, Pier 20 East River, 10 ships; Richard P. Buck & Company, 29 South Street, 10 ships; and C. G. Endicott, 93 West Street, 7 ships.

In the steamship field a few names still well known were operating coastwise, West Indian, and South American vessels in the early 1890s. Among these were the Red D Line, C. H. Mallory & Company, and New York and Cuba Mail Steamship Company (Ward Line). Other operators included the Ocean Steamship Company (Savannah Line), Pacific Mail Steamship Company, Morgan Louisiana & Texas Railroad & Steamship Company (Morgan Line), Cromwell Steamship Line, W. R. Grace & Company, and United States & Brazil Mail. Pacific Mail Steamship Company had seventeen ships, and C. H. Mallory & Company operated eleven. New York and Cuba Mail Steamship Company and Ocean Steamship Company had seven ships each.

Vessels belonging to railroad, ferry, or tugboat companies were all American-flagged. Among operators of such ships were the Pennsylvania Railroad Company, the Central Railroad of New Jersey, Chesapeake & Ohio Railway, Cheney's Towing Company at the foot of West Twentieth Street, New York Central & Hudson River Railroad, and the Philadelphia & Reading Railroad, with ten steam and three sailing ships.

Organizations operating vessels in Hudson River and Long Island Sound waters included the Albany Day Line, Iron Steamboat Company, Maine Steamship Company, New England Terminal Company, New Haven Steamship Company, Providence and Stonington Steamship Company, People's Line, and Metropolitan Line.

However, although the annual exports of the nation's own produce exceeded a billion dollars in value, the American flag was never before such a rarity on the North Atlantic ship lanes. The nineteenth century closed with foreign ships carrying about ninety per cent of American imports and ninety-four per cent of her exports.

CHAPTER X

International Rivalry—1901-39

THE SUPERLINERS

T HE NINETEENTH CENTURY gave way to the twentieth without any appreciable effect on the Port of New York. The early 1900s were little more than a continuation of the 1860-1900 period. Steam had proved its superiority over sail, yet only five years before 1900 more than seventeen hundred sailing vessels had entered the Port. This figure indicated the last great effort of sail to compete with steam. The race for speed and size went on, but the opening years of the twentieth century offered few startling developments in this phase of shipbuilding and shipowner competition. The Spanish-American War had given rise to speculation concerning its effect on the Port's business, and some shipping men had envisioned an almost automatic boom. Nothing of the sort occurred.

Since the European trade of the North Atlantic routes was dominated by foreign-flag shipping, American ships were fighting for trade positions chiefly in the Western Hemisphere. In 1895 and in 1900 more American-flag ships entered the Port of New York from Cuba than from any other country. Second place in 1895 and 1900 went to American ships returning from England, but by 1910 these had dropped to fourth place. This indicated the steadily tightening grip which the British were exerting on the transatlantic trade. British ships were taking a leading part in the business of the Port of New York, whereas American ships were playing an insignificant role in Liverpool and London.

Total port tonnage in American-flag shipping dropped steadily. Only 16.9 per cent of the Port's foreign commerce in 1895 was transported in American bottoms. By 1900 the percentage had dropped to 13.97, and the year 1910 saw a further drop to 10.79.

Chelsea Piers Erected

The Chelsea Piers, nine large docks extending from Twelfth Street to Twenty-second Street on the Hudson River, were built by the city between 1902 and 1907 at a cost of fifteen million dollars. They were planned to berth the largest ocean liners of the time. The construction of the Transatlantic Steamship Terminal (Piers 88, 90, and 92) between Forty-eighth and Fifty-second streets in 1936, designed for the *Normandie*, the *Queen Mary*, the *Rex*, and other huge liners, failed to lessen the importance of the Chelsea docks. Piers 53, 54, and 56, during the 1930-40 period for example, were leased to the Cunard Steamship Company; the first for $45,375 a year, and the other two for $84,700 a year each. The French Line rented Pier 57 for $84,700 annually, while the International Mercantile Marine Company paid the same annual rental for each of four of the piers, and $45,375 a year, during this period, for the last one, Pier 62.

1914

In the summer of 1914 the attention of the Port was centered on Europe, threatened with a general war. Germany's magnificent *Imperator* arrived in New York on June 3, establishing a new speed record; after the war this ship flew British colors as the *Berengaria*. The *Oceanic* docked on the tenth, carrying its usual quota of notable travelers. Marine disaster added a touch of excitement: the pilot boat *New Jersey* was rammed during a fog and sank; a few days later the Hamburg-American steamer *Pretoria* rammed the *New York* of the American Line, and both limped into port.

On July 28 Austria declared war on Serbia, and events in Europe moved swiftly. On August 1 Admiral Dewey declared that a world war would pave the way for a great American merchant marine. Two days later Germany declared war on France. Hamburg-American's docks were heavily guarded. A German cruiser was sighted off Sandy Hook; the darkened *President Grant* slipped into port, and the *Kronprinz Wilhelm* left the harbor to begin the run for her home port. Great Britain made its declaration against Germany on August 4, and the Port of New York again faced the problem of trade disruption caused by war.

Confusion in the Port

The Panama Canal was opened to traffic on August 15. Commerce with Europe practically ceased. The New York Stock Exchange closed; bankers refused to accept bills of lading as collateral. Marine-insurance rates rocketed, and prices of domestic and imported goods soared. Committees to consider the situation sprang up everywhere. Unemployment resulted as workers in the export field were laid off or put on part time. Longshoremen and teamsters were thrown out of work. Thousands of alien reservists crowded steamship offices and consulates, trying to get back to Europe.

The harbor was an extraordinary sight. Not since the days of Jefferson's embargo preceding the War of 1812 had there been such a mass of ships riding at anchor or made fast to docks. In Jefferson's day most of the shipping had flown the American flag. Now ships flying the flags of many countries were stretched from Ellis Island to Tottenville. Manned by crews of nations at war, they lay for months side by side. Yet, as the New York *Press* put it at the time, "They lie in amity; the mantle of this nation covers all alike. . . Here are British tramps and German liners, Russian emigrant ships and French freighters, Austrian hookers and many others, their ensigns all fluttering. Some may grow weary of inaction and slip out past Sandy Hook, to brave the dangers of destruction or capture. How many will be afloat a year from now?"

But war business from Europe soon reversed the picture. Imports and exports rose so rapidly that the Port of New York seemed incapable of handling the sudden freightage increase. Drays and trucks often clotted the waterfront arteries, adding greatly to the cost of transportation. Other ports were being developed by the Federal government, however, and some of the war traffic was soon diverted to them, particularly incoming freight. Laborsaving machinery and methods, bridges and tunnels, and better port organization were needed.

Various individuals and groups charged city officials with lack of port-consciousness. Particularly was this criticism directed against the mayors between 1902 and the period just before American participation in the European war. Despite this apathy and other factors alleged to be retarding development, the Port began to expand and profit greatly as a result of the war. Most of the trade with the Central Powers had been lost because of the Allied blockade, but trade with the Allies, and the neutral countries deprived of their normal sources of supply, more than compensated for the loss. Allied orders increased immensely after the first year of war had depleted stocks. The Port of New York was in a strategic position to gain from this war trade. This position, as well as the recovery from the loss of Central Powers' commerce, is revealed in the following table:

VALUE OF NEW YORK EXPORTS

1913	$ 917,936,000
1914	833,394,000
1915	1,792,335,000
1916	2,790,403,000

American Seamen's Conditions Improved

While coastwise shipping was by law exclusively American, only about ten per cent of the country's foreign commerce was carried in American bottoms. American steamships registered for foreign trade in

1914 amounted to but 725,000 gross tons. Several months after the outbreak of the war Congress enacted legislation allowing foreign-built ships owned by Americans to be transferred to American registry. This added nearly 750,000 gross tons of shipping to the United States tonnage, much of which New York gained.

Less than ten per cent of the personnel of the country's merchant marine were American citizens. The merchant seaman's lot was not an enviable one. Working conditions aboard ships were bad, and the hours were unreasonably long. Controlling the maritime labor market were crimps who, in the modern sense, were boardinghouse operators who also acted as independent ship-employment agents. Even the seamen's trade unions permitted hiring through such agents, and a seaman often found himself working for wages already signed over to the crimp.

The founder of marine trade unions in New York and president of the International Seamen's Union was Andrew Furuseth, a Norwegian sailor who emigrated here during his youth. Furuseth saw that seamen's conditions first must receive the benefit of Federal legislation before any cooperation from steamship owners could be hoped for. Following years of lobbying in Washington, he obtained the aid of Senator Robert M. La Follette, and after a long fight, backed at last by all labor organizations, the Seamen's Act of March 4, 1915, was passed. The La Follette Act abolished arrest and imprisonment for desertion in foreign ports, which was a long step forward; a sailor could now quit a ship in protest against unfair labor practices or ill-treatment.

The legislation improved safety regulations, standardized working hours, gave the men better food, increased the number of rated men in ships' crews, required larger living space in crews' forecastles, and made all forms of corporal punishment by the officers a penitentiary offense. The law also protected wages from assignment to creditors, which put a damper on the crimps' activities and led to an improved hiring system.

One of the chief aims of the Seamen's Act had been to raise the wage level on American vessels, but the low wage scale of foreign ships' crews touching American ports was a complicating factor, as it tended to keep American seamen's wages down. The law prohibited the jailing of foreign seamen for desertion in this country and allowed them to quit their ships here if dissatisfied with conditions. This loss of protection to foreign-ship operators was designed to induce them to better conditions and raise wages on vessels calling at American ports. According to a report by the United States Shipping Board in 1918, the aim was partly achieved.

Before the passage of the law wages out of American Atlantic ports, including New York, ranged from twenty-four dollars to thirty-five dollars a month for able seamen. The first two years of the war did not appear to bring about any wage increase. Three months after the Seamen's Act had been passed wages were increased to forty-five dollars a month, and the pay of European seamen rose to the American level. By 1918 the average monthly wage was seventy-five dollars, plus bonuses for crews operating in war zones.

Shipping Board Created

After the uncertainties of late 1914 and early 1915 shipbuilding responded to demand; existing yards flourished, and new ones were laid out. Yet the 1915 output was only 155,000 gross tons. In 1916 Congress set up the United States Shipping Board to regulate rates and practices of ocean shipping. It also appropriated fifty million dollars for the building, purchasing, chartering, and operating of vessels.

Huge profits were made by shipowners. Before the war it cost twenty-five cents to ship one hundred pounds of cotton to England; two years of war sent this cost to five dollars. In 1914 it cost eighty-eight cents a ton monthly to charter ships for transatlantic service; in 1915 the price was $7.37 a ton. In 1917 it rose to thirteen dollars a ton if outside the war zone, to twenty-one dollars a ton on the New York-Genoa trade, and to twenty dollars a ton on the New York-France trade.

Seizures and Sinkings

As the war spread and gained momentum and the British blockade tightened, Great Britain again demonstrated that her notion of freedom of the seas differed sharply from that of the United States. The War of 1812 had been fought over this issue, but, in the peace following that conflict, Britain had conceded none of her "rights." Now, more than one hundred years later, British warships were again seizing American vessels carrying materials which His Majesty's government had declared contraband. That these vessels were dealing with neutral countries seemed to make no difference to Britain. She charged that, since her enemies were receiving materials of war through neutral countries, she had no alternative but to seize ships bearing such cargoes. This position was also adopted by the French, who likewise interfered with American shipping under similar circumstances.

The United States government protested this interference with American shipping to neutral ports. Notes were exchanged as tempers flared. The *John D. Rockefeller, Brindilla,* and *Platuria* were among the vessels whose names figured prominently in the press during this period. America's protests came to nothing. United States mail was rifled, and it was charged that American trade secrets had been stolen. Exporters to the neutral countries soon found that approval by the British Embassy was the only safeguard for shipments, so far as the Allied blockade was concerned.

When finally the United States entered the war this issue was put aside. Before that, however, resentment against British and French tactics had been replaced by a similar feeling toward the Germans. Allied interference with neutral trade had resulted in property loss. Now Germany announced a policy that spelled probable loss of life as well as of property, and she emphasized her position by means of a notice appearing in New York newspapers of May 1, 1915.

The Lusitania

Beneath the Cunard advertisement announcing the sailing of the *Lusitania* from New York there appeared a statement by the Imperial German Embassy warning the public that all enemy vessels were liable to destruction in the war zone. Travelers sailing on them, the embassy stressed, did so at their own risk. Although this announcement gained wide publicity, few of the *Lusitania*'s passengers canceled sailing.

On Friday afternoon, May 7, 1915, the *Lusitania* was torpedoed ten miles off the Old Head of Kinsale, southeast tip of Ireland. According to an eyewitness account:

"We saw what looked like a whale or a porpoise rising about three quarters of a mile to starboard. . . . Immediately a white line, a train of bubbles, started away from the black object. ...It ...struck under the bridge. . . . We all hoped for the fraction of a second it would not explode. But the explosion came clear up through the upper deck, and pieces of the wreckage fell clean aft of where we were standing . . . The boilers exploded immediately. The passengers all rushed at once to the high side of the deck—the portside. There was such a list to starboard that all boats on the portside swung right back inboard and could not be launched."

Within 20 minutes after the submarine U-20's torpedo struck her the *Lusitania* disappeared beneath the surface of the sea. Of the 1924 passengers and crew aboard, 1198 were lost, 124 of them being Americans.

This sinking angered the American public, especially along the Atlantic seaboard. War with Germany seemed probable. But three days later President Wilson made his "too-proud-to-fight" speech, and a crisis was averted. An exchange of notes between the United States and Germany followed, during which time several American vessels were torpedoed and many Americans went down with British, French, and Italian ships. Finally Germany gave a conditional pledge to restrain her submarine warfare, and from May 4, 1916, to January 31, 1917, she sank no ships under circumstances outlawed by the United States.

Explosions on Ships and Ashore

Explosions aboard ships began to engage the attention of New York's officials. On January 3, 1915, a mysterious explosion occurred on the *Orton*, docked in Erie Basin. During the following three months so many bombs were found and so many fires broke out on vessels bound for Allied countries that the public as well as shipowners clamored for action. The difficult job of running down the ship saboteurs in New York was assigned to the New York Police Department's Bomb Squad. On October 1915 the first break came when a purchase of TNT was traced to a bombing ring, which had in its possession twenty-five sticks of dynamite, four hundred and fifty pounds of potassium chlorate, four hundred detonating caps, two hundred bomb cylinders, and four finished bombs. Military experts declared the bombs to be mechanically perfect. They were designed for attachment to a ship's rudder, whose motion wound up a mechanism that eventually set off the explosive, of which there was enough in each bomb to sink a ship.

Because most of the men arrested in this ring were of German descent, three of the Bomb Squad were assigned to German saloons lining the Hoboken waterfront. They gained the confidence of dock workers and German seamen whose ships lay idle at the piers. In April 1916 the detectives succeeded in smashing the bombing ring. The *Friedrich der Grosse* had been used as a workshop, and a German agent had supervised the making of the bombs. This agent estimated that cargoes worth ten million dollars had been destroyed on thirty-six ships.

The prevention of sabotage ashore was even more difficult. Hardly a week went by without a mysterious fire or explosion in some factory producing ammunition or other war supplies for the Allies.

The chief terminal in America for the transfer of munitions to Allied ships was on Black Tom, a mile-long peninsula in the Port of New York, extending from the New Jersey shore toward the Statue of Liberty. Warehouses, trackage, and piers were owned by the Lehigh Valley Railroad Company. Freight cars were run to the northern part of

Black Tom, where their contents were unloaded upon barges and transported to ships. Black Tom was guarded by six railroad watchmen and private detectives hired by the Allies. However, watchmen seldom challenged the bargemen who passed, and the unlighted terminal could easily be reached by boat.

On Saturday night, July 29, 1916, there were thirty-four carloads of munitions in the yard. These contained more than two million pounds of high explosives. In addition, there were ten barges, most of them loaded. At 12:45 A.M. guards noticed flames coming from a munitions car. They turned in an alarm and fled. One hour and twenty-three minutes later there was a terrific blast, followed soon by another and seemingly heavier one. Both were heard as far away as Philadelphia. Windows were blown in by the terrific concussions; skyscrapers were shaken; many slumbering persons were thrown from their beds, and dazed crowds filled the streets under a sky lighted by the conflagration. The major blasts were followed by a series of smaller shell explosions. Fragments of metal were thrown as far as Governors Island. Ellis Island buildings were badly damaged, and their occupants were quickly removed. The Black Tom terminal was completely destroyed, but only two persons were killed, owning to the early-morning hour of the explosion. The property loss amounted to twenty-two million dollars.

United States Enters the War

On the last day of January 1917 Germany informed the United States of her decision to resume unrestricted submarine warfare. Receipt of this news in New York disrupted industrial and shipping activity. The stock and commodity markets declined; marine-insurance rates soared; sailings were canceled; the Port was virtually closed; the watch on interned German ships was doubled, and the Navy Department ordered destroyers out to reinforce the neutrality patrol.

Throughout this tense period the sinking of the British liner *Lusitania* was kept in the minds of Americans; emotionalized, it personified the German submarine blockade of the British Isles and meant "wanton murder" rather than war. Actually twenty-three months elapsed between the *Lusitania* disaster and America's entry into the war; four United States vessels had been sunk by Germany before the *Lusitania*, and nine American ships between the latter and the American war declaration. When Germany announced its unrestricted submarine warfare in tightening its blockade of the British Isles on February 1, President Wilson lost all patience and broke off diplomatic relations with Germany on February 3. The United States declared on April 6, 1917, that a state of war existed with Germany.

America's first war need was ships. A total of one hundred and twenty-three German and Austrian vessels had been seized and transferred to American registry, and private vessels were being commandeered for government purposes. However, since it was believed that all of these could be sunk within a few months by German U-boats, the United States decided upon one of its most important contributions to the winning of the war. This was shipbuilding. The program involved a succession of concrete, steel, iron, wood, and even composition ships. Shipbuilding was put on a mass-production basis; one of the largest shipyards in the country was in the New York area. This was the Submarine Boat Corporation at Port Newark, which employed fifteen thousand persons.

Wartime Organization of the Port

Wartime organization of the Port of New York resulted in the expenditure of millions of dollars on new piers and other improvements. Yet America's entry into the war put such a strain on the Port that breakdowns occurred. In addition, a severe coal shortage in 1917 and 1918 resulted from railroad congestion at the Port. Thousands of freight cars waiting to be unloaded jammed New York terminals. In other parts of the country empty railroad cars were as scarce as unused ships in New

York, where the oldest hulks were made seaworthy and luxurious yachts were converted into naval craft.

The Port's main handicap was lack of unified control. In 1917 the first step in creating the Port of New York Authority was taken. This was the appointment, by the states of New York and New Jersey, of a Harbor Development Commission to determine the best means of facilitating commerce. The commission's findings, together with the program it formulated, aided in the better organization of the Port during the critical war years.

Fifteen million dollars had been expended by the government on Port Newark Terminal, a stretch of reclaimed swampland. This development was first used as a supply base for the War Department's Embarkation Service but later abandoned. President Wilson created the War Board for the Port of New York, with Irving Bush as executive officer. The Bush Terminal at South Brooklyn was taken over by the government at the beginning of 1918, and its vast warehouse space and well-equipped berthage became the Embarkation Service's Army Supply Base. Army supply shipments increased from sixteen thousand tons in June 1917 to eight hundred thousand tons in November 1918. Yet the Port's export and import figures for the two years reveal a drop in its share of the nation's totals:

	Value of NY Exports	% of Total U.S. Exports
1916	2,790,403,000	50.8
1917	2,901,138,000	48.1
1918	2,560,857,000	41.6
	Value of NY Imports	% of Total U.S. Imports
1916	1,257,185,000	52.5
1917	1,361,662,000	46.1
1918	1,294,415,000	42.6

Troop Movements and Harbor Defenses

One of the most thoroughly German cities in America, Hoboken, became the embarkation center for American troops sent to fight the Germans. The six Hudson River piers of the German lines were taken over by the Embarkation Service, and an embarkation camp was erected within marching distance of the piers. This was Camp Merritt, near Tenafly, New Jersey.

Three quarters of all troops sent to France embarked from the Port of New York. Most of these men had never seen an ocean-going vessel, and ferryboats were sometimes mistaken by them for transports. Festive departures were banned by the War Department. Nobody was allowed on the piers on sailing days. Welfare workers were finally granted access, and departing soldiers were occasionally served coffee and sandwiches.

By the end of 1917 more than one hundred and ninety thousand men had embarked for France. In the spring of 1918 ways were found to get twice as many soldiers into a ship, so that thousands sailed daily during the summer. The average round-trip time for transports was shortened from fifty-two days in the spring of 1917 to thirty-five days in 1918. Cargo ships required about seventy days. During the war more than two million American troops were carried safely overseas. No transports were lost on the eastward run, and only three were sunk on the return voyage.

New York Harbor was defended by warships and a system of forts. Fort Hancock was at Sandy Hook, Fort Tilden at Rockaway Point, Fort Wadsworth and Fort Tompkins on Staten Island, and Fort Hamilton on the Brooklyn shore flanked the Narrows. In the Upper Bay was Fort Jay on Governors Island. Two forts commanded the Long Island entrance to the East River, and four guarded the eastern entrance to the Sound. After America's entry into the war a huge steel net was placed across the mouth of the harbor, and obsolete guns of the various forts were replaced.

U-Boats off the Port

The German submarine U-151 damaged shipping along the coast from the Delaware capes to Newfoundland. Yet the U-151 and five other German submarines sent to American waters failed to accomplish their purpose, for the stream of soldiers across the Atlantic, as well as transatlantic and coastal shipping, was not seriously disorganized at any time by underseas warfare. Credit for this was due primarily to the convoy system, under which the Atlantic coast was divided into six naval districts, each having hunt squadrons, mine sweepers, and seaplanes.

The sinking of the United States armored cruiser *San Diego* off the coast of Long Island was attributed at first to a German submarine. The *San Diego* was zigzagging into New York during the morning of July 19, 1918, ten miles southeast of Fire Island, when a violent explosion ruptured her hull below the water line. Of the 1189 men aboard, three were instantly killed. The wireless was put out of commission. The gun crews were ordered to "fire at anything that looks like a submarine," and the gunners fired at random until orders were passed to abandon ship. Later a Naval Court of Inquiry held that the sinking was caused by a mine. Six lives were lost and six men injured.

Postwar Peak in Shipping

Upon the termination of the war, the United States Embarkation Service became the Debarkation Service. New York was the center of this enormous activity. Warships, cargo carriers, and vessels just completed were pressed into service. During thirteen months hundreds of ships landed troops at New York, and all but a few of these ships flew the Stars and Stripes. Thousands of the war dead were also brought back, most of them reaching American soil through the Port of New York.

The Port had held onto its huge share of the nation's commerce, chiefly through a large increase in imports. The table below summarizes the 1918-20 growth:

	Value of NY Exports	% of Total U.S. Exports
1918	$2,560,857,000	41.6
1919	3,456,329,000	43.6
1920	3,283,873,000	39.9

	Value of NY Imports	% of Total U.S. Imports
1918	$1,294,415,000	42.6
1919	2,064,654,000	52.8
1920	2,892,621,000	54.7

The demand for ships did not abate. By June 30, 1919, more than 5,500,000 tons had been delivered, with about 8,000,000 more still due. The shipbuilding peak was reached in 1920 when vessels totaling 3,660,000 tons were launched. On January 1, 1920, the American flag flew on more than 2500 ocean-going ships of 1000 tons or larger. These vessels totaled 9,500,000 tons, 62 per cent of which were owned by the United States Shipping Board. High rates made it profitable to operate almost any kind of ship on any ocean route. Scores of new services were started to small ports. Ships were precious, a vessel built in 1900 for $175,000, for example, being worth $575,000 in 1920.

Those were days for dreams of maritime greatness, and many believed that the American merchant marine was to regain the dominant position it had held in the clipper days. But it remained a dream. The ships and the money were available in huge quantities, but the love of the sea and the fierce determination to make the American flag supreme upon the seas seemed no longer to be characteristic of the American people. Industry, not the sea, was now their consuming interest, and particularly was this true of New Yorkers, whose wealth was no longer derived directly from South Street.

The Port of New York Authority

The Port of New York Authority was created in April 1921 as a self-sustaining public corporation, which would solve Port problems cooperatively in spite of the state line that divides the district. For more than two years preceding the signing of the bistate compact, however, there were sharp public debates and much political opposition to the plan of combining New York's and New Jersey's resources to secure a centralized and coordinated control of the Port.

When local opposition had been overcome the respective legislatures authorized commissioners to sign the compact between the states of New York and New Jersey, and the new project was ratified by Congress in August 1921. In February 1922 the legislatures adopted a comprehensive plan that gave the Port Authority, governed by six commissioners from each state, broad powers with which to aid in the future development of the Port.

In general terms, the Authority was to "promote and encourage the movement of domestic and foreign commerce by land and water, through the port and between the port and other localities; and improve existing facilities and provide new facilities for the movement of such commerce."

The comprehensive plan involved the improvement of waterways, tunnels, highways, bridges, and terminals; the building of new bridges, tunnels, and terminals; the coordination of both trucking and railroad-terminal facilities; and the layout of the Port in transportation belts so that direct routes and terminals could be placed in a manner that would prevent traffic congestion. In May 1924 the New York legislature amended the plan for the development of the Port of New York, giving the Authority additional powers. For future Port planning, the Authority was given power to hold hearings, investigations, or inquiries, to compel the attendance of witnesses, to procure the advice or testimony of corporations, to administer oaths, and to issue subpoenas.

Since that date the Port Authority has constructed the Lincoln Tunnel under the Hudson River at midtown, the George Washington Bridge over the Hudson at 179th Street, three bridges between Staten Island and the New Jersey mainland (the Outerbridge Crossing, the Goethals, and Bayonne bridges), and the Inland Terminal No. 1, which has been called New York's first "union station for package freight." Although the Holland Tunnel was built by an earlier commission, the Authority refinanced and now operates it.

The Port Authority finances its projects by the sale of its own bonds. Interest, amortization, and operating costs are paid by the proceeds of tolls, and all Port facilities are held in trust for both states.

In addition to its construction activities, the Port Authority carries on an extensive program as a planning and advisory agency. It has conducted continuous research on questions of pier and harbor development, channel improvements, arterial highways, airports, markets, union terminals, and allied subjects. The Port Authority has upon many occasions cooperated with other agencies in studying such projects as the Foreign-Trade Zone constructed by New York City on Staten Island and the new naval dry dock for the Port of New York now under construction at Bayonne.

The Port Authority, being charged by New Jersey and New York with the duty of protecting the Port's commerce, appears on behalf of the Port of New York at hearings before the Interstate Commerce Commission on questions of transportation rates and officially champions the Port of New York before the United States Maritime Commission and other regulatory bodies. Such port-protection activities involve the presentation of briefs and oral arguments at hearings and have as their aim the prevention of any attempt by a competing port to divert traffic from New York through manipulation of transportation rates or inequitable service charges. The Port Authority has also been active in advocating uniformity as to transportation rates and procedures for all communities lying within the Port of New York district as established by the 1921 treaty.

Rum Row and Hijackers

The 1920s, which witnessed constructive developments such as the Port of New York Authority, also saw the strange effect of the national prohibition law on the Port. Rumrunning, which actually dates back to colonial times, again became a colorful part of the local maritime scene and developed swiftly into an illicit business of vast magnitude. This smuggling was brazenly defiant in its early stages, when shiploads of liquor were landed within the Port itself. Later a stricter enforcement of the law led to the phenomenon known as Rum Row. Ships riding deep with liquor anchored outside the three-mile limit off Sandy Hook, and small craft went out to them at night to run cargoes ashore. The Coast Guard battled these fast ship-to-shore motorboats, but the battle was a losing one, chiefly because the rumrunners could buy faster boats over-night, whereas governmental red tape delayed purchase of new Coast Guard craft to meet the increasing speed of rumrunning boats.

After a few years the government announced that the three-mile limit would no longer apply to the liquor supply. Territorial waters were extended in this respect to twelve miles off the coast. Rum Row adapted itself to the new conditions by moving just beyond the new limit and continuing to outrun the Coast Guard. Then a new threat arose to plague the rumrunners. The hijacker came on the scene. He preyed on both the rumrunner and bootlegger, capturing cargoes of liquor and disposing of them at enormous profits because he had little overhead other than pay roll. The merchandise and the cost of transporting it from foreign bases cost the hijacker nothing.

A raid on one of the rumrunning rings in the New York District gave an indication of the extent to which the bootlegging business had developed. This ring had its headquarters in an old mansion at Atlantic High-lands. To defend the building against hijackers, the ring had sheath-ed the lower walls with sheet steel, behind which expert marksmen waited with machine guns, tear-gas bombs, and other weapons. Within the house was a high-powered radio equipment, through which instructions were issued in code to the ring's fleet of six steamships and more than twenty speedboats. This efficiently directed organization ran about ten thousand cases of liquor into New York each week before Federal agents smashed it.

In the latter years of prohibition Rum Row was broken up to the extent that ships no longer anchored in groups to await the swift blockade-running speedboats. Instead they would radio their positions to shore, and the ship-to-shore craft would decode these messages and then go out forty or fifty miles to meet their supply ships. Cargoes were landed in New Jersey, Brooklyn, Long Island, and even at Manhattan piers.

The major activity of the Coast Guard during prohibition was its war on the rumrunners. It had about thirty cutters and other patrol boats attached to the Port of New York. None was assigned exclusively to prohibition enforcement, but all engaged in it at one time or another. The same was true of its personnel. In the New York District, which extended from Delaware to Rhode Island, about three thousand coast-guardsmen were active.

Development of the United States Lines

A European service was inaugurated in 1920 by a private organization known as the United States Mail Steamship Company, which put fifteen vessels into service. In August 1921 this company's financial difficulties resulted in the taking over of its vessels by the government. They were then operated by the United States Shipping Board as the United States Lines. The names of seven of the vessels were changed to the "President" series.

By the fall of 1923 the Shipping Board had disposed of several United States Lines vessels, including some sold to the Dollar Line. To replace these the Shipping Board acquired five transports from the Army Transport Service. These were reconditioned and run as the American Merchant Lines under the management of J. H. Winchester and Company.

Paul W. Chapman & Company bought the United States Lines from the government in 1929. The deal involved eleven vessels. In August 1931 the Chapman Company turned over the *Republic* to the Army Transport Service in exchange for the *Cambrai* and the *Somme*. The Chapman fleet then consisted of twelve vessels.

There was another change in ownership in 1931, when the International Mercantile Marine Company took over the United States Lines from Paul W. Chapman & Company. The fleet then consisted of ten commissioned vessels and two building at Camden, N.J. The latter were the *Manhattan* and the *Washington*. Two of the former Chapman vessels were turned back to the Shipping Board and laid up in Chesapeake Bay, together with other decommissioned Shipping Board vessels.

Outstanding Ships

In the period 1900-39 New York was introduced to one notable ship after another. The *Oceania*'s 17,274 gross tons constituted a waterfront wonder at the beginning of the century, remained in service for years, and was a favorite with the traveling public until the outbreak of the first World War. Meanwhile the first *Mauretania* and the *Lusitania* appeared in 1907. Both ships made record crossings from Queenstown to Sandy Hook. The *Mauretania* continued in service long after the *Lusitania* had been torpedoed. Originally a coal burner, she was converted to oil in 1922. In 1935 she was scrapped.

For about five years after her launching the *Mauretania* was Queen of the Seas in size as well as in the affection of those who traveled aboard her. Then the first of the prewar floating palaces appeared. This was Hamburg-American's *Imperator* of 1912. With a tonnage of fifty-two thousand, quadruple-screw propulsion, and six decks, she was the maritime wonder of her day. The *Imperator* had accommodations for 714 first-class passengers, 401 second-class, 962 third-class, and a steerage capacity of 1772.

The Titanic

In the same year that the *Imperator* was launched the British made another important bid for New York trade with White Star's luckless *Titanic* and her sister ship, the *Olympic*. These were smaller than the *Imperator*, although equally luxurious.

The *Titanic* was 852 1/2 feet long, 92 1/2 feet beam, with a tonnage of 46,329. Her height from keel to bridge was 104 feet; she had 8 steel decks, a cellular double bottom, and 16 watertight compartments which, it was believed, rendered her unsinkable. If the sides were punctured one or more of these compartments were supposed to be closed off by steel bulkheads, operating from the bridge by a switch controlling electromagnets or by hand, locally, thus shutting off the flooded section.

While making her maiden voyage to New York the "unsinkable" *Titanic* struck an iceberg with terrific force on the night of April 14, 1912, and sank early on the fifteenth. The collision took place off Cape Race, Newfoundland. Of the 1513 lives lost out of a total of 2224 on board, 103 were women and 53 were children.

Improvements resulting from the *Titanic* disaster were a shifting from the northern to the southern lane; better regulation of wireless patents, over which Marconi and De Forest had fought bitterly; and the establishment of a Coast Guard ice patrol to watch for dangerous icebergs floating southward from the Arctic Ocean. The White Star Line called in the *Titanic*'s sister ship, the *Olympic*, to have her hull strengthened.

The Vaterland

The *Titanic* disaster did not seriously retard the race for speed and size. Two years later Hamburg-American made still another bid for North Atlantic supremacy with its *Vaterland*. She was six thousand tons bigger than the *Imperator*, had more than enough lifeboat equipment to take care of her passengers and crew, possessed a maximum horsepower of ninety thousand, boasted even more luxury than her predecessors, and was bigger and longer than any ship up to that time. She made three trips before the World War began; then her owners decided to intern her in New York. When the United States entered the war she was seized, renamed the *Leviathan*, and became a famous transport.

After the war the *Leviathan* was completely reconditioned, converted from coal to oil, and, after a period of unprofitable operation by the United States Lines, tied up to a dock in Hoboken until 1938, when she was sold to be broken up for scrap.

The Aquitania

Again the German threat, which had been concentrated in the *Vaterland*, was met by the British with Cunard's *Aquitania*, one of the best-known vessels plying between New York, Southampton, and Cherbourg. She was smaller than the *Vaterland*, but her increased emphasis on safety and luxury turned much of the passenger trade toward her. The *Aquitania* arrived in New York June 5, 1914, on her maiden voyage. Shrieking whistles and dipping colors welcomed the new vessel as she steamed up the harbor after a brief halt at quarantine. Fog and ice had forced her to reduce speed during part of the trip. After she had docked there were several gay ceremonies aboard, and a large department store featured the latest gowns from Paris "just off the *Aquitania*"

The *Aquitania* marked a pause in the construction of superliners until 1929, when North German Lloyd's *Bremen* was launched. The *Bremen* arrived in New York on July 22, having set a new record for the westward crossing—4 days, 17 hours, and 42 minutes. The *Bremen* has a tonnage of 51,731, a length of 899 feet, and a beam of 102 feet. Her sister ship, the *Europa*, 49,746 tons, arrived in the Port in March 1930.

That same year White Star reverted to the "small-but-comfortable" type of ship with its 26,943-ton *Britannic.* She proved to be merely an interlude in the race for primacy in size and luxury. Later her service was augmented by the *Georgic.*

The Italian Line entered the "super" field in 1932 with its *Rex* and *Conte di Savoia*. The *Rex* is quadruple-screw, 51,062 gross tons, 880 feet in length, and with a beam of 102 feet. She won the world's speed record for the passage between Gibraltar and New York in 1933 and held it for two years. The *Conte di Savoia* is also quadruple-screw with a tonnage of 48,502; length is 820 feet, beam 95 feet. Her gyro-stabilizers, reducing any rolling motion, constitute her main contribution to modern sea travel. The first large passenger ship to be so stabilized, the *Conte* is reported to be greatly superior in comfort to a non-stabilized vessel.

The Pilsudski *and the* Batory

Another shift back to the "small-but-comfortable" type of ship occurred in 1934, when Poland's Gdynia-America Line brought out the *Pilsudski* and the *Batory*. The former was destined to be sunk in 1939 during the second World War. These were motor ships, powered by Diesel engines, and ran between New York and "Poland's own port," Gdynia. Many marine experts regarded these oil-burning, motor-driven ships as more modern than their larger turbine-driven contemporaries. Their New York docks were on the New Jersey side of the North River, just opposite the stronghold of Cunard White Star in Manhattan's West Twenties. Two important mergers had taken place in 1934—Cunard with White Star and North German Lloyd with Hamburg-American.

The Normandie

In the latter years of this period of intense international rivalry a high point in the race for speed and size was reached with the construction of the French Line's 83,423-ton *Normandie*. This $55,000,000 superliner arrived in New York June 3, 1935, having made the run of 2971 miles from Bishop's Rock, off Plymouth, to Ambrose Lightship in 4 days, 3 hours, and 13 minutes. The *Rex*'s average speed on the Gibraltar-New York run had been 28.92 knots; the *Normandie*'s on the North Atlantic crossing was 29.94 knots. Prior to either of these performances North German Lloyd's *Europa* had held the record, which she established in June 1933 at an average speed of 27.92 knots.

The *Normandie* was greeted with one of the greatest demonstrations in the maritime history of the city. Crowds thronged the Staten Island and Brooklyn waterfronts. Battery Park was crowded for hours before the ship's appearance in the Upper Bay. Tugs, ferryboats, and sight-seeing vessels massed at Staten Island. French and American flags were dropped on the liner's deck by a squadron of military planes as she came abreast of Ambrose Lightship and broke out the speed-record pennant. Many New Yorkers turned out during the next few days to inspect the new speed queen. She had a permanent motion-picture theater seating 380, a garage for ten cars with a special lift, a first-class dining room 300 feet long, decorated with glass paneling, a swimming pool 112 feet long by 30 feet wide, all kinds of specialty shops, eleven decks connected by elevators, and many other luxury features. She accommodated 848 cabin passengers, 670 tourists, and 454 third class. Officers and crew numbered 1345.

On her first eastbound trip the *Normandie* also broke all records, establishing herself as the speed queen of the North Atlantic. She was the fastest liner afloat until Cunard White Star's *Queen Mary* wrested the Blue Riband from her, and she remained the world's biggest ship until the *Queen Elizabeth* was launched in 1939.

World's Fastest Passenger Ship

The *Queen Mary* was built at Clydebank, Scotland, in 1936 and has a gross tonnage of 81,235. The great liner has a length of 975 feet—nearly five times the length of the *Britannia*, the first Cunarder—and a beam of 118 feet. She made her maiden voyage from Southampton to New York in 1936, arriving in port on the first of June. The *Queen Mary* established new records that year, lost the Blue Riband to the *Normandie* in 1937, and regained it in 1938. The ship is driven by single reduction-geared turbines, operating four propellers, the largest cast for any ship up to the time of the building of the *Queen Elizabeth*. The propelling machinery develops 200,000 horsepower, 50,000 for each shaft. There are accommodations for 2075 passengers and a crew of 1200.

World's Biggest Ships

According to *Lloyd's Registry of Shipping*, 1939-40, the world's biggest ten ships are:

Name	Built	Country of Registry	Gross Tonnage	Length	Breadth	Depth
				(in feet & 10ths of feet)		
Queen Elizabeth	1940	Great Brit.	85,000	987.0*	120.0*	70.0*
Normandie	1935	France	83,423	981.4	117.9	57.6
Queen Mary	1936	Great Brit.	81,235	975.2	118.6	8.5
Bremen	1929	Germany	51,731	898.7	101.9	48.2
Rex	1932	Italy	51,062	879.9	97.0	30.7
Europa	1928	Germany	49,746	890.2	102.1	48.0
Conte di Savoia	1932	Italy	48,502	914.6	96.1	32.4
Aquitania	1914	Great Brit.	44,786	868.7	97.0	49.7
Ile de France	1926	France	43,450	763.7	92.0	55.9
Empress of Britain	1931	Great Brit.	42,348	733.3	97.8	56.0

The dates when these vessels were built and the order of their size attest the keen rivalry among Great Britain, France, Germany, and Italy in developing the superliner. Of the largest ten ships, Great Britain took the lead with four; France followed with two, Germany two, and Italy two. The Netherlands became size-conscious and closely trailed the largest ten in 1938 with the *Nieuw Amsterdam*, a 36,287-gross-ton vessel, with a 713.7-foot length and an 88.3-foot beam.

Some Steamship Lines of the Period

In January 1938 the Red D Line, one of the oldest American-owned and -operated companies, which had long been plying between New York and Venezuela, was absorbed by the Grace Line. The Panama Mail Steamship Company, which had become famous after the California gold-rush days for its mail and passenger service between Panama, Central America, and San Francisco, ran between New York and San Francisco after the opening of the Panama Canal. It, too, was absorbed by the Grace Line. The Grace Line continued its services between New

* No survey of the *Queen Elizabeth* was made before she sailed in 1940 for America. Dimensions given are from architect's plans.

York and Caribbean and South American ports. This line carried passengers and mail as well as copper, gold, iodine, vanadium, and other metallic cargoes. Its new turbo-electric ships were first built with subsidies granted under the Jones-White Act and later with loans from the Maritime Commission. These sturdy ships replaced older vessels and extended the passenger and freight facilities on the run from New York to the west coast of South America.

Foreign operators also experienced changes. During the 1914-18 war the vessels of the Atlantic Transport Company were active as troopships. Lamport & Holt's "V" ships, running to the east coast of South America, terminated their careers with the sinking of the *Vestris* in 1928. The Red Star Line, famous for its cattle and livestock boats, was absorbed by the Holland-America interests. The ships of the Arnold Bernstein Line were specially constructed to carry assembled automobiles. When the German government seized the company and Bernstein was forced to leave Germany, his line was sold to the Holland-America Line. In 1939 Bernstein established a line running between New York and Scandinavian ports.

The Panama Railroad Steamship Company included in its fleet three speedy passenger-freight vessels which were among the finest of their type afloat. The New York and Cuba Mail Steamship Company operated the Ward Line's ships, known to every traveler by sea to Veracruz or Havana. The early ships of this line were used as transports in the Spanish-American War.

Moore-McCormack's house flag was a familiar sight in the harbor. Founded by tugboat operators, the company operated a service to Scandinavian and Baltic ports (American Scantic Line) and later started services to the east coast of South America (American Republics Line). Many of the line's older vessels were sold to Brazil and replaced by C-2- and C-3-type fast freighters designed by the Maritime Commission. The line's new pier at the foot of Canal Street was specially fitted to handle grain in bulk, hides, coffee, and heavy machinery.

Developments in the 1930s

The enormous expansion of facilities during the first World War had carried the Port of New York through the profitable 1920s to such heights that, as the 1930s dawned, a Port Authority bulletin declared the Port to be "the largest, most frequently used, and best-known port in the world."

More steamship tonnage was using the Port than was calling at any other—about forty-three million tons entered and cleared in 1930. During that year a ship arrived or departed every ten minutes of daylight hours. Steamship services out of the Port included one hundred and fifty-nine foreign routes, thirteen intercoastal to Pacific ports, fourteen coastwise to Gulf and Atlantic ports, and seventeen to New England.

The speed with which the Port could handle big liners had been repeatedly demonstrated. The Cunard liner *Berengaria* had docked at nine in the morning and sailed again at midnight after unloading one thousand passengers, nine hundred sacks of mail, and freight, and then reloading. The French liner *Ile de France* had arrived and sailed again within fourteen hours. To accelerate such movement the Port now maintained a customs force of thirty-seven hundred employees.

There were fifty ship-repair yards in the Port. Extraordinarily fast repair jobs had been carried out at piers. The *Mauretania* and *Veendam* were among the vessels that had undergone unusual repairs at their piers.

Five hundred steamship piers and deep-water berthage totaling seventy miles of side wharfage were available. During the 1920s more deep-water steamship berthage had been added to New York's already developed waterfront than existed in the entire Port of New Orleans. In 1931 even greater expansion was being planned or was under way.

The City of New York was building or planning to build seven piers with a total of more than two and one half miles of wharfage. The Port of New York Authority and Jersey City were planning for four piers on the west bank of the Hudson River, all more than one thousand feet long and having berthing slips from three hundred to four hundred feet wide.

Storage space in the Port district was equivalent to a two-hundred-story skyscraper built up solidly on a four-acre plot. In 1930 the Pennsylvania Dock & Warehouse Company in Jersey City was placed in operation. It then had a capacity of four hundred thousand square feet of refrigerated storage, and an ultimate capacity of two million square feet in dry storage. In the same year the Lackawanna Terminal of the Delaware, Lackawanna & Western Railroad was also opened in Jersey City. It had one million square feet of floor space. The Bayway Terminal at Elizabeth, N.J., which was an addition to the Elizabeth Terminal, added two million square feet to its plant. The Port Authority constructed for its own use the huge Port of New York Authority Building covering the entire block bounded by Fifteenth and Sixteenth streets and Eighth and Ninth avenues. This enormous structure, containing all modern freight-handling facilities, houses the Union Inland Terminal.

Mechanization of Waterfront

New York's waterfront had undergone many physical changes, particularly in the handling of cargoes. During the packet and clipper days, when South Street was at its height, man power sufficed to handle cargoes.

The steam engine had been successfully applied to Hudson River navigation and even to transatlantic traffic, but its use in cargo handling was infrequent. Moreover, labor was cheap and plentiful, and the comparatively small ships of the period could not load cargoes too large to be handled at a profit by men alone.

Then the development of the steamship got underway, and, as steel was applied to shipbuilding in the 1880s, the sizes of vessels became such that cargoes could no longer be unloaded or stowed by hand, especially since increasing labor costs made purely manual loading and unloading prohibitively expensive. This resulted in cargo-handling machinery.

Electricity has since been applied to a high degree. Particularly is this true of such huge freight-handling plants as those of the Bush Terminal and the New York Dock Company. One of the uses to which electricity has been put with marked success is in the electromagnet. One of these can handle more scrap iron, metal, or structural steel in a single operation than scores of men could move in the same period of time. The invention of the gasoline engine has also speeded water-front movement. Motor trucks, tractors, and cranes mounted on tractors have contributed greatly to the handling of cargo. Steam also plays its part, especially in the operation of winches and cranes. As a result of the increased ease of handling heavy or bulky goods, the warehousing of various products, such as foodstuffs, has been vastly expanded and improved.

Seatrain, a Highly Mechanized Development

In striking contrast with this manual operation is the seatrain vessel, which eliminates longshore handling entirely. The idea back of this was to ship goods in the freight cars in which they had been originally loaded. A special type of ship was designed and given the name of seatrain. In general appearance it looks something like a high-sided tanker. It is four hundred and eighty feet long, sixty-three and a half feet at the beam, and has four decks, all served by one large hatch extending across the vessel amidships. Each of these decks contains four rows of standard-gauge railway tracks, so that a total of one hundred freight cars can be accommodated by a seatrain ship. The freight car is lifted from the siding to a seatrain track in the cradle hoisted by a special crane, secured to prevent movement, transported to port of destination, unloaded onto land tracks, and sent thence to its destination. Prior to June 1941 when the navy took over two of their vessels, Seatrain Lines operated five of these ships in services between New York and Cuba, New Orleans, and Texas City. Terminal facilities in the Port of New York are maintained in Manhattan and Hoboken.

The seatrain vessel was wholly an American maritime industrial idea created during the depression. Advantages claimed for it include increased protection against fire and contamination and much greater speed in discharging and reloading. A seatrain ship can discharge and reload in ten hours, as against several days for an ordinary vessel carrying the same amount of freight. Shippers of perishable commodities under ventilation or refrigeration, as well as of liquids in large quantities, are among the more important users of these unique vessels.

End of the Period

The 1900-39 period was brought to a close with the dramatic sailing of the *Bremen*; the German invasion of Poland, which began the European war of 1939; and the Presidential Proclamation of Neutrality, restricting American vessels from ever-widening war zones.

The *Bremen* had arrived in New York on August 28, 1939, when the world was waiting for Hitler's decision with respect to Poland. Officials of the Hamburg-American North German Lloyd, the *Bremen*'s operators, had planned to send their crack liner back to a German port without passengers, in order to avoid the concentrated British naval power on the high seas between the *Bremen* and safety in a home or neutral port. Suddenly the United States Treasury Department decided to subject the *Bremen* (as well as the French liner *Normandie* and others) to a thorough inspection. This had been decided upon, it was announced, in order that the Customs Service could notify the Collector of the Port that the *Bremen* was within the law, so far as gun emplacements, legitimate crews, and proper cargo were concerned.

German officials here and abroad complained that, since the *Normandie* was to be examined first, the *Bremen* was being subjected to a delay which meant steadily increasing danger for her, in the event that war should break out in Europe. Despite all objections, however, the *Bremen* was searched so carefully that an official of the line furiously exclaimed: "Now they are searching the empty swimming pool!" President Roosevelt pointed out that similar search was being carried out aboard the British *Aquitania*, the French *Normandie,* and other ships. Finally United States Attorney-General Frank Murphy summed up the search by declaring: "There will be no repetition of the situation in 1917, when a democracy was unprepared to meet the espionage problem."

For two days the *Bremen* was held at her pier while every inch of her was searched. Then on the night of August 30 the crack liner sailed. "As twilight fell," the New York Times reported, "the liner *Bremen*, her long reaches of deck empty, save for an occasional white-coated steward or blue-clad officer, slipped away from her West Forty-sixth Street dock with a band playing German airs. Unlike many other occasions of the past, when the two immense buff-colored stacks were illuminated by piercing floodlights and the cabins were filled with passengers eagerly looking forward to whatever lay before them in European resorts, the great liner slipped almost furtively down the river, with every light extinguished except the running lights required for navigation." Her black-out in operation, the liner disappeared into the darkness and began the elusive dash to outstrip British cruisers, eventually arriving at Murmansk, Soviet Russia. The *Aquitania,* released at the same time, arrived safely in England.

On September 3, 1939, Great Britain declared that she was at war with Germany. Two days later President Roosevelt announced America's neutrality and proclaimed that the Neutrality Act, as amended in 1937, was in force; but on November 3 a new Neutrality Act was passed in a special session of Congress in the form of a joint resolution which virtually placed an embargo on United States merchant ships to belligerent ports or waters, although it repealed the arms embargo and opened the munitions industries and trade to the belligerent powers.

President Roosevelt signed the joint resolution on November 4. One of several presidential proclamations, also signed on the fourth, defined the combat area at the time. The President, in an explanatory statement, said that the area took in "the whole Bay of Biscay, except waters on the north coast of Spain so close to the Spanish coast as to make danger of attack unlikely. It also takes in all the waters around Great Britain, Ireland, and the adjacent islands, including the English Channel. It takes in the North Sea, running up the Norwegian coast to a point south of Bergen. It takes in all the Baltic Sea and its independent waters."

There was immediate protest by the shipping companies in the Port of New York. At the same time the harbor began to show the absence of ship movements. Vessels were tied up. Aerial views of piers up and down the Hudson River and the Upper Bay showed many idle ships.

The New York Custom House made a desperate effort to interpret the new law for American shippers, who were demanding new trade routes and charging that they were being legislated out of business, while foreign ship operators were demanding the utmost secrecy in sailing permits and information on ports of call. News of frequent torpedoings showed that their alarm was not exaggerated. All the while the Maritime Commission worked swiftly to create new trade routes to South America, South Africa, and to points in the Pacific.

The Port now faced a crucial year—1940—and for the second time in the century had to cope with the special problems growing out of European war and widespread blockade.

CHAPTER XI

The Port Today and Tomorrow—1941 and the Future

T HE OUTBREAK of the twentieth century's second major war late in 1939 saw no repetition of the paralyzing confusion that existed in New York Harbor after the declaration of hostilities in 1914. Not only was the Port better prepared, having made extensive plans in anticipation of that contingency, but many European countries, particularly Great Britain, France, and Germany, had made arrangements in advance to take care of any of their ships caught in the harbor by a sudden war declaration.

The 1939 Neutrality Act was considered by many to be a devastating blow to New York shipping, and the year 1940 was viewed with apprehension. Chairman Bland of the House of Representatives Committee on the Merchant Marine estimated that the loss sustained by the nation through the legislation would amount to nearly three hundred million dollars and that from fifty-eight hundred to sixty-three hundred seamen would be unemployed.

The American-flag service to the war zones, now discontinued, had employed about ninety cargo vessels. The service had been developed over a period of twenty years at great cost and with government aid. The volume of American trade in the prohibited areas had amounted to approximately three billion dollars in 1937—about forty per cent of the total foreign commerce of the United States.

The same Neutrality Act which made it impossible for American sailors to enter belligerent areas immediately placed a premium on foreign seamen in the New York maritime labor market. Sailors had to be found to man the freighters which were transporting supplies and war materials to the Allies. Norwegian seamen were recruited from whaling ships already in United States ports. Netherlands recruits came from the reserve of five hundred men of the *Nieuw Amsterdam,* laid up at her Hoboken pier. The New York *Times,* June 9, 1940, reported that "although Belgian and Danish seamen were still idle on ships tied up in the harbor, Norwegian and Netherlands sailors are making more money than they were before their countries were invaded."

Scheduled Sailings Shrink

Within a month after England and France had declared war on Germany fewer than thirty ship lines maintained regular sailing schedules. The *Official Steamship & Airways Guide* left blank spaces for British- and French-owned lines and merely stated, "Schedules not available this month." The four pages usually devoted to the Transatlantic Passenger Conference Sailings to and from Europe were also blank, with a boxed explanation, "This Joint Schedule will be reinstated when the present situation becomes more settled." The lines of British registry so affected included the Anchor, Cunard White Star, Cairn, Thomson, Furness Bermuda, Furness Red Cross, Furness Prince, Furness West Indies, and the Booth Lines. The splendid motor ships of the Gdynia-America Line had disappeared from the harbor before the conquest of Poland was completed; the regular sailings of the Hamburg-American North German Lloyd ceased the same day that German cruisers began to shell Danzig; the Belgian Line and two British freight companies, the Silver Line and the Barber Line, withdrew their ships from regular schedules.

Shipping soon lost its normal appearance. The de luxe liners of the seas no longer came into port. Cunard White Star's *Queen Mary* was tied up at her pier and painted a dull lead gray. Her sailings were canceled. The same line's *Mauretania* was soon covered over with a dirty-gray color. The French Line kept its fleet leader, the *Normandie*, tied at her pier in the North River and sent its *Ile de France* to the municipal piers at Staten Island. The harbor police maintained a day-and-night watch over these leviathans. Visitors were no longer allowed aboard, and sight-seeing along the waterfront was discouraged.

The Port took on a wartime appearance in 1940. Camouflaged British and French vessels moved cau- tiously in and out of Sandy Hook, arriving early in the morning after breaking convoy and sailing late in the afternoon or at midnight. Most of the British ships were black-hulled and black-funneled, with brown superstructures. The French went in for wave patterns and battleship grays. Stern deck guns were covered with canvas at first and then openly displayed; anti-aircraft guns pointed skyward; depth bombs lined their taffrails, and paravanes (mine cutters) flanked their bows under water. The Allies' flags were small, hardly visible, and often deliberately soiled in order to make identification difficult.

An indirect effect upon shipping was the suspension of the issuance of passports—except in special cases —for travel to nations within the war zone. This turned thousands of people who had planned on European trips for vacations to reading advertisements and booklets on the delights of cruises in American waters. South America proved attractive. Traffic greatly increased on lines to Caribbean and South American ports. At the beginning of the year neutrals like the Holland-America Line put their ships on schedules to handle tourist trade diverted to the West Indies. The Grace Line, wholly American in ownership and registry, reported having booked more than four thousand passengers for Caribbean and South American cruises. The Swedish and the Norwegian-American lines joined in this lucrative passenger traffic on "neutral ships to neutral ports." Bermuda traffic fell out of the hands of the British, and a large part of it was carried on steamers of the United States Lines.

British Blockade

Direct shipments to Germany after September 1939 were prevented by the British blockade. However, the effect on American trade was less serious than it had been in 1914, for 1939 exports to Germany had been less than three and one half per cent of total national exports, as compared with fifteen per cent in 1914.

In January 1940 Great Britain announced that some trade with the Reich through the blockade would be permitted to American businessmen in "very exceptional cases." Britain's Minister of Economic Warfare replied to a series of questions through the American Embassy and stated that Americans could make applications for exemptions from the provisions of the Orders in Council for the seizure of all German exports. Such applications had to contain full information as to consignee, consignor, origin of goods, contract terms, and the like. If granted, the British authorities notified the applicant and gave instructions to the customs and naval authorities.

However, the British blockade of German exports had already brought an official American protest—as similar blockades had all through American history. On December 8, 1939, the United States government characterized the blockade as an interference with legitimate trade. Great Britain waited until February 22, 1940, before making formal rejection of the protest, declaring the blockade justifiable and proper legal reprisal against Germany's practice of mining and torpedoing Allied and neutral shipping.

Many American shippers were making it easier for British officials to expedite the passage of their ships by applying for navicerts more quickly. In February 1940 these passports for cargoes began coming in at the rate of twelve hundred weekly for all American ports.

The *Scottsburg*, out of New York, the first freighter carrying a cargo fully covered by navicerts, passed through the Mediterranean contraband-control base early in February with phosphates for Italy and mules for Turkey. It was held up only two and one half hours, whereas other United States vessels with unguaranteed cargoes were held up as long as twenty-three hours. Owners of these last ships complained that they were detained much longer than Italian ships. The British Ambassador to the United States asserted that the ships contributed to the delay by failing to allow a British check of cargo before they left the United States.

The British insisted that they wanted to do everything possible to minimize difficulties while they were trying to prevent contraband from getting through to Germany. In handling German exports to the United States, if no larger amount of money was involved and the German goods could not be purchased conveniently elsewhere, the British allowed the goods to proceed. Scientific German machines, drugs not obtainable elsewhere, and certain machine parts were usually not touched.

In March two Allied economists arrived to explain the blockade and its functions and to receive suggestions from the United States for reducing friction between this country and Britain and France induced by the blockade.

Bringing Americans from the War Zone

After the beginning of the war the repatriation of Americans scattered abroad became a serious problem for the government. Many ships were taken from their regular runs to handle the war refugees, most of whom were disembarked at the Port of New York. The torpedoing on September 3, 1939, of the British liner *Athenia,* which carried about three hundred Americans, had focused attention on the danger to Americans traveling in the war zones. The *Iroquois* of the Clyde-Mallory coastwise line was pressed into service and made a trip to the British Isles in order to bring back American citizens. The homeward voyage held the attention of the American public after an assertion by Germany that the *Athenia* had struck a mine and that Great Britain had also planned to blow up the *Iroquois* and place the blame on Germany.

These allegations were denied by the British Admiralty in a statement declaring that no mine fields existed in the waters involved.

The coast guard cutter *Campbell* and two destroyers from the United States Neutrality Patrol were dispatched to pick up the *Iroquois* at sea and protect her from attack. Captain Chelton of the *Iroquois* did not notify his passengers of the German warning until after the arrival of the convoy. Escorted by the cutter and the destroyers, as well as by five navy flying boats, the *Iroquois* continued on her course, arriving at New York on October 11, 1939, without further incident.

The liner *Manhattan* was among the first ships employed to bring back Americans from the war zones. On her first trip in February 1940 she was held up forty-four hours by the British; on the second, she was stopped for twenty-seven hours eastbound and nine hours westbound. On June 11 she arrived with 1907 refugees, a record number. She had waited eighteen hours at Genoa to catch latecomers from Germany, Norway, Denmark, Belgium, Poland, and elsewhere.

On June 9 the *President Roosevelt* brought 723 refugees to port from the British Isles. The ship was crowded to twice its normal capacity. On June 21 the *Washington* came home with 1787 passengers fleeing the war areas. The *Washington* had encountered a U-boat off Portugal, and at one time all passengers had been ordered into the lifeboats.

The exodus continued through July. On the fourteenth the *Washington* returned from another trip to the British Isles with 1609 passengers, all but 273 of whom were American citizens; more than 600 of the passengers were children. On the twenty-ninth the *Exmouth,* second-last ship of the American Export Lines to leave the Mediterranean, arrived in port.

In addition to the American ships, many foreign-flagged ships took part in the service: the *Volendam*, the *Scythia,* the *Britannic*, the *Cameronia,* and others. The *Volendam*, on July 2, brought 223 passengers, 79 of whom were children being removed from England for the duration of the war. Many were en route to homes in Canada, Australia, and New Zealand. All ships carrying refugees out of England were convoyed by warships out of Liverpool through the danger zone.

British and French Liners Leave Port

The Germans, profiting by their World War experience, had moved all their ships from the harbor within two months of the war declarations. The English and the French, however, with the *Queen Mary, Mauretania, Normandie*, and *Ile de France* tied up, had to face the problem of the future of these valuable ships.

On March 20, 1940, both the *Queen Mary* and the *Mauretania* were made ready to leave the Port. Officials maintained their usual silence concerning the activities of ships in wartime, although it was generally assumed that they would be used as troopships. The *Mauretania* was the first to sail. With lights dimmed, she left her West Fourteenth Street pier at eight o'clock in the evening. The *Queen Mary* left her West Fiftieth Street pier the following morning. Later the *Mauretania* was reported at Panama; she was expected to make a transit of the Canal on her way to Australia, guarded by British cruisers. The arrival of the ship at Honolulu confirmed the belief that she was to be used in transporting troops between Australia and the Near East, where the British were massing forces. The *Queen Mary* was eventually reported seen off the Cape of Good Hope, and it was assumed that she, too, was to be used in the transportation of Australian or New Zealand troops.

On May 5 the *Ile de France*, painted black and gray, sailed at nightfall with a cargo of war materials and having aboard members of the French Purchasing Commission. She was reported bound for an unnamed port in the English Channel. The *Normandie* remained tied up at her pier throughout the year—problems of ownership and disposal further complicated by the defeat of France and her withdrawal from the war alliance with Great Britain.

World's Greatest Ship Arrives

The year 1940 saw the arrival in port of the world's greatest ship, Cunard White Star's *Queen Elizabeth*, and the largest ship ever built in this country, the *America* of the United States Lines.

The *Queen Elizabeth*, which arrived early in March, represents Great Britain's latest entry in the contest for the fastest North Atlantic crossing, which has featured the period between the two great wars. The maiden voyage of the *Queen Elizabeth* was one of the strangest ever made—marked by a secret departure, with the crew ignorant of the destination throughout most of the voyage, a complete absence of the usual formalities for both departure and arrival, and a run through seas made perilous by mines and torpedoes.

The *Queen Elizabeth* was the first ship to arrive with a magnetic mine neutralizer. This consisted of two electric cables strung around the hull just below the superstructure. Mystery has surrounded the device since its introduction, but it is said that the cables exert an electrical force calculated to neutralize the magnetic attraction of the hull of a ship. Since magnetic mines are exploded by a mechanism sensitive to the magnetic force emanating from the metal of a ship, any vessel so equipped should, in theory at least, be able to pass safely through a field of these mines.

After their introduction belligerent and neutral vessels carrying the mine neutralizers painted large yellow crosses on their hulls. These markings, just beneath the superstructure, warned other vessels not to come too close because the device sometimes put the compasses of near-by ships out of adjustment.

The *Queen Elizabeth* showed a dingy gray paint instead of the gleaming white her superstructure would have had in times of peace. The superliner remained tied up at her West Fiftieth Street pier, heavily guarded, until November when she left port. Officials of Cunard White Star did not disclose her destination.

On July 29 the new liner *America*, queen of the American merchant marine, arrived at the Port of New York. The *America* is the largest, most luxurious, and the fastest ship ever constructed in the United States. She carried eight hundred passengers, guests on this initial trip from Newport News, Virginia. The *America* was accompanied on her run up the Bay by a fleet of coast guard cutters, police boats, and two fireboats. Airplanes wheeled overhead.

A comparison of the specification of the two vessels is enlightening. The *Queen Elizabeth*, with a tonnage of 85,000, has a length of 987 feet (nearly the height of the Empire State Building) and a beam of 120 feet. She has a sharp bow, giving a streamlined effect. The ship has fourteen decks, only two smokestacks, and no ventilating funnels. Owing to advances in building engines for power, she needs only twelve high-pressure boilers. The *Queen Elizabeth* is expected eventually to lower the Atlantic crossing record now held by the *Queen Mary*.

The *America* is 723 feet long and has a beam of 93 feet, 3 inches. The displacement is 35,440 tons. She is powered by two sets of triple-expansion turbines capable of developing 34,000 shaft horsepower, will attain a speed of 22 knots, and has a cruising radius of 9400 miles. The ship, which has a capacity of 1200 passengers and carries a crew of 643, cost $17,500,000.

American Lines

Reminiscent of the old clipper days was the sailing of the *Flying Cloud* in January 1940, inaugurating a new South American route for the Moore-McCormack Lines. Named for the famous clipper, this modern version of the speedy cargo carrier made the initial trip of a fortnightly sailing schedule with stops at Pernambuco, Bahia, and Rio de Janeiro. Fifty-nine of these steel merchant vessels were under construction in 1939; forty were launched in that year and twenty-five put into service. Some of the names—*Donald McKay, Challenge, Red Jacket,* and *Nightingale*—are reminders of the time when the United States merchant marine was supreme.

The *Queen Mary*

The Yankee Clipper, La Guardia Airport, New York

The *Exchequer*, built by the Maritime Commission, is a good example of the new type of streamlined freighter. By welding the hull together, the overlapping of plates was eliminated, and the ship was expected to carry greater loads at faster speeds and with lower fuel consumption than the old-style freighter. The *Exchequer* has a deadweight tonnage of 9820, an over-all length of 465 feet, a beam of 69 1/2 feet, and a draft of 33 1/2 feet. Cruising speed is rated at 16 to 17 knots. Built for the American Export Lines, the *Exchequer* was never delivered to the steamship company but instead was turned over to the navy for use as a transport.

During the year many active American ship lines were operating out of the Port of New York despite the war. The service was rather uncertain, some of it abandoned for lack of trade, in other cases increased in order to explore new trade possibilities.

At the end of the year active lines included eight from New York to the United Kingdom, a weekly service to Portugal, three sailings a month to Greece, a fortnightly service to Spain, and occasional sailings to Petsamo, Finland. The shipping service to East Africa and South Africa was well maintained with twelve sailings a month, and service to the east coast of South America was also in good condition, although there was an excess of cargo space on the southbound run.

Service to India and China was maintained with eight sailings a month via Good Hope, and service to the Philippines, Shanghai, and the East Indies by two American-flag lines and four foreign-flag lines via the Panama Canal was active and regular.

The Baltimore Mail extended its New York-to-California service with four ships to the Far East, including in their runs the ports of Cristobal, Balboa, Manila, Hong Kong, and Singapore. This line has among the ships in its fleet the well-known *City of Baltimore, City of Newport News, City of Los Angeles*, and *City of San Francisco*.

The *Manhattan* and *Washington* of the United States Lines, taken from the Mediterranean route after Italy entered the war, and of course excluded from the North Atlantic service by neutrality legislation, were now put into a new de luxe service between New York and California. Permission for this service had been granted by the Maritime Commission after the American Hawaiian Steamship Company had opposed it on the ground that the new venture was damaging to their intercoastal service. The *Washington* returned to the Port with 375 passengers on August 28 to complete the first round trip in the company's new service. During 1940 the *America* was first employed in twelve-day cruises to the West Indies. Early in 1941 she was scheduled for two trips in the California-New York service, then was expected to return to the West Indies run, her future operations uncertain until war conditions clear.

The Clyde-Mallory Line, which had maintained a New York-to-Texas service for more than seventy years, announced in March 1940 that it would establish a new service between New York and Houston, which replaced Galveston at the Texas end of the run. This was the first fast freight-and-passenger service between these cities. The first trip was made late in May. There were five ships on the new run; the *Algonquin* and the *Seminole* made stops at Miami in each direction, and three cargo ships stopped at Charleston, South Carolina. This service continued throughout the year but was to be abandoned early in 1941, when the Moore-McCormack Lines also withdrew from the Gulf route.

Maritime Commission

The United States Maritime Commission has been given power to charter, transfer, sell, or block the sale of ships in the merchant marine, as well as to contract for reconditioning old and building new ships. Passage of neutrality legislation, however, made performance of some of these duties difficult. In January 1940 efforts to transfer eight United States Lines ships to Norway were blocked by the State Department, on the ground that it would have been a breach of neutrality. However, in February eight old ships of this line, seven of them cargo vessels, were sold to Belgium for four million dollars, the transaction having been consummated after a long delay.

In February five concerns made bids to the Maritime Commission for twelve ships of the Pioneer Lines to be used in the transpacific service. Intercoastal shippers feared a shortage of ships as a result of the expanding war purchases; it was charged that operators were making sales, with the authority of the Commission, on a scale that threatened the interests of the shippers. Organized opposition to further approvals by the Commission developed in Washington. However, interested shipping men denied that there was any shortage for normal purposes and contended that operators should be given every opportunity to dispose of old carriers, if they guaranteed to order replacements at once.

In April it was reported that ninety American vessels, totaling 364,014 tons, had been sold or transferred to Great Britain with the approval of the Maritime Commission. In addition to other legal powers assigned to the Commission, in May it was empowered to adjust ship subsidies and further given broad powers to be used in emergencies resulting from the war.

By November a total of 425 British, Allied, and neutral vessels had been reported lost since the beginning of hostilities, and at this time the Commission was openly in the market for ships. The Black Diamond Lines was urged to sell eight ships to Great Britain. These vessels were out on charter and were being operated by the Isthmian Line. Britain was expected to buy fifteen old vessels to replace losses. The Commission's report on the construction of new ships showed two hundred ships six months ahead of schedule and to be completed by the middle of 1941.

The War and Foreign Trade

In spite of the embargo on American vessels in the war zones, the widening of the British blockade, and the countries lost to American foreign trade because of the war, exports from the Port of New York during 1940 were in sufficient quantity to suggest a growing war boom. During the calendar year the value of exports shipped from New York amounted to $1,944,817,000, which was 48.3 per cent of the total

United States export valuation ($4,021,564,000). A three-year comparison shows the sharp increase caused by the war:

Year	NY Exports	US Exports	% of NY to US
1938	$1,126,260,152	$3,094,440,000	36.4
1939	1,294,013,366	3,177,344,000	40.7
1940	1,944,817,000	4,025,416,000	48.3

The Port's nearly two-billion-dollar export figure for 1940 is in excess of the total United States export figure for 1933—$1,674,994,000—and is far above the Port's export figure for 1914, which was $833,394,000. Exports in 1915 were valued at $1,792,335,000. The valuation figure for 1940 is well below the war-boom figure for 1916, which had risen to $2,790,403,000. During the year almost all of Europe's share of the Port's export trade—with the exception of that of the United Kingdom—was eliminated piecemeal as the German grip on the Continent tightened. This was in sharp contrast with 1916, when all of Europe except those parts controlled by the Central Powers was open to American trade.

The 1940 figure becomes even more suggestive when it is taken into account that these export totals represent twelve of the first sixteen months of the war, while the 1915 figure—much smaller—represents twelve of the first eighteen months of World War I.

The Port's import figure held to a steady rise from 1938 through 1940, although the proportionate increase was below that of the exports. The valuation of 1940 imports was $1,241,818,000, which was 48.8 per cent of the nation's total, and ninety-two million dollars more than it had been in 1939.

In comparison with the World War years, New York's imports for 1940 were worth fifteen million dollars less than her 1916 imports and fell below the 1917 imports by one hundred and twenty million dollars. They were fifty-two million dollars less in valuation than the 1918 imports.

Port Clearances in the Foreign Trade

Vessels clearing the Port in the foreign trade during 1940 totaled 7503 ships with an aggregate net tonnage of 25,205,128. Using 1917 and 1938 as contrasts, the calendar year 1938, a peacetime recession year, showed an increase over the World War I year of 727 ships cleared in the foreign trade. The number of ship clearances in 1940 showed an increase of 1420 over 1939, a part of which was due to increased war trade, and an increase of 1736 vessels since 1938.

On the other hand, the aggregate tonnage showed a gradual falling off since 1938. The 1940 tonnage in the foreign trade dropped two and one half million net tons below the 1938 figure, while it failed to meet the 1939 figure by one and a half million tons. Two large factors in the 1940 drop were the removal from the transatlantic trade of the great liners with their tonnages of forty-five thousand to eighty-three thousand and the return of small, slow, World War I freighters to the trade in the submarine-blockaded areas. The following table shows clearance figures for four selected years:*

	1917	1938	1939	1940
Vessels cleared in the foreign trade	5,040	5,767	6,083	7,503
Net tons:	15,817,087	27,718,332	26,939,542	25,205,128

Tonnage Prices

The price of vessels began to rise almost immediately after the outbreak of war. The ship market had been inactive before the war, and backwater channels were crowded with old ships out of commission. A freighter that sold for eight or ten dollars a deadweight ton before September 1939 could be resold for fifty-five dollars a ton in February 1940. New York ship brokerage companies became extremely active, and tonnage prices soared as agents of foreign governments tried to buy ships.

---

* The figures for each year include totals for ships sailng direct to foreign ports, ships going via other domestic ports with residue cargo to discharge, and ships going via other domestic ports to lade—the totals include both foreign and American ships.

By the end of 1940 the British, almost the sole remaining purchasers of vessels in great numbers, managed to keep the price range down near sixty-five dollars a ton, but it was predicted that if their shipping losses increased, the price of tonnage would eventually go far above the 1940 high.

Charter rates for vessels also rose during 1940. Although they varied widely in different trades, the rates in the South American trade shifted from eighty cents a ton before the war upward to points between five dollars and a half and seven dollars a gross ton per month. The latter routes, where ship tonnage was needed toward the end of 1940, were affected by this rise, as vessels returning in ballast were unprofitable at such high charter rates.

According to the Department of Commerce, export trade to Latin America had increased markedly during the last four months of 1939, after the war had isolated European sources of supply, and the increase continued through 1940. American shipments to Latin-American republics had been valued at less than forty million dollars for August 1939 but increased to seventy-one million for December of that year; they showed an average monthly total of sixty-three million in the first six months of 1940 and of fifty-eight million in the last six months of the year. The Port of New York handled a large portion of these exports. In June 1940 the Port shipped sixty-seven per cent of the nation's exports to South America and forty-eight per cent of the national exports to Central America.

1940 Port Compared with 1917

In 1940 the Port of New York was far better equipped to solve the problems growing out of a European war than it had been in 1917. The Port now had adequate facilities to handle the great traffic load—these included terminals, piers, warehouses, bridges, tunnels, tugs, lighters, and cranes—and was able to coordinate its facilities and use them effectively in relation to the roads, rails, and ships of the national transport system. This coordination of port facilities and the country's transport system—especially railroads—was perfected as a deliberate preparation for the impending war conditions.

Thus, with the 1917 port paralysis still in mind, the war had hardly begun when harbor-traffic coordinating committees were organized and set in motion by the steamship companies, the Port of New York Authority, the railroads, and the motor-transportation companies. The three main committees were the Emergency Port Committee, composed of shippers, Port authorities, and steamship companies; the Association of American Railroads, which formed a committee headed by a Port-traffic manager; and the Steamship Pier Trucking Committee, which maintained cooperation of all motor-truck companies operating in and out of the greater Port. While the railroad committee has borne the greatest responsibility for cooperation under greater traffic pressure, the trucking committee has mastered a new problem which did not confront the Port during the last war. In the event that this country goes to war again, the army or the navy would set up its own machinery for traffic coordination in the Port of New York.

Export shipments through the Port in 1940 increased more than fifty per cent in value over the previous year. Despite this increased load, the machinery of the Port functioned smoothly. On the waterfront twenty miles of new steamship berthage had been added since 1918, and there were 189 steamship piers as compared with 116 in 1917. Because of the increase in cargoes, additional pier space was solicited by many of the large steamship companies. The newest city pier, at the foot of West Twenty-fourth Street, a WPA project costing $1,333,000, was completed in May. In addition, new ship-rail terminals had been established, and terminal space had been expanded by five million square feet. The daily movements of motor trucks had increased from seven thousand in 1920 to twenty-five thousand in 1940.

The Association of American Railroads reported in June an average unloading at the Port of 815 cars daily, as compared with averages of

715 cars daily for the previous five months. The railroads had modernized their equipment, and the Port now had nearly one thousand modern railroad-owned lighters and an equal number of independently owned craft of the same type. These were in addition to older lighters.

Marine Division Handicapped

One government service especially handicapped by war conditions was the Marine Division of the United States Weather Bureau. In normal times this agency received radio reports daily from approximately four hundred ships at sea. More than half of this number sent four reports daily as to their exact positions and the prevailing weather conditions. The others sent one or two similar reports daily. When ships found it expedient to keep their whereabouts unknown because of war conditions, their use of the outgoing radio ceased. However, the forecast radioed twice daily to all ships at sea from the station in Whitehall Street, New York, suffered little in accuracy.

Coast Guard

The United States Coast Guard celebrated its one hundred and fiftieth anniversary in August 1940. In 1790, under the title of the Revenue Cutter Service, it was a ten-boat and eighty-man affair. In 1915, when its name was changed to the Coast Guard, it had three hundred craft and a personnel of more than eight hundred commissioned officers, several thousand petty officers, cadets, and enlist-ed men, manning two hundred and fifty shore stations. Until 1915 its principal duties remained in the field of customs regulation and maritime-law enforcement, based on the act of 1789.

As the nation grew other duties were added to those initially assigned to the Revenue Service. Some of these were declared by statute and some were assumed. Two of the assumed important duties, almost from its inception, were the saving of life and property at sea and the aiding of vessels in distress.

The Coast Guard enforces the Federal statutes governing customs and the prevention of smuggling, navigation and merchant shipping, suppression of mutiny and piracy, prevention of oil pollution, harbor rules and regulations governing anchorage and movements of vessels, immigration, quarantine, and neutrality.

In 1939 the Lighthouse Service was consolidated with the Coast Guard. In that capacity it contributes to safety in New York Harbor. This means manning and provisioning eighteen lighthouses, three light-ships, and tending innumerable light, whistle, and bell buoys.

The main lighthouses having an important tie-up with Coast Guard operations are the Navesink, Sandy Hook, Fire Island, and Montauk. Of these, Navesink Light is the largest. Situated on a high wooded ridge in the Navesink Highlands of New Jersey, it is the strongest light in the country and the first of the New York harbor lights to be seen by navigators of ships approaching from the south or the southeast. Trans-atlantic steamers on inbound voyages first sight the Fire Island Light on the south shore of Long Island about thirty-five miles nearer Europe than the Navesink Light. The Sandy Hook Light, at the entrance to New York Harbor, is on the sand bar for which it is named. This is the harbor's oldest lighthouse. It was erected by the colony of New York in 1764 on land in the colony of New Jersey. The structure still stands although the original equipment is gone. Montauk Light, on the east-ernmost tip of Long Island, and the Block Island Light mark the entrance to Long Island Sound.

The lightships have an interesting history. A scant ten miles offshore from Fire Island Lighthouse is Fire Island Lightship. This ship was anchored in its present position in 1886 to mark the place where a sunken Cunard liner was a hazard to navigation. By the time the wreck had been removed the lightship had become such a traditional beacon to incoming ships that it was permanently maintained. A sunken ship also caused the establishment of another of the lightships. This is the *Scotland*, which is anchored just off Sandy Hook; it is named for the wrecked steamship *Scotland* whose hulk, since removed, it first marked. A third lightship is the *Ambrose*. It marks the parting of two dredged channels—the Ambrose and the Gedney—which are the main deep-water entrances for marine commerce into the Port of New York.

A secondary function of the Coast Guard in New York Harbor is to keep marine traffic lanes free of obstructions—these include harbor boats, fishermen in small craft, and cross traffic—and to keep moored vessels within the harbor areas assigned for anchorage purposes.

The duties of the Coast Guard were greatly increased during the winter of 1939-40 by the extension of neutral waters from twelve miles offshore to three hundred miles. This greatly enlarged the area to be patrolled.

The Coast Guard also operates a school on Hoffman Island, under the auspices of the United States Maritime Commission, for the purpose of training non-commissioned officers for service in the American merchant marine.

New York Harbor

The predominant feature of New York Harbor is its size. There is a water frontage of 771 miles and docking facilities, measured around piers and slips, of nearly 350 miles. The city owns more than 25 per cent of the approximately 900 piers along the developed frontage.

The Lower Bay provides the harbor's main entrance. It has an area of one hundred square miles and is well protected from ocean storms. The Narrows, a deep tidal strait about one mile wide and two miles long, leads to the Upper Bay, which extends from the Narrows to the Battery, a distance of about five miles. Its area is seventeen square miles.

The Hudson and the East rivers branch off from the Upper Bay, the Hudson on the west, extending northward between Manhattan and New Jersey. The East River, actually a strait, is between Manhattan and Long Island and leads to Long Island Sound. Manhattan's insularity is maintained by another strait, the Harlem River, which connects the Hudson and the East rivers.

Newark Bay, also a part of the harbor, is situated west of the Upper Bay and is joined with it by a short strait called Kill van Kull. Another strait, Arthur Kill, connects the Lower Bay with Newark Bay. New Jersey's Hackensack and Passaic rivers flow into the bay.

Among the harbor's great natural advantages are the relative lack of ice during the winter months, the absence of true ocean fog, the comparatively small rise and fall of the tides, and the presence of natural ship channels.

It has been necessary from time to time, however, to make channel improvements by dredging. Large shoal areas are in the Lower Bay and along the eastern and western shores of the Upper Bay. In the early days ocean vessels, usually of shallow draft, had no difficulty in navigating the natural entrance channels. As the size and draft of ocean steamships increased, the natural depths of channels had to be increased to accommodate them.

All the waters of the harbor are under the control of the War Department of the United States government, and all improvements throughout the harbor have to be made under authorization of Congress. The first appropriation for the improvement of Gedney Channel, which leads from the ocean into the Lower Bay at Sandy Hook, was made in 1884. The dredging of the channel through the Sandy Hook bar was completed in 1886.

The dredging of Ambrose Channel—originally called East Channel—was commenced in 1901 and was not completed until 1914, although the channel was in use by 1907. This important channel connects the ocean and the Narrows through the Lower Bay. Three years after its completion Congress authorized the dredging of Anchorage Channel—forty feet deep and two thousand feet wide—which was an extension of Ambrose Channel through the Upper Bay. This was completed in 1929.

Since nearly two thirds of the ships entering the harbor through the Lower Bay dock at Hudson River terminals, the Hudson River Channel is vastly important. This channel extends from deep water in the Upper Bay to the northern limits of Manhattan. The first improvements were made in 1875. A project begun in 1935 provided for a forty-foot channel extending from Fifty-ninth Street to a point about one thousand feet north of the Battery, another forty-foot channel to deep water off Ellis Island, and a third channel thirty feet deep along the Weehawken-Edgewater waterfront. In order to make provision for superliners such as the *Queen Elizabeth, Queen Mary,* and *Normandie,* this project and those designed for the improvement of Ambrose and Anchorage channels were modified in 1937. The new plans call for a channel two thousand feet wide from the sea to Fifty-ninth Street, a mean low-water depth of forty-five feet at West Fortieth Street and of forty-eight feet at West Fifty-ninth Street.

The New York and New Jersey channels are of great utility, as they serve a vast industrial section where great quantities of petroleum and petroleum products are stored, refined, and prepared for distribution. These channels extend from Gedney Channel through the Lower Bay and Raritan Bay, around Staten Island, then through Arthur Kill, Newark Bay, and Kill van Kull to the Upper Bay. The volume and value of commerce along this waterway in 1937 was in excess of thirty-seven per cent of the Port's total commerce in that year. Depths for these channels range from thirty to thirty-two feet, but plans have been made to provide a uniform thirty-five-foot depth for the entire length of the waterway.

Rail Transportation of the Port

Next to the ships, no other agency contributes so much to the greatness of the Port as the railroads, and no other port in the world has better railway facilities for handling raw materials and merchandise in large quantities. The Port is served by twelve leading trunk lines, operating nearly forty thousand miles of main track and connecting the city with all parts of the country. Only one of these great rail systems, the New York Central, has direct access to Manhattan with freight service; the others have their terminals in other boroughs or across the Hudson in New Jersey.

The New Jersey trunk lines make delivery of freight to Greater New York by means of lighters. The roads have developed a highly efficient system of free lighterage with the lighters, car floats, and barges either self-propelled or tug-powered, and transporting freight from terminal to warehouse or pier. By this means the roads have overcome the difficulty presented by the numerous waterways, which otherwise would isolate many sections of the Port and deprive them of rail facilities.

Harbor craft owned by railroads include self-propelled tugs, steel car floats capable of carrying twenty-four freight cars at a time, covered and refrigerated barges for the protection of perishable and packaged goods, and derrick lighters for handling automobiles and machinery. There is more mobile derrick equipment and other freight-handling machinery on harbor craft, piers, and docks than in any other port in the world.

The aggregate of freight-car and other lighters and the number of tugs to propel them naturally vary from year to year, but it is conservatively estimated that the number averages about two thousand regularly, and ninety per cent of them ply daily between New Jersey railroad terminals and various other points in the five boroughs. In addition to the tugs, lighters, and car floats, nearly all the railroads operate ferryboats for passengers and freight. The City of New York owns and runs a fleet of ferryboats for various purposes—carrying passengers and vehicles, taking visitors to institutions, and transporting goods and supplies to municipal institutions on East River islands.

Many of the nine hundred piers in the harbor are owned by the principal railroad and terminal companies. The scope of the terminals is large and varied, including facilities for the storage and handling of all kinds of commodities. Railroad docks occupy an extensive part of the

Hudson River shore line, and a coordinated system of docks, ware-houses, lofts, and transportation facilities offers an efficient distribution to all five boroughs. Deliveries are made at all piers, warehouses, and waterfront industries within the free-lighterage area.

The railroads maintain regular fast-freight schedules to and from all important cities of the country, delivering export freight from the interior to shipside in record time. An unusual service permits freight to be forwarded and billed to the Port without specific designation of pier and steamship delivery. The exporter can then charter steamship space and notify the railroad of the point of delivery.

The Port's facilities for dry docking are unsurpassed in this country. If a ship is damaged above the water line the repairs are made at the regular dock, but if a ship requires repairs to the hull, there are dry docks for all but about a dozen of the largest ships. In 1940 construction was begun on a dry dock that will accommodate a forty-five-thousand-ton battleship.

There are fifty floating docks, two commercial graving docks, and four navy graving' docks which can be used by merchant vessels when no commercial dry dock is vacant. These dry docks are suitable for ships ranging in size from two hundred to twenty-seven thousand tons. Floating grain elevators that can run up along-side of a ship and unload tons of grain in a matter of minutes are one of the features that make for the speedy turn around of the cargo ships.

Pilot Service

The New York and New Jersey Pilots' Associations, which rank high in such services, achieved this rating solely on the individual efforts of the men engaged in this specialized work. Henry Hudson spent days in his small boat avoiding the shoals in the Lower Bay before reaching Manhattan Island. Later, when the Ambrose Channel had been dredged, currents and tide made it mandatory that ships be guided by experts to keep from going aground or otherwise interfering with the ever-increasing harbor traffic. New York insisted upon the use of licensed pilots even before it became a state. Now the Federal government prohibits ships from passing inward from Sandy Hook without a licensed pilot on board.

Prior to 1895 the pilots were individualists; the first to reach an incoming ship got the job of piloting it. By 1895 there were thirty pilot boats cruising a six-hundred-mile course outside the harbor. Some had two pilots on board; others carried as many as twelve. On days when there was an inrush of ships many of the pilot boats would have to anchor off Sandy Hook, because the dash to one ship would carry many pilots off the course of other ships. Finally the idea of organization took hold, and in 1895 the New York Pilots' Association was formed. The New Jersey pilots organized also within a few months. The two combined, and all pilots were put on regular routine.

One boat is maintained off Sandy Hook with a sufficient number of pilots on board to handle ordinary traffic. As a pilot leaves to take a ship in, his place is usually filled by the pilot of an outgoing vessel. The incoming pilot, after having completed his task of getting a ship to her berth, reports to the headquarters of the association in lower Manhattan.

The apprenticeship of a pilot is a more rigorous course of probation than any official body would dare set up. At least ten years of hard work are required before a man can become a full-fledged pilot.

In spite of the long hard climb for the beginner, piloting often runs in families; there are a number of father-and-son pilots. The young man serves his initial apprenticeship for at least two years—shining brasswork, scrubbing decks, and performing other maintenance work.

For the next eight years he serves as an apprentice pilot at forty dollars a month, pulling the oars in the pilot boat's dinghy, putting the pilot aboard the incoming vessel, and taking him off departing ships. In his spare time he studies charts, harbor navigation, shoals, depth variation, and the like. After a period during which he accompanies the experienced pilot while the latter performs his duties, the apprentice pilot becomes watch officer or captain of one of the three pilot vessels. At the end of ten years he is examined by the harbor authorities; he must know the harbor floor by memory; he must know offhand every buoy and land-mark, and in effect his mind must be a large geodetic map which instantly gives the depth at any point in the harbor and its many channels.

Having passed the examination, he is given a license to pilot small vessels—ships of not more than eighteen-foot draft. From then on he is re-examined every few years and licensed to pilot progressively larger ships. After perhaps twenty years of irreproachable service he is finally allowed to pilot the huge transatlantic liners in and out of New York Harbor.

Federal Supervision

The Federal government has many services and bureaus whose duties are closely related to various functions of the Port of New York. The three best known to the public are the Immigration and Naturaliza-tion Service, which administers the laws relating to the admission, exclusion, and deportation of aliens; the Bureau of Customs, which administers the powers and duties pertaining to the importation and entry of merchandise into, and the exportation of merchandise from, the United States; and the Public Health Service, which works to prevent the spread of human contagious and infectious diseases and administers the foreign and domestic quarantine laws.

The Public Health Service has established a quarantine station at Rosebank, Staten Island, on the Narrows just north of Fort Wadsworth. The station itself is not elaborate, consisting mainly of a building where the health officers meet and berthage for the quarantine service's vessels—three tugs and a launch. When these boats are on duty they fly the regulation quarantine service flag—the Service Corps device in blue on a yellow field—from the forestay.

A daytime observer at the Rosebank station sights each ship as it passes through the Narrows and notifies the health officers, who board their launch and proceed to the vessel when it anchors just offshore from the station. Vessels coming into quarantine fly a yellow flag or bunting at the foremast head; the flag is struck when a vessel is released. Ships arriving after dark drop anchor and wait until daylight; all ships on hand then are inspected in the order of their arrival, with the exception of fruit and passenger vessels, which receive preference. Vessels in distress always receive preference and may be inspected after daylight.

If an incoming vessel has a ship's doctor who is a fully accredited physician approved by the Public Health Service, the quarantine officers will accept his guarantee that ship, passengers, and crew are free of contagious or infectious diseases, and the vessel is allowed to proceed to its dock.

If a ship has a quarantinable disease aboard the person or persons suffering from it are removed to a city hospital where such cases are treated. The remaining passengers, officers, crew, and the pilot are detained aboard the ship a sufficient time to cover the period of incubation of the disease germ, if in the opinion of the quarantine officers they have been exposed to the disease. They are inspected twice daily by physicians, and while in quarantine the different groups are isolated from one another. At the end of the quarantine period, if no further traces of the disease are found, the quarantined persons are released and the ship cleared.

In 1937 the Public Health Service initiated medical clearance by radio for certain passenger ships—a striking departure from historic practice—which enables such vessels to dock well in advance of their usual time. An eligible vessel approaching the Port must make radio application for clearance not more than twenty-four, nor less than twelve, hours before it expects to arrive in New York. Passengers and crew are examined by the ship's doctor who reports his findings by wireless to the health officers ashore. Ships that are granted clearance by radio pass through quarantine and go directly to their docks.

This service is confined to passenger ships in service between New York and European ports and passenger vessels in regular service between New York and Bermuda or ports in the West Indies as well as vessels engaging in seasonal cruises to these points. Passenger ships in service between New York and certain ports of Central and South America are also included radio clearance is not compulsory.

Ships that are ineligible for radio clearance include cargo vessels, vessels known to carry or suspected of carrying quarantinable diseases, vessels with commercial shipments of birds of the parrot family, and any vessel ordinarily eligible which does not carry a qualified doctor familiar with contagious and infectious diseases.

There are other routine services. Engine, hull, and similar inspections are made for the promotion of safety at sea, as well as to establish whether there have been any taxable repairs or additions to ships while abroad. Agricultural products are also inspected. Subject to this are fruits from the tropics that might carry parasites which would imperil the well-being of homegrown oranges, peaches, pears, apples, and other fruits.

Vegetables are likewise subject to inspection, and the produce of other nations is placed under a ban whenever its condition warrants such action. Animals are more closely scrutinized; a special quarantine station is maintained for animals, and suspected livestock is kept there.

The customhouse at the Port of New York is the headquarters for the Customs District of New York, which includes the subports of Newark, Perth Amboy, and Albany; all of Long Island, several counties of New Jersey, and more than twenty counties in southern New York State.

Customs officials meet all incoming ships in the harbor, boarding them when they are stopped at the quarantine station. All imported merchandise is subject to customs entry, examination, and appraisement. The merchandise is subject to duty or free of duty, according to rates provided for by the various tariff acts.

Unless directed otherwise by the Secretary of the Treasury, ten per cent of all imported merchandise must be examined by the official appraiser in order to determine its character, value, and classification.

Customs men are again active when ships leave. Until recent years the United States, having no duties on exports, did not require their examination by officials of the Bureau of Customs. However, in 1940 Congress passed the Export Control Act, designed to control the exportation of materials used in the prosecution of war. The aim of the act was twofold: to prevent the extension of American aid to certain belligerent powers, and to retain at home the materials essential to national defense.

Administration of the provisions of this act meant an important change in the functions of the New York Customs Service—a historic shift of emphasis from import to export. The customs men are now furnished with lists of the types of merchandise that require examination and checking—for example, the kind of oil used by airplanes—and they must ascertain whether such shipments in any way violate the provisions of the Export Control Act.

The detection of contraband goods on board any vessel sailing from the Port is in the hands of the Customs Agency Service (equivalent to a maritime secret service), which is maintained at New York and other ports by the Bureau of Customs in Washington.

The four administrative customs officers at the Port of New York, appointed by the President, are the Collector of Customs, the Appraiser of Merchandise, the Comptroller of Customs, and the Surveyor of Customs; practically all other employees come under civil service classification.

Municipal Services

Unlike the Bureau of Customs and the Immigration and Public Health Services, which are under Federal supervision, the police and fire services of the harbor are maintained by the City of New York. The municipal police department operates a fleet of eleven high-powered launches, which night and day patrol five hundred and eighty miles of the city's waterfront. These launches range in length from twenty-two to sixty feet.

Two-way radio apparatus has been installed on two of them, while the remainder use short-wave receivers similar to those on police cars.

The waterfront gangs of thieves and smugglers, who constituted such a serious problem in past years, have largely disappeared from the harbor as a result of the efficient activities of the harbor police and their surveillance of the piers and the merchandise stored thereon. Today whatever criminal acts the police investigate are usually of a petty nature—the theft of compasses, clocks, binoculars, and other equipment from motorboats or launches moored in the city's waterways.

Many of the activities of the harbor police are not concerned with law violations at all. They recover bodies from the harbor and bay—the great majority of these are suicides or the victims of accidental drownings, although a few are eventually listed as unsolved homicides—and effect a considerable number of rescues from drowning. In the winter the harbor patrol often has to extricate small craft caught in ice packs, and occasionally marooned persons are taken from floes headed for the sea. Barges and other craft that might go adrift and float down the river, creating hazards to normal shipping, have to be made secure by the harbor police.

Police launches patrol the waters from Arthur Kill (separating Staten Island from New Jersey) to Execution Light, near the city's northeast boundary on Long Island Sound, and from the Hudson River to Coney Island. The crew of a launch varies from four to six men, generally in charge of a sergeant. The personnel of the harbor squad consists of one captain, three lieutenants, seven sergeants, and more than one hundred and fifty patrolmen. Many of the harbor police are former members of the navy or the merchant marine.

The City of New York's first harbor police force was organized in February 1858. At that time it consisted of a squad of husky policemen who manned a fleet of five rowboats. They patrolled the Manhattan pier ends and even rowed over to New Jersey when necessary, in pursuit of waterfront thieves and river pirates.

The Marine Division of the New York City Fire Department operates ten fireboats equipped with modern fire-fighting equipment and with ship-to-shore radio telephone. Four of the boats are oil burners; four use coal; one, the *John J. Harvey*, is gasoline-electric propelled. The latest addition to the fleet, the *Fire Fighter*, which the city acquired in 1938 at a cost of one million dollars, is powered by twin sixteen-cylinder Diesel engines. Of 583 tons' displacement and drawing 9 feet, 3 inches, the *Fire Fighter* is 134 feet in length, with a beam of 32 feet. She is able to attain a speed of 17.2 miles an hour. Her four two-stage centrifugal pumps can supply 20,000 gallons of water a minute at 150 pounds' pressure, or 10,000 gallons at 300 pounds, more than enough pressure to reach the top deck of any liner. Her bow "gun" is capable of shooting 6500 to 10,000 gallons of water a minute for a distance of several hundred feet.

In addition to the ten fireboats, there is the *Smoke*, a tender which has a small pump capable of supplying 125 gallons of water a minute at 60 pounds' pressure. The *Smoke* has a draft of only $3^{1/2}$ feet, despite its 53-foot length and 7-foot beam. The tender is also supplied with equipment for fighting chemical fires. In addition to carrying firemen to and from the scene of a fire, she fills an important role in ship, dock, and warehouse fire, where her shallow draft and small over-all dimensions allow her to "get in" and fight the blaze where her larger sisters of the fleet cannot go.

Although primarily concerned with the saving of life and property endangered by waterfront and harbor fires, the Marine Division firemen engage in other emergency activities. Like the police of the harbor patrol, they are called upon to rescue persons, and sometimes animals, from floating ice cakes, the victims of collisions and other marine disasters, and potential victims of drowning. One of their biggest jobs, rounding up "breakaways" (car floats, barges, and other craft whose lines have broken), is called a "river rodeo" by those firemen.

More than four hundred firemen, many of them ex-sailors, comprise the personnel of the Marine Division, which is under the command of a deputy chief and three battalion chiefs. Fireboat pilots, who are federally licensed, receive a salary of thirty-five hundred dollars a year, five hundred dollars more than the ordinary fireman. Fireboat engineers, who are duly licensed marine engineers, must also take the regular training courses and examinations for firemen.

As in other divisions of the municipal fire department, the Marine Division operates on the three-platoon system, officers and men working in eight-hour shifts. Although pilots and engineers must stay on board the fireboats at all times while on duty, other firemen remain in the firehouse, except when on call or when other duties, such as cleaning and polishing of equipment, require them to be on board the fireboat.

When on call the *Fire Fighter* and the *John J. Harvey* carry a complement of three engineers, one pilot, eight firemen, and an officer in command. Other boats of the fleet carry from five to eight firemen, engineers, a pilot, and chief officer. The pilot controls the boat in much the same way that a chauffeur controls an automobile. He is sometimes referred to as the "chauffeur." With the exception of the *Fire Fighter* and the *John J. Harvey*, all the fireboats are named for former mayors of the City of New York.

The Marine Division of the New York City Fire Department can trace its origin back to the year 1800, when the city's first fireboat, the *Floating Engine*, was launched. It was a large scow with a sharp bow and square stern and was propelled by twelve oarsmen. She carried hose, hooks, and other equipment and mounted a large and comparatively powerful hand-operated pump. From her station at the foot of Roosevelt Street, East River, the *Floating Engine* responded to ship, dock, and waterfront fire alarms, working in conjunction with the regular shore engine companies.

America's First Free Port

The first Foreign-Trade Zone, or Free Port, in the United States is now operating at five of the City of New York's piers at Stapleton, Staten Island. While still in the experimental stage, the project is proving increasingly successful. The municipal piers at Stapleton were built between 1920 and 1921 during the administration of Mayor Hylan.

The Celler Act, which was passed by Congress and approved by President Franklin D. Roosevelt on June 18, 1934, provided for the establishment, operation, and maintenance of foreign-trade zones in ports of entry of the United States. Section three of the act provides:

"Foreign and domestic merchandise of every description, except such as is prohibited by law, may, without being subject to the customs laws of the United States, except as otherwise provided in this act, be brought into a zone and may not be manufactured or exhibited in such zone but may be stored, broken up, repacked, assembled, distributed, sorted, graded, cleaned, mixed with foreign or domestic merchandise, or otherwise manipulated, and be exported . . ." In 1936 the chairman of the Foreign-Trade Zones Board, Secretary of Commerce Daniel C. Roper, granted the City of New York the privilege of establishing, operating, and maintaining Foreign-Trade Zone No. 1 at Stapleton.

The zone area includes piers 12 to 16 and the adjacent inland territory, a total land, pier, and water area of about ninety-two acres. The landside of the zone is enclosed by a high wire fence and the waterside guarded by an electric-eye system. Located at the entrance to the Upper Bay, adjacent to adequate anchorage, and served by direct railroad connections, it is provided with dockage for ocean-going vessels and lies within the bounds of the free-lighterage limits of the harbor. The physical equipment of the piers is the last word in modern scientific freight handling. There is ferry service to Staten Island from Manhattan, Brooklyn, and New Jersey, and the zone is made more readily accessible by the four bridges, three vehicular and one railroad, that connect New Jersey with Staten Island.

The zone was originally operated directly by the city from February 1, 1937, to May 10, 1938. A private corporation was then awarded the contract for soliciting and handling business under the supervision of the Commissioner of Docks, and this plan is currently (1941) in effect. The proceeds from operation are divided between the city and the zone corporation, according to a sliding scale.

The Foreign-Trade Zone provides considerable facilities for the storing of foreign goods that may be held on consignment or for importation or transshipment duty free, without the expense of bond and for the mingling of domestic and foreign goods and assembling of cargoes with a minimum of customs supervision.

Maximum service at minimum cost is being furnished to exporters, importers, and merchants, which benefits purchasers of and dealers in foreign goods and manufacturers and exporters of domestic goods. The zone management strives to maintain fair and reasonable rates, and serious consideration is given to all questions of operation and rates.

Plants have already been established for handling Argentine canned beef, the processing of tungsten ore, cleaning peas, marketing of Sumatra and Java tobacco, and many other commodities. Work has been provided for from 200 to 800 people per day. Vast cargoes of war material have been assembled at the zone.

THE FUTURE PLANS

Tunnels to Relieve Traffic

One of the projects of the Port of New York Authority is the construction of a freight tunnel under the waters of the Upper Bay from New Jersey to Brooklyn. If this railroad tunnel accomplishes the expected results, lighterage traffic in the harbor will be greatly decreased. The congestion in New Jersey freight-receiving terminals makes delivery difficult in Manhattan and Brooklyn. The proposed freight tunnel is expected to facilitate the flow of traffic to Brooklyn. From that point it also could be carried into Manhattan over five bridges—Brooklyn,

Manhattan, Williamsburg, Queensboro, and Triboro—and through two tunnels—the Queens-Midtown and the Manhattan-Brooklyn, which is now under construction.

Another menace to quick movements of ocean ships in the harbor is the freight barge. This unwieldy craft is dependent upon a tug for mobility. It is used for the transportation of cargoes from inland and nearby coastal points.

Future Changes

The first attempts to establish a pattern of intersecting runways for seaplanes on the surface of the harbor adjoining La Guardia Field—in February 1940—created excitement among masters of tankers and steamers plying the East River route to New England and Long Island ports. The more imaginative foresaw disaster—heavily laden air clippers crashing into excursion boats or fifty-ton airships landing at great speed and colliding with ships carrying cargoes of high-test gasoline. But their fears did not materialize, and it is possible to conceive of a time in the near future when the air clippers now landing passengers from Lisbon at La Guardia Airport will be landing many times the present number of passengers and from all the leading countries of the world.

In view of this, plans have been outlined for the creation of an artificial island in the harbor, to occupy the flats south of Governors Island, built of fill excavated from the Battery-Brooklyn tunnel. Other proposals have been made from time to time, including a similar man-made island off the New Jersey shore between the Statue of Liberty and Staten Island. La Guardia Airport, large as it is, will not long be able to clear the air traffic of the future.

It has been predicted that ocean liners in the future will dock at piers in Jamaica Bay, within a half-hour of the open ocean. In the eyes of these prophets, Jamaica Bay, instead of becoming a big industrial and commercial center, will become an immense water-air-land terminal for passenger and express service, with speedy streamlined trains and the newly constructed circumferential highway to take the increased three-way traffic to any part of the City of New York or the United States.

Other visionaries like to recall the dream of Collis P. Huntington and Alexander J. Cassatt, the railroad magnates, who planned fast train service from special docks at Montauk Point, Long Island, to other parts of the country. It has been calculated that such a service could have passengers in Pittsburgh before the same ship could land them at the present North River piers. However, the Port is attractive to shippers and passengers just because of its proximity to the City of New York.

As planned today the world's greatest port bids fair to continue along the lower banks of the Hudson and around a greatly developed Upper Bay. The natural advantages of this area, as apparent to the early Dutch navigators as to our own present-day army engineers and the planners of the Port of New York Authority, make it certain that the facilities of New York Harbor will be constantly improved and that the active center of the Port will not change its situation for many years to come.

The story of the rise to greatness of the Port of New York has been told against a background of continuous growth that, in a little more than three hundred years, has turned a tiny trading post into a world metropolis visited by all the great ships of the world, the recipient of nearly every type of cargo, from rough metals in bulk to the exotic and refined products of far countries, and at one time or another a debarkation point for people of nearly every tongue and nation.

During this three-hundred-year period governmental control passed from the Dutch to the English and then to the native Americans; ship styles changed—the swift and graceful sailing packets and clippers were superseded by primitive steam vessels, and these developed into the efficient cargo and passenger steamships and motor ships of today. Many striking figures appeared in the different eras—Kieft, Stuyvesant, Andros, Kidd, Washington, Astor, the pirates of the late seventeenth century, adventurous China traders, the privateers of the War of

1812, the rough but able officers and crews of the clipper ships, and the inventors and financial backers of the pioneering in steam.

Holding all these together—the main theme—has been this continuous and vital growth, which went on despite the unfortunate loss of world position by the American merchant marine and which typifies in so many ways the remarkable growth of the nation, from its initial position as an imperial colony to its present status as a world power.

Epilogue

1941—Present

By BARBARA LA ROCCO

ABOUT A WEEK before *A Maritime History of New York* was released the United States entered the Second World War. Between Pearl Harbor and VJ-Day, more than three million troops and over 63 million tons of supplies and materials shipped overseas through the Port.

The Port of New York, really eleven ports in one, boasted a developed shoreline of over 650 miles comprising the waterfronts of five boroughs of New York City and seven cities on the New Jersey side. The Port included 600 individual ship anchorages, some 1,800 docks, piers, and wharves of every conceivable size which gave access to over a thousand warehouses, and a complex system of car floats, lighters, rail and bridge networks. Over 575 tugboats worked the Port waters. Port operations employed some 25,000 longshoremen and an additional 400,000 other workers.*

Ships of every conceivable type were needed for troop transport and supply carriers. On June 6, 1941, the U.S. Coast Guard seized 84 vessels of foreign registry in American ports under the Ship Requisition Act. To meet the demand for ships large numbers of mass-produced freighters and transports, called Liberty ships were constructed by a civilian workforce using pre-fabricated parts and the relatively new technique of welding. The Liberty ship, adapted by New York naval architects Gibbs & Cox from an old British tramp ship, was the largest civilian-made war ship. The assembly-line production methods were later used to build 400 Victory ships (VC2)—the Liberty ship's successor. Eighteen months after the U.S. entered the war, shipyards were producing ships faster than the enemy could sink them. By 1944 the United States had the largest Navy in the world.

Harbor defenses were controlled by Harbor Entrance Control Posts at Fort Tilden in Rockaway, Fort Wadsworth in Staten Island and at Fort Hancock at Sandy Hook. A notice to mariners issued on December 10, 1941 stated that "A mined area covering the approaches to New York Harbor has been established. Incoming vessels will secure directions for safe navigation from patrol vessels stationed off Ambrose Channel Entrance." The U.S. Navy Net Depot in Bayonne, New Jersey erected a submarine net across the Narrows. The tenders stationed at the net had no propulsion, therefore had to be moved by tugs when the net was ordered opened or closed. Lookouts observed the entrance to the port from 100 foot tall towers at Fort Tilden and Arverne in Rockaway. German submarines began to cross the Atlantic and assault American shipping. The U-boats had no need to enter New York Harbor, using the lights from the city for direction; they lay in wait offshore for merchant ships to leave port. In 1942 an enemy submarine sank the British tanker *Coimbra* just 61 miles east of Ambrose light. U-boats laid mines in the Lower Bay below the Narrows. Mines washed ashore at the beaches of Coney Island, Rockaway, and Monmouth. Improvements to New York's limited harbor defenses were quickly implemented, including magnetic detection loops laid along the bottom of the harbor in Ambrose Channel to detect U-boats that could not be detected by the newly developed radar system and underwater listening equipment called "hydrophones."+

On January 3, 1944 an explosion aboard the U.S. Navy destroyer *Turner* rocked the port. *Turner* had just returned from her third tour of duty and was anchored off Sandy Hook, New Jersey waiting to go to Brooklyn Navy Yard for repairs. A second explosion ripped the bottom

* NYS Historical Survey of the State Museum conducted by Historian Joseph F. Meany titled Port in a Storm: The Port of New York in WWII.

+ "War Diary" of the Eastern Sea Frontier from Dec. 1941- Sept. 1943 out of the vessel and she sank below the surface taking 15 officers and 138 crewmembers. 165 survived. There was a lot of speculation at the time that the *Turner* had been torpedoed by a U-boat, but it was determined to be an accidental detonation of ammunition onboard the vessel.

The Port's merchant fleet facilitated the greatest sealift in history between the homeport and the fighting forces spread throughout the globe. Sandy Hook Pilots safely guided three times the usual number of vessels bound to Europe for the war effort. Under the command of Rear Admiral Michael Moran, a fleet of over 100 tugs, both Moran Towing and other New York operators, were critical to the success of the invasion at Normandy on D-Day where they hauled components for artificial harbors known as Mulberries across the English Channel and towed damaged ships to Great Britain for salvage or repair. The tugboat captains and their civilian crews, were awarded citations for "meritorious service and courageous devotion to duty" by the War Shipping Administration.

Many large famous luxury liners were procured for wartime duty as supply carriers and transport ships. The Cunard White Star fleet transported more than three million troops and over eleven million tons of cargo during the war years. When war ended, ships such as the *Queen Mary*, *Queen Elizabeth* and *Aquitania* contributed to war relief by transporting some 200,000 war brides to the United States. The first war bride ship to cross the North Atlantic was Moore-McCormick Lines' S.S. *Argentina* which sailed into New York Harbor on February 4, 1946, in what was called "the Diaper Run" with 452 war brides, 173 children and one war groom.

The huge New York Naval Shipyard on the East River, popularly known as the Brooklyn Navy Yard, was the premier shipyard in the world and the largest industrial complex in New York State. The Navy Yard, established by the federal government in 1801, was the site for the construction of Robert Fulton's steam frigate, the *Fulton*, launched in 1815 and the *Maine*, whose sinking sparked the Spanish-American War.

In 1938, about ten thousand men worked at the Navy Yard, one-third of whom were W.P.A. workers. Activity peaked in 1944 when over 70,000 civilian workers were employed at the shipyard—a workforce that was 30 percent female personified by "Rosie the Riveter." Earnings surpassed $4.2 million weekly. The wartime Brooklyn Navy Yard produced over 5,000 ships, many aircraft carriers, cruisers and battleships, including the *Arizona*, lost at Pearl Harbor; the *Iowa*, the most powerful ship of its day; and the *Missouri,* on whose deck the Japanese surrendered on September 2, 1945.

In addition to the Brooklyn Navy Yard, the Port of New York had an additional thirty-nine active shipyards. Bethlehem Steel built major destroyers on Staten Island near Mariner's Harbor. During WWII, there were 47 destroyers, 75 landing craft, 5 cargo vessels and 3 ocean-going tugs built at the Staten Island Yard. Caddell Dry Dock and Ship Repair serviced warships and commercial vessels on the Kill Van Kull. In Brooklyn, Robbins Dry Dock converted vessels for wartime service and Sullivan Dry Dock & Repair Company laid down submarine chasers. In 1943, Todd Shipyards in Brooklyn near Erie Basin had about 20,000 employees who handled 3,000 ships and built 24 LCI's (Landing Craft Infantry) designed with flat-bottom hulls and two gangways to disembark troops from both sides of the bow quickly from ship to shore for amphibious assaults. After the war, demand and the work force scaled back at shipyards throughout the Port of New York. Bethlehem Steel was closed. Todd Shipyards performed ship conversion and repair work for the military and private industry until 1980 when it closed.

Staten Island's Stapleton piers, America's first free port, were a major embarkation point and port of call for hospital ships during the war. Once in port, wounded servicemen were taken by train to the military hospital on Staten Island. After the war the port once again became a free trade zone but use declined and the piers were demolished in the 1970s. During the 1980s, the Navy proposed to build a "homeport" at Stapleton as a base for docking Navy war ships. The project closed in

1994 before its completion due to budget cuts. The city renovated the 36-acre site in recent years. Development plans, including a proposed speedway racetrack, are currently under review.

Activity at Brooklyn Navy Yard continued throughout the Cold War, building America's first angled-deck aircraft carrier in 1952 – the U.S.S. *Antietam* (CVA 36). The Kitty Hawk class aircraft carrier U.S.S. *Constellation* (CV 64) was commissioned in Brooklyn on October 27, 1961. The carrier was celebrated as "America's flagship" because of its namesake the three-masted frigate *Constellation* which was the first ship launched by the U.S. Navy in 1797. The New York Navy Yard was decommissioned in 1966 to become an area for private manufacturing activity. It still contains three ship repair docks, vessel berthing businesses and the city's oldest graving dock, which has been in continuous use since 1851. Caddell Dry Dock is today the oldest operating shipyard in the Port offering six dry docks where the company annually services over 300 vessels.

Maritime Training

All of the Liberty and Victory ships needed trained officers and crews to operate them, consequently Maritime education became an essential activity in the Port. Hoffman Island in New York Harbor was opened as the first Merchant Marine training station in 1938. About 2200 apprentice seamen were enrolled in 1943 and a Radio School for officers also functioned on the island. A year after Pearl Harbor, the nation's largest training facility for unlicensed seamen opened at Manhattan Beach on the eastern tip of Coney Island, now the campus of Kingsboro College. The station had an annual output of more than 35,000 seamen. In 1943, Hunter College's Bronx campus, now Lehman College, was placed in commission as the boot camp for Coast Guard (SPARS) and Navy (WAVES) women. Hunter trained 1900 SPARS and 3300 Marines that year, and a total of 80,000 WAVES went through basic training at Hunter through October 1945. In early 1945 the Coast Guard combined training for males and females at its station in Manhattan Beach. Hunter College was officially decommissioned on February 1, 1946.

North German Lloyd Steamship Lines office at 45 Broadway was taken over by the War Shipping Administration and housed the country's largest Coast Guard Enrollment Center where about 21,000 men enrolled between 1942 and 1944.

The prewar population of experienced mariners was increased four-fold through the Maritime Service training programs. In 1940 the entire U.S. merchant marine, from ocean liners to tow boats included some 65,000 men. By the end of WWII that number had risen to 250,000 and the various merchant marine academies were consolidated to the former Walter Chrysler estate in Kings Point, Long Island.

The nation's oldest commercial maritime institution at Fort Schuyler in the Bronx provided officer's training for war service. Founded aboard the U.S.S. *Mary* in 1874, where 26 cadets attended the then New York Nautical School, it moved to its present campus in 1934 and was renamed Maritime College. In 2004 the college, now part of the State University system, welcomed the largest incoming class in its history—close to 400 students. The school continues to supply trained officers through the city's only Navy and Marine Reserve Officer Training Corps as well as providing skilled seamen for civilian service. Maritime College consistently has a 100 percent graduate placement rate. The school now offers a first of its kind program in port and shipping security. On the Hudson River, Davidson Laboratory at Stevens Institute of Technology in Hoboken, NJ, founded in 1935, is today one of the world's leading centers for the study of naval architecture, ocean engineering, and marine environmental engineering.

Superliners

French Line's *Normandie* had been laid up at Hudson River Pier 88 since 1939 because of the war in Europe. The liner was painted a dull wartime gray and renamed U.S.S. *Lafayette* during conversion into a troop ship. The *Normandie*, the gem of the French Line fleet was the world's largest liner—a position she held for five years—and the fastest having earned the Blue Riband for five record-breaking crossings. At three o'clock on the cold morning of February 9, 1942 a workmen's torch set off a fire which quickly spread. Eyewitnesses reported that the winds carried the smoke across midtown Manhattan obscuring the Empire State Building. An estimated 800,000 gallons of water were pumped aboard the burning ship by FDNY fireboats. Twelve hours after the blaze began, rising tides and water from the fireboat pumps caused the ship to keel over onto her port side. Eighteen months after the fire, the *Normandie* was slowly floated from the bottom and then towed to a dry dock in Brooklyn. In November 1943, the $60,000,000 ship of extreme beauty was sold to the Lipsett Scrapyard in New Jersey for $161,000. The U.S. paid the French government $24,000,000 in compensation for the *Normandie*. The great liner contributed to the war by providing valuable dive and salvage training that helped to establish the Navy Salvage Service.

The first jet aircraft crossed the Atlantic in 1958. By 1965 airlines carried 95 percent of the transatlantic traffic, replacing the gigantic passenger liners. The Blue Riband speed record lost its past status as the new heroes of long-distance travel were the Boeing 747 or "Jumbo" jets. Lines increasingly focused on cruise travel and new ships were designed with less first-class accommodation but maximum facilities for tourists.

Only nine of 25 of Holland America Line (Netherlands America Steamship Co.) ships survived the war. In 1963 the City of New York lured Holland America from Hoboken with a new terminal at Pier 40 that was capable of accommodating four oceangoing ships at once. It was the most costly pier and largest shipping terminal in the Port, handling both passengers and freight operations. Holland America liners made a record fifty voyages to the Pier in 1964. The company moved operations to the just-completed Passenger Ship Terminal in 1974 and Pier 40 was closed. The company by then had suspended transatlantic service and was focused full time on tourist cruise travel. Holland America was purchased by Carnival Lines in 1989. The entrance hall at Pier 40 still has a Delft tile mural featuring four of the *Rotterdam* liners.

The United States Lines flagship, the *United States*, was the biggest American-built passengership and the fastest. On her maiden voyage, July 3, 1952 departing from New York Pier 86 bound for Le Havre and Southampton, the red, white and blue crowned superliner broke the *Queen Mary*'s 14 year hold on the revered Blue Riband by over ten hours. The *United States* was the first grand American transatlantic liner and the last of the great superliners. *United States,* designed by renowned New York naval architect William Gibbs, was built using large amounts of aluminum which provided extreme weight savings over vessels of similar size. Her construction was a joint effort between the U.S. Navy and United States Lines and was heavily subsidized by the U.S. government underwriting $50,000,000 of her $78,000,000 cost. The ship never turned a profit. United States Lines sold her sister ship the *America* to Chandris Lines in 1964. *United States* was withdrawn from service in 1969 marking the end of U.S. flagged service on the North Atlantic. She was sold to the Federal Maritime Administration in 1973, and changed hands many times over the years. United States Lines declared bankruptcy in the 1980s. In 2004, the *United States* was purchased by Norwegian Cruise Line to serve as a U.S.-flag ship in their "Homeland Cruising" program.

The Cunard house flag was lowered aboard the RMS *Queen Elizabeth* in 1968. She was sold at auction and on January 9, 1972 in Hong Kong harbor the great ship succumbed to fire. In May 1969, the *Queen Elizabeth 2* entered service and remained the last great transatlantic liner and the flag-ship of the Cunard Line for thirty-five years. Carnival Cruise Lines purchased Cunard Line in 1998. In August of 2002, the *QE2* logged a record 5 million miles at sea. The *Queen Mary* made her last transatlantic crossing on September 16, 1967. The venerable liner cruised to the town of Long Beach, California to begin her new role as a museum, hotel and conference center. Inaugurated January 2004, the RMS *Queen Mary 2* is the largest, longest, tallest and most expensive passenger liner in the world. The *QM2* is five times larger that Cunard's first ship, *Britannia* (230 ft.) and 113 feet longer than the original *Queen Mary*. On April 22, she arrive for the first time in Port of New York and was soon joined by her sister ship the *QE2*, the ship she would replace. On April 25, the two ocean liners made history as they departed together from the port to sail across the North Atlantic. It was the first time in Cunard's 164-year history that two ships made a transatlantic voyage in tandem. Cunard is the last of the prestigious Old World lines to carry on the tradition of regular transatlantic sailings.

The 1992 NYC Comprehensive Waterfront Plan reported: "Ocean-going cruise ship activity once helped define New York City's image; only 14 cruise ships, generating about 200 trips annually, now call at the Port Authority Passenger Ship Terminal. Cruise Ship activity is unlikely to expand." There has since been a great resurgence in cruise ship activity. New York is now the fifth busiest pleasure cruise port in the United States with over a dozen lines carrying a million passengers in and out of the port each year. In January 2004, Norwegian Cruise Line announced it was deploying *Norwegian Dawn* out of New York year round. It was the first cruise ship to be based at the Port of New York in decades.

This year, Carnival and Norwegian signed a 13-year deal with the City of New York to bring 13 million cruise passengers to the Port through 2017. Royal Caribbean has begun operating *Voyager of the Sea* at its new Cape Liberty Cruise Port in Bayonne. The city will refurbish the New York Cruise Ship Terminal piers 88, 90 and 92, (last renovated in the 1970s) in addition to establishing cruise berths in other Manhattan and Brooklyn ports.

Ocean Shipping

From the early nineteenth century through the 1950s, the Port of New York was the busiest port in the world. The metropolis of

Greater New York was the largest in the world with a population of 12.3 million people by the mid-twentieth century. It was also the world's largest center for manufacturing, wholesaling and shipping as well as the world's financial and corporate capital. The years that followed the war represented the zenith in prosperity for the Port. Foreign commerce was on the rise. The world economy was recovering from the effects of the war and there was little foreign competition for American shipping.

Almost as soon as it reached its high point, the Port of New York began its decline. Competition from other seaports and other forms of transportation posed a great challenge to the seaport. This coupled with changes in maritime technology, specifically containerization, had a decisive effect on the Port beginning in the 1960s.

On 26 April 1956 the first containership, the *Ideal X* made history when it sailed from Port Newark in New Jersey down the Atlantic Coast through the Gulf of Mexico to Houston with 58 reinforced boxes strapped to its deck. It was the brain-child of North Carolina trucker Malcolm Mclean who first advanced his novel idea to the railroad companies, was rejected and subsequently tested the concept in shipping after having acquired the Pan Atlantic and Waterman steamship companies. Mclean converted two ships to carry containers which could then be mounted on truck chassis. His vision soon became the industry standard. In 1960, the company was renamed Sea-Land Service Ltd. and in 1966 the company's SS *Fairland* inaugurated the first transatlantic service sailing from Port Elizabeth, New Jersey to Rotterdam in the Netherlands—a port Mclean had custom-built to handle containers. When Mclean sold his share in Sea-Land for $160 million in 1968, it was the world's biggest container carrier.

Before containerization, cargo handling had changed very little since the clipper ship era when brawny dockworkers moved hefty loads of loose cargo, called break-bulk, by net, grappling hook, and muscle piece-by-piece to and from the ship's hold and shore side warehouses.

It was a cumbersome, sluggish and costly process. Ships might remain in port for days. The men who worked the docks were casual laborers selected for work in longshore gangs at a morning 'shape-up' or 'call.' The post war years had been riddled with dock strikes, racketeering and corruption. The drama that played out on the Port's waterfront was depicted in the New York Sun's 1949 Pulitzer Prize winning series "Crime on the Waterfront" by Malcolm Johnson, and later in Bud Shulberg's novel "Waterfront" which became the film "On the Waterfront."

Standardized units increased efficiency and productivity while reducing the number of workers a stevedore needed to load and unload cargo. From the 1950s to the 1970s, productivity rose 400%. It took one-fourth the number of longshoremen to move much more cargo. Three years after Malcolm Mclean began shipping containers out of Port Elizabeth, the International Longshoremen's Association reached an agreement with the New York Shipping Association—which represented shipping concerns—to receive a guaranteed annual income, "so long as they showed up at the hiring hall daily and accepted available jobs." Whether the jobs were available or not, all longshoremen that showed up at the hall were paid. At its peak in 1983, the guaranteed income program cost the Port $65 million.

The majority of goods that arrive by supertanker or containership are moved in Port by large barges or pushed by tugboats. Throughout much of the twentieth century, most ocean shipping called at Manhattan and Brooklyn. Freight had to be transferred on barges and lighters across the harbor to link with rail lines in New Jersey. These so-called "brown water" industries, coastal and inland flat-bottomed workboats such as tugboats, barges and towboats still provide an essential link in moving petroleum and other products throughout the Port. A major consolidation took place in the harbor tug trade in the post-war years. Big operators went through a period of growth and geographic expansion. Reinauer, founded in 1923 and headquartered on Staten Island, is one of the few remaining family-operated companies. It specializes in the transport of petroleum and chemicals and today operates 30 tugboats and the Erie Basin Bargeport in Red Hook, Brooklyn. Moran, the oldest and today the world's largest towing company, moved its headquarters from New York to Connecticut. McAllister Towing, founded in the 1860s, is another family-owned company and the only one still based in Manhattan.

U.S. Flagged Fleet

The U.S. flagged fleet, comprised of American owned vessels operated by U.S. citizens, presently consists of only about 260 ships; a drop of 50 percent since 1991. Today, just four percent of U.S. trade is carried on U.S. ships. All U.S. flagged ships, commercial and military, are manned by US citizen merchant mariners. Maersk Sealand is the largest U.S. flag operator in the world. Other big haulers include Horizon Lines (formerly CSX)—recently bought-out by The Carlyle Group, American Ship Management, and Waterman Steamship.

In 2003, President George W. Bush reauthorized the Maritime Security Program (MSP) to "mandate establishment of a fleet of active, militarily useful, privately-owned vessels to meet national defense and other security requirements and maintain a U.S. presence in international commercial shipping." The program supports American flagged merchant ships engaged in commercial foreign trade. In exchange, the ships, their crews, and all intermodal assets are made available as needed to the Department of Defense for military support services.

The Jones Act or cabotage law restricts cargo moving between U.S. ports to vessels that are U.S.-owned, -built and -crewed. Similar U.S. cabotage laws reserve the movement of passengers and the performance of marine services such as dredging, towing and salvage to U.S. -owned, -built and -crewed vessels.

After nearly 25 years of declining shipbuilding of non-military vessels in the U.S., construction and orders for new boats and ships are on the rise primarily due to MSP and growth of the Jones Act fleet. The new millennium has seen unprecedented growth. Approximately 140 commercial vessels of all types with a market value of more than $4.4 billion are under construction in American shipyards. Included in that total are the first large U.S. flag cruise ships in more than 40 years. Contracts are pending for another 150 vessels.

Port Geography Shifts

In its prediction of future trends, *A Maritime History* envisioned a port that would "continue along the lower banks of the Hudson and around a greatly developed Upper Bay. ...and that the active center of the Port will not change its situation for many years to come."

The writers had not foreseen the revolution containerization would set off. From the start, containers reduced the cost of shipping and profoundly changed how general cargo moves in the port. While the traditional break-bulk freight was concentrated on the Brooklyn and Manhattan waterfronts, containerships required more spacious docks and landside areas as well as truck and rail linkages. In 1962, the first containerport in the nation was constructed by the Port Authority at Port Elizabeth near Port Newark.

The investment in containerization technology on the Jersey-side of the harbor altered the geography of the Port and by the 1970s maritime-related industries begin to fade on the New York-side of the harbor. In 1960, New York City handled 75 percent of the port's cargo; by 1990 its share had dropped to 15 percent. Most, if not all, port activities were consigned to the periphery of the harbor where there was better access to rail and interstate roads. The traditional break-bulk cargo terminals of Manhattan, Brooklyn, Hoboken and Jersey City relocated to specialized terminals at Port Elizabeth, Newark, Red Hook and Howland Hook. Cargo numbers more than doubled since 1994 to over four million units in 2003.

Today, Port Elizabeth handles 60 percent of containerized traffic. Howland Hook, built on the north shore of Staten Island by American Export Lines and sold to the city in the 1970s, was reactivated as a full service containerport in 1996. It is the fastest growing terminal in the Port.

The largest port on the Eastern Seaboard of the United States, New York today is the third largest port in North America (ranked behind Los Angeles and Houston) and one of the top fifteen ports in the world. The Port is the nation's largest petroleum and auto port. Between 1991 and 1999, imports and exports through the port rose from 12 million metric tons to 18 million metric tons (approximately 2200 pounds). In announcing the Port's 2003 record-breaking year, New York Governor George E. Pataki said, "The Port of New York and New Jersey continues its historic role as a centerpiece of the economy in New York and the entire region. In 2003, more than 78 million tons of cargo passed through the port. They include everyday items that we take for granted from petroleum products to a year-round supply of fresh fruits and vegetables."

Ninety-five percent of U.S. commercial imports and exports are delivered by sea, most of it traveling the world sealed in standard-sized 20 foot containers. Containerships are the largest vehicles in the world: faster, cheaper and safer than old freight carriers; newer vessels can cruise at 26 knots, displace 100,000 tons when loaded and can turn around in their own length. The Panamax containerships, so named because the vessel can fit through the Panama Canal, carry 4,000 TEUs (20-foot equivalent units). The next generation known as the post-Panamax ships, with beams exceeding 106 feet and an overall length of more than 1,000 feet, are 50 percent larger and capable of carrying in excess of 12,000 TEUs. The size of a containership determines its carrying capacity and larger ships offer tremendous cost-savings, estimated at 40 percent from reduced insurance, fuel and labor costs.

The Port of New York and New Jersey is the central supply hub for distributing petroleum products, such as heating oil, diesel fuel, gasoline and kerosene, throughout the eastern states. Commercial shipping carried approximately eight million barrels of petroleum products worth about $465 million up the Hudson to ports upriver in 2003. Oil terminals are concentrated on the Staten Island and New Jersey waterfronts on Newark Bay, Arthur Kill and Kill Van Kull. Port Mobil facility, a 203-acre site located on the Arthur Kill shore of Staten Island, has 39 above ground tanks with the capacity to hold 2.9 million barrels of petroleum products.

Port Improvements

Throughout the last half of the twentieth century to the present, the Port of New York and New Jersey has been in a race with other East Coast seaports for dominance in international marine trade. This is the driving force behind the investment in infrastructure improvements including terminal expansion, modernization of cargo handling facilities, deepening navigation channels and enhanced inland transportation. At stake is maritime commerce and jobs that studies show will grow as much as eight times during the next 40 years.

The main channels in the Port of New York and New Jersey have a depth of 40 feet. Bigger ships demand deeper channels. A study by Louis Berger Group in 2004 found that "as channel depth decreases, cargo losses and added costs for serving New York harbor rise exponentially." Current plans call for deepening all major channels in the harbor first to 45 feet and then to 50 feet by 2009. These channels include Ambrose, Anchorage, Port Jersey, Kill Van Kull/Newark Bay, Arthur Kill and Bay Ridge. The challenge for deepening channels in recent years has been the handling of dredged material which historically had been dumped at an ocean site located six miles off of Sandy Hook, New Jersey, called the Mud Dump. Dredging disposal and other environmental challenges are addressed in the Comprehensive Port Improvement Plan (CPIP), an initiative to help develop a more environmentally protective and economically sustainable port.

The Port of New York and New Jersey has an extensive intermodal network that connects marine and petroleum terminals to three local airports, multiple rail connections with two railroads, and an expansive interstate highway system that facilitates cargo movement to a population of 20 million locally and a consumer population of over 80 million. In the metropolitan area, less than two percent of freight travels by train. Most containers transit the Port by truck—an estimated 15,000 trucks per day, most entering into New York City over the George Washington and Verrazano bridges. To help reduce truck traffic, the development of improved intermodal links that involve water, highways, rails and airports is a priority. The Port Authority of New York and New Jersey launched the Port Inland Distribution Network (PIDN) in 2002 which calls for using rail, barges and short-sea shipping to an airport-type system of hub and inland feeder ports. The pattern is post-Panamax ships call at the hub port in New York harbor to discharge their cargo which is then transferred by barge to second tier feeder ports like Albany, Bridgeport and Providence. Currently, the PIDN is operating between New York City and Albany.

Marine terminals in the Port are operating at close to capacity. Port redevelopment and new terminal construction are necessary to increase throughput capabilities. Port Elizabeth, the largest container port in the world through the 1970s, is today the largest cargo handling complex on the East Coast occupying 2100 acres that contains terminals run by Maersk Sealand, the world's largest container shipper and the successor to Sea-Land. The terminal is upgrading to prepare for the next generation megaships and adding direct ship-to-rail transshipment capability. Howland Hook is doubling landside capacity by 2006 and improving rail connections and on-dock rail services with the reactivation of the Staten Island Railroad which links directly to the North American rail network.

Brooklyn offers deep water facilities and the shortest distance to the open sea. The waters off Red Hook are 65 feet deep and reach depths of 150 feet in Bay Ridge. American Stevedoring handles break-bulk cargo at its Red Hook piers. A new 350-acre port is planned for Sunset Park, at the South Brooklyn Marine Terminal. The city recently revitalized car float operations at the 65th Street rail yard in Brooklyn to improve freight movement. The Port's only remaining rail-freight carrier, the New York Cross Harbor Railroad, provides daily rail-barge service across the harbor between Brooklyn and Jersey City.

One-hundred years ago the Pennsylvania Railroad floated a plan to construct a rail freight tunnel under the Upper Bay connecting Brooklyn and New Jersey. Regional planners sought to implement the plan in the 1920s and again as a matter of security in 1941. The scheme has recently been revived as a solution to truck congestion. Studies show a tunnel would divert 8.6 million tons of freight from truck to rail.

The Port Authority of New York New Jersey

The Port Authority of New York, serving region since 1921, changed its name to The Port Authority of New York and New Jersey in 1972 to more accurately identify its role as a bi-state agency. It operates many of the busiest and most important transportation links in the region. No other port authority in the world manages such a diversified portfolio of activities, infrastructures and terminals. While the Port Authority is a public organization, it functions like a private corporation; rather than taking tax money it produces its own revenue streams.

In 1948, New York's three major airports, Newark, La Guardia and John F. Kennedy came under the jurisdiction of the Port Authority. In the 1950's and 60's the Port Authority built the Bus Terminal and a second deck on the George Washington Bridge. During this era, many Brooklyn Piers were rebuilt and the world's first containerport was developed on Newark Bay. The agency also operates the Lincoln and Holland tunnels; the three bridges between Staten Island and New Jersey; the PATH (Port Authority Trans-Hudson) rail system; the Downtown Heliport; Howland Hook Marine Terminal; and the Brooklyn Piers/Red Hook Container Terminal.

In the 1970's and 80's, the Port Authority built the towering World Trade Center as a global center dedicated to international trade. The project was initially championed by David Rockefeller in 1961 as a way to energize the downtown business district. The complex was erected on a 16-acre site in Lower Manhattan, stretching from Church Street on the east to West Street on the west, and from Liberty Street on the south to Barclay and Vesey streets on the north. Minoru Yamasaki designed the center consisting of two 110-story office towers (1&2 WTC), a 47-story office building (7 WTC), two 9-story office buildings (4 & 5 WTC), an 8-story U.S. Custom House (6 WTC), and a 22-story hotel (3 WTC), all constructed around a central five-acre landscaped Plaza. Completed in 1972, the two towers, each rising over 1360 feet, were the tallest buildings in New York City and the tallest in the world, until the Sears Tower in Chicago overtook them in 1974.

On the morning of September 11, 2001, two hijacked jet airliners piloted by terrorists hit the towers of the World Trade Center causing the buildings to collapse. There were 2830 people killed and ten major buildings destroyed or subject to partial collapse.

USCG

The Navy was given control of the Coast Guard in November 1941. During the war, convoy escort and port security were the Guard's principal duties. On shore armed guardsmen patrolled beaches and docks. The Coast Guard helicopter unit was headquartered at Floyd Bennett Field where the Sikorsky helicopter rotary wing was developed.

Coast Guard Activities New York is today the largest operational field command in the U.S. Coast Guard, controlling an area that stretches from Long Branch, New Jersey to New York City and up the Hudson River to the Canadian border. The unit is responsible for oversight of New York Harbor, including search and rescue, licensing of ships and crews, harbor patrol, maritime safety and anti-terrorism operations. It also maintains a fleet of cutters, seagoing tenders and ice-breakers to maintain waterways for the safe passage of maritime traffic.

In 1968, the Coast Guard acquired Governors Island, just off the south tip of Manhattan and abandoned the Lighthouse Depot on Staten Island. While under the Coast Guard, Governors Island hosted the 1986 relighting of the Statue of Liberty. In 1988, President Ronald Reagan met with Soviet Premier Mikhail Gorbachev to negotiate a disarmament agreement in one of the last summits of the Cold War. And in 1993, it was the meeting place of United Nations-sponsored talks to restore democratic rule in Haiti. Governor's Island was decommissioned in the mid-1990s and the USCG unit took up residence at Fort Wadsworth on Staten Island.

From Fort Wadsworth's vantage over the Narrows, Activities New York operates the Vessel Traffic Service (VTS) a surveillance system consisting of radar sensors and cameras installed throughout the harbor. It is one of only four such facilities in the country, originally designed 15 years ago in response to the Exxon-Valdez catastrophe to prevent collisions and spills. In the wake of the September 11 attacks, the VTS system is being upgraded to include an Automatic Identification System (AIS) which receives information via Global Positioning Satellites from transponders installed in the holds of commercial vessels calling on the Port. The AIS allows the Coast Guard to track vessels up to 30 miles from the harbor identifying name of vessel, cargo, point of origin, destination and speed.

The biggest port security operation since WWII was established in New York Harbor after the attacks of September 11. Within minutes of the strike, Activities New York closed the harbor and secured the terminals. USCG active duty, Reservist and Auxiliary (the volunteer arm of the Coast Guard) members mobilized to direct a waterborne evacuation of almost a million people from Manhattan Island and coordinated relief efforts at Ground Zero. On March 1, 2003, the U.S. Coast Guard officially became part of the new Department of Homeland Security.

The Coast Guard retains responsibility for lighthouses, bell buoys and hundreds of aids to navigation in New York Harbor. Most lights are automated today and no longer require much upkeep. On December 11, 2003, the last of the Coast Guard civilian lighthouse keepers passed away at the Coney Island Lighthouse. Frank Schubert, 88, served at Governors Island light from 1944 to 1961, when he took up residence at the Coney Island Light in Sea Gate for next 42 years.

Municipal Services

The *Fire Fighter* had just entered service when *A Maritime History* was written. In the years since, *Fire Fighter* has distinguished itself as the most decorated fireboat in New York City Fire Department history. It is the only fireboat honored with a Gallant Ship Award—the highest tribute the country gives for heroics at sea—which it received for rescuing 30 seamen from a fire caused by the *Esso Brussels* and *Sea Witch* collision. The incident occurred June 1, 1973, the *Esso Brussels*, loaded with crude oil, was at Stapleton anchorage awaiting docking space at the Bayway refinery when the U.S. flag containership *Sea Witch,* traveling at 14 knots, experienced a steering failure and veered into *Esso Brussels'* starboard side, causing her cargo oil to spill and burn on the water. Both vessels, engulfed in flames, were carried by the ebb tide and drifted beneath the Verrazano Bridge, where flames shot up stopping traffic on the bridge.

Large fires had been a regular occurrence on the waterfront in the era when break-bulk cargo sat in the holds of wooden ships on wooden docks and wharves. The advent of containerization and concrete piers and warehouses reduced the frequency of fires. Fireboat priorities shifted to water rescues, which now comprise 40 percent of fireboat responses. New York City's active fireboats responded to over 2400 calls in 2000.

All FDNY fireboat captains hold a Coast Guard harbor pilots license. The Marine Unit has a fleet of seven boats including fireboats and tenders. Fireboats currently operating are *John D. McKean* (1954), docked at Marine 1 Gansvoort Street; *Governor Alfred E. Smith* (1961), *Kevin C. Kane* (1992), and the small fireboat *Smoke II* at Marine Company 6 at the Brooklyn Navy Yard; and *Fire Fighter* (1938) at Marine Company 9 docked at Stapleton piers on Staten Island.

The collapse of the towers on September 11, 2001 ruptured water mains in Lower Manhattan so fire trucks were left without water pressure to combat the raging fires. On the west side of the World Trade Center, fireboats took up position on the Hudson River seawall to pump water directly from the river to fire trucks—the *Fire Fighter* (20,000 gallons per minute capacity) docked at Vesey Street, the *Smoke II* (2,000 gallons per minute capacity) and *Kevin Kane* (6,500 gallons per minute capacity) docked in North Cove, and the *John D. McKean* (19,000 gallons per minute capacity) docked at Albany Street. Retired fireboat *John J. Harvey* (18,000 gallons per minute capacity) returned to active service and joined the other large vessels. The fireboats were instrumental in suppressing the fires pumping nearly 60,000 gallons of water a minute twenty-four hours a day over the course of the next three days. Fuel and supplies were provided by the *Hayward*, the Army Corps of Engineer's vessel. The *John J. Harvey* and her civilian crew of volunteers remained on duty to aid the relief efforts for several days.*

The Harbor Unit of the Police Department patrols the waters surrounding New York City in a fleet made up of four 50-foot and five 30-foot Kenny Hanson class patrol launches equipped with 13-foot Boston Whalers. The Harbor Unit is primarily responsible for enforcing the law, rescue and recovery missions, waterfront security, and now adds anti-terror to its duties. The unit is located at the South Brooklyn Marine Terminal at 58th Street in Sunset Park. Its Scuba Unit has about 27 divers, all male, who make over 1,000 dives annually. It is the only full-time police dive team in the country. Scuba maintains an air-sea rescue team at Floyd Bennett Field in Brooklyn.

---

* FEMA Technical Report: Fireboats Then and Now, May 2003

Ferries

In the late-twentieth century, the construction of bridges and tunnels as well as the subways sharply reduced the need for ferries. The opening of the Verrazano Bridge in 1964 supplanted the 69th Street Bay Ridge, Brooklyn to St. George, Staten Island ferry. Three years later, the last of the cross-Hudson ferries ended service. The sole ferry service by the late 1960s was the publicly-operated Staten Island Ferry, the city's oldest and largest ferry service, with daily ridership of approximately 70,000 today.

Cross-Hudson ferry service was non-existent for close to two decades. In 1986, entrepreneur Arthur Imperatore, the owner of a trucking company saw ferry service as a way to attract buyers to the redeveloping New Jersey riverside. Imperatore initiated the Port Imperial Ferry between Weehawken, New Jersey and West 38th Street, Manhattan where company buses then transported riders over routes to midtown and downtown. The ferry was renamed New York Waterway and operates without subsidy carrying passengers aboard a fleet of double-deck, bow-loading passenger ferries capable of 35 knots and higher. By 1991, seven ferry routes were carrying more than 16,000 passengers daily. Ridership in 2000 reached 32,000, now its 60,000 a day.

The ferry market in New York Harbor was growing by 2000. Sea streak, sister company of Hoverspeed which operates ferries across the English Channel, joined the cross-Hudson route. Ridership surged more than 50 percent after September 11, 2001, when bridges and subways were shut down. New York Water Taxi launched service to landings around New York City in 2002. The bright yellow taxi-style vessels are environmentally friendly, with low-emission engines and hulls that minimize wakes and disruption of aquatic life. The Port Authority of New York and New Jersey will invest in a ferry service between Lower Manhattan and JFK Airport by 2005. To enhance LaGuardia Airport connections, a fast ferry will also run between Manhattan and a new LaGuardia ferry terminal.

Five major projects are underway or planned to rejuvenate and develop ferry terminals including: the enhancement and expansion of the Whitehall terminal—fire-damaged in 1991; transformation of the St. George ferry terminal in Staten Island (the current dull looking structure built in 1951 replaced the original terminal destroyed by fire in 1946); a new terminal at Pier 79 on West 39th Street; and improvements to the Port Imperial terminal in Weehawken and the historic Hoboken terminal in New Jersey. Work is also planned on numerous Water Taxi landing slips along the East River and Hudson River.

Excursion Boats

The fuel shortages during World War II curtailed most excursion boating. In 1945, a group of Irish boaters pooled resources and fleets to offer tours that circle the island of Manhattan departing from at Pier 83. The company would later take the name Circle Line. In 1953 the operator took over the Statue of Liberty Ferry service. Circle Line did not operate without competition, but managed to buy-out or overtake most rivals. Hudson River Day Line set up at nearby Pier 81 and was purchased by Circle Line in 1963. A partner in the original investment group, Jeremiah Driscoll broke away to start Panorama Sightseeing which operated from the Battery up until 1969. Fairwater Cruises, originally established to link Manhattan and Flushing, Queens for the 1964 World's Fair, operated around-Manhattan sightseeing boats from the Battery for two seasons. Seaport Line, started up at the redeveloped South Street Seaport in 1985 and was taken over by Circle Line five years later.

In 1991, 32 operations with 65 vessels were providing excursion boating in the port. In 2004, the century long tradition of the Hudson River Day Liner was revived by New York Cruise Lines, the parent company of Circle Line, World Yacht, and The Beast Speedboats.

9/11 Sealift

On September 11, 2001 the waterways provided the only escape route for hundreds of thousands of workers in lower Manhattan. The USCG Activities New York coordinated the largest rescue mission on American soil since Pearl Harbor directing an armada of more than 100 vessels, both public and private. John Snyder, senior editor of Marine Log reported the response of New York's maritime fleet in the article "Ferries to the Rescue After World Trade Center Attack," (Oct. 2001) excerpt below:

"...soon we could see a swarm of vessels—ferries, dinner boats, tugs and small private craft—shuttling thousands of evacuees across the Hudson River from downtown Manhattan to various points of safety in New Jersey. Larger vessels were also on station including a Sandy Hook pilot boat, a Coast Guard cutter and a spill response vessel. The Coast Guard estimated that one million New Yorkers were evacuated from Manhattan by water. The response by vessel operators was nothing short of phenomenal.

Because of their bow-loading design, NY Waterway's ferries were pressed into service as waterborne ambulances. The vessels were used to medivac injured firefighters across the Hudson to Colgate. In all, NY Waterway ferries carried about 2,000 injured.

With all of Manhattan's arteries shut down and its subways at a standstill, NY Waterway put 22 of its 24 ferries in "load and go" service at piers in lower and Midtown Manhattan, taking a total of 158,506 evacuees to points in Jersey City, Hoboken and Weehawken, N.J., as well as Brooklyn and Queens.

Also pitching in, were a number of dinner and tour boat operators. "We moved about 30,000 people on our six boats," says Peter Cavrell, senior vice president of sales and marketing for Circle Line. "It wasn't any kind of coordinated effort. We just started doing it." Continues Cavrell, "In its own small way, Circle Line is a symbol of New York. We just wanted to do our part."

Excursion vessel operator Spirit Cruises began shuttling evacuees from Chelsea Piers across the Hudson River to the Lincoln Harbor Yacht Marina in Weehawken, N.J. Spirit used its three dinner boats, the 625-passenger *Spirit of New York*, 500-passenger *Spirit of New Jersey* and 350-passenger *Spirit of Hudson*. Steve Schwartz, Spirit Cruises' regional director, says some 8,000 passengers were moved during a 2 hour period.

On September 14, the *Spirit of New York* was given special permission to dock at North Cove Yacht Harbor [at the World Financial Center], where it was used as a floating rest stop to distribute food donated by many of the area's fine restaurants, including the TriBeCa Grill. It remained on station for 72 hours.

Marine Spill Response Corp. *Responder* remained on station at North Cove Yacht Harbor for three days to provide a rest area for firefighters, police and volunteers working in the rescue effort.

According to the American Waterways Operators (AWO), virtually every tugboat company in and around New York committed all of their resources to evacuating disaster victims in response to the Coast Guard's call. About 35 tugs, stationed at spots designated by the Coast Guard throughout lower Manhattan, aided in the evacuation effort from about 10 a.m. on September. 11 to 3 a.m. on September 12."

Preservation

In the second half of the twentieth century burgeoning development and neglect threatened countless maritime relics throughout the city. The demolition of Pennsylvania Station in 1963 increased public awareness of the value associated with the city's architectural and cultural heritage. Citizen advocacy on the part of individuals passionate about preserving the historic legacy of the seaport reclaimed many maritime historic sites and structures as cultural, recreational, and educational resources.

Navy veteran Peter Stanford had the idea to create a maritime museum to chronicle the city's seafaring past. In 1967, he launched South Street Seaport Museum in a storefront at 16 Fulton Street with the help of Jakob Isbrandtsen, a shipping magnate of American Export Lines, whose father's cousin A. P. Moller had formed the great Maersk Line. Within a few decades, the museum negotiated a 99-year lease with the city to rescue five blocks of buildings and three piers—piers Stanford had originally claimed by squatter's rights. It secured landmark status and assembled one of the largest fleets of historic ships in the hemisphere. The Coast Guard donated the first vessel—the *Ambrose* Lightship. The museum's Melville library under the care of Norman Brouwer grew to be an important repository of nautical books, photographs and ship's documents. In recent years, the museum expanded gallery space through the rehabilitation of the Schermerhorn Row Counting Houses on Fulton Street. It draws about 10 million visitors annually to the seaport district. To ease financial strain, the museum is currently in the process of selling many of the historic vessels and transferring the library's collection to storage to help pay the bills.

Artist and mariner, John Noble campaigned to preserve Sailor's Snug Harbor from developers. The first home for retired seamen in the United States opened on the shores of the Kill Van Kull on Staten Island in 1833. The sanctuary was privately endowed by Captain Robert Randall, a man who made his fortune from the sea and willed it support "as asylum or home for aged, decrepit seamen." At its peak, Snug Harbor housed more than 1000 retired seamen and contained 60 buildings, including two hospitals and a church. The population of residents, called Snugs, diminished by the 1950s and the property fell into a state of disrepair. Mayor Robert Wagner turned down an offer from the institution's board to accept the site for free. In the 1970s, Mayor John Lindsay purchased the 83-acre property for $7 million. It reopened as the Snug Harbor Cultural Center in 1976. Today, it contains twenty-six historic buildings including five Greek-revival structures; one occupied by the Noble Maritime Collection featuring works of the artist who helped rescue the property; works in which Noble strived "...to make a rounded picture of American maritime endeavor of modern times."

The Intrepid Sea-Air-Space Museum on the Hudson River on Manhattan's west side began with a battle-scarred aircraft carrier and the strong will of philanthropist Zachery Fisher, who spent $24 million of his own money in order to save the *Intrepid*. The ship was retired from active duty in 1974 and on the verge of being scrapped. Mr. Fisher established the Intrepid Museum Foundation to transform the vessel into an educational museum and memorial to those who served in defense of their country. The 900-foot-long *Intrepid* decked with 25 aircraft and flanked by the guided missile submarine *Growler* forms the core of the Museum opened to the public in 1982, and annually hosting 500,000 visitors.

The Ellis Island Immigration Center had been used as a detention center for enemy aliens in WWII and closed in 1954 after millions of immigrants had entered America through its doors. It was a vital part of America's immigrant history; over 100 million Americans can trace their ancestry in the United States to the Registry Room on Ellis Island. In 1965, Ellis Island became part of Statue of Liberty National Monument. An ambitious restoration effort was mounted and the Ellis Island Immigration Museum opened to the public in 1990.

Roland Betts, owner of the Texas Rangers and Silver Screen Studios, thought Sky Rink where his daughter practiced skating was too small and the column-free space at Chelsea Piers would make an ideal ice skating rink. Chelsea Piers were originally constructed in 1910 as docks for the famed White Star and Cunard Lines. The Hudson River piers served as a troop embarkation point during WWII. The last tenants, the United States and Grace lines, relocated to New Jersey in 1967. By the mid-1980s the piers were shabby, collapsing and slated for demolition. The NYC Tow Pound was at Pier 60; a sanitation truck repair shop at Pier 59; and Customs Impound at Pier 62. Betts won a bid for the structure in 1992 and opened the Chelsea Piers Sports and Entertainment Complex in 1995. The three piers and headhouse stretching from West 23rd Street south for five blocks were transformed into a public waterfront and huge recreational center featuring two Olympic-size skating rinks.

On the Hudson River flanking Chelsea Piers at West 23rd Street Pier 63 Maritime is a privately owned 320-foot Erie-Lackawanna barge that at one time carried freight cars across the river from New Jersey. The barge is owned by John Krevy and since 1989 has been a base for preservation of historic vessels. The centerpiece of the pier is the *Frying Pan* lightship and *John J. Harvey* fireboat. Nearby is the restored Baltimore & Ohio Float Bridge at Pier 66a, where railroad cars transferred onto barges from 1954 to 1973.

The historic vessels now under restoration at many Hudson River Park piers provide a hands-on glimpse of life aboard ship. The *Pegasus* tugboat, built in 1907, was designed to serve waterside refineries and terminals of Standard Oil, as the *Esso Tug No.1*, she plied the waters of the New York Harbor docking ships and moving lighter barges of petroleum products. In 1953 she was sold to McAllister Towing for further use as a harbor tugboat and renamed the *John E. McAllister*. Hepburn Marine bought her in 1987, brought her back to New York as the tugboat *Pegasus* where she was continued to engage in towing and transport work. The tug was retired in 1997 and preservation efforts began immediately under the direction of Captain Pamela Hepburn. *Pegasus* is docked at Chelsea Piers. Other historic vessels under preservation on the Hudson include the ferryboat *Yankee* at Pier 25 and the steamship *Lilac* at Pier 40.

The Historic House Trust of the City Parks Department was created in 1989 to preserve and promote 22 historic house museums located in New York City parks. Many of these are waterfront homes that provide insight into the storied past of the Port and the people who populated Old New York. Gracie Mansion on the East River overlooking Hell Gate is named for Archibald Gracie a Scottish shipping magnate who bought the property in 1798. It is now the official residence of the mayor. Merchant's House Museum, built in 1831, is the only 19th century family home preserved intact in New York City. It was home to Seabury Tredwell, an importer and wealthy city merchant with a business on Pearl Street, near South Street Seaport. On Staten Island, the Seguine Mansion overlooking Prince's Bay was built in 1838 by a successful bay oysterman.

The former Coast Guard Lighthouse Depot on Staten Island, which had supplied lighthouses for more than a century, was abandoned in the late 1960s when the USCG took up residence on Governor's Island. The property suffered from years of weather damage and vandalism. In the 1980s, public outcry led to preservation of the historic buildings.

Plans are underway to restore the ten acre historic site as the National Lighthouse Museum. Four buildings have been placed on the National Register of Historic Places and the Administration Building received City Landmark status. Construction has begun on many of the structures including repair of the 850-foot pier to berth the Museum's lightship, the *Nantucket-112*.

On Jan. 31, 2003, President Bush returned Governors Island to the City of New York for $1. Two historic fortifications and their surroundings became a national monument under the jurisdiction of the National Park Service. Presently, the Governors Island Preservation and Education Corporation is charged with developing long-range plans for the island, which may include a campus of the City University of New York, a park and space for commercial development.

Many reminders of New York City's historic seafaring past are in the recycled buildings located throughout Lower Manhattan. One that has remained intact, Fraunce's Tavern has stood at 54 Pearl Street since it was built in 1762. It was here that George Washington gave his farewell address. When the U.S. Customs Service moved to the World Trade Center in 1973, the Custom House stood vacant for almost a decade until its rescue and reuse as the Museum of the American Indian. The entrance to the Cass Gilbert designed building is flanked by sculptures representing the four continents. The Rotunda ceiling of the U.S. Customs House at One Bowling Green is embellished with eight views of activity in the Port of New York painted by WPA-commissioned Reginald Marsh. Frederick Dana Marsh, Reginald's father, created the nautical-themed tiles that were installed at the Broadway-Nassau subway station in 2000. The 1913 tiles were salvaged from the old Marine Grill in the McAlpin building on Herald Square. The Post Office at 25 Broadway was originally built in 1921 as the Cunard Line building, as is suggested by murals in its main hall. The signs above the Citibank Building at One Broadway designate "First Class" and Cabin Class" leftover from when it was the United States Line Building.

Waterfront Renewal

A Maritime History of New York opens by shedding light on why the city and the port naturally developed along the harbor. The harbor is a large natural system—an estuary, where land meets water and freshwater mixes with seawater. Estuaries are diverse ecosystems that form the foundation of the coastal food chain. This estuary nature forms the fabric of the port and endows New York City with a wealth of fish, shellfish, birds, plants species, and other wildlife. The seaport that grew on its shores has been the keystone of the city's progress and a catalyst of economic growth for four hundred years.

Over the centuries, the tasks of the port often clashed with the nature of the harbor. "A conflict between developing the waterfront for commerce and developing it for public use has been with us since 1811 when the plan for Manhattan was laid out. Commercial use, considered incompatible with recreation, was given clear preference. Later, in 1835, in a discussion about the potential development of Stuyvesant Cove for a park, it was argued that it would be a waste of 'a great front for shipping on the East River'."*

A Maritime History predicted in 1941 that a major seaport would be built on Jamaica Bay. As early as 1878, the city government floated plans for a seaport on the bay because of its close proximity to the open sea. By the 1930s pressure mounted to develop a port to rival Rotterdam and Liverpool. In a letter to Mayor La Guardia dated July 18, 1938, then Parks Commissioner Robert Moses expressed his desire to preserve Jamaica Bay's 18,000 acres of water, marsh and meadowland. Moses' plan called for transferring the bay and all lands surrounding it to the Parks Department, "for recreational use, including protection of scenery and waters; encouragement of swimming, fishing, boating and preservation of wild life; public use of the meadowlands adjoining Cross Bay Boulevard, including Big Egg Marsh..." Ten years later, Jamaica Bay and the bounding lands were conveyed to the Parks Department. Robert Moses created Jamaica Bay Wildlife Refuge which in the 1970s was

* New York City Comprehensive Waterfront Plan: Reclaiming the City's Edge, 1992
NYC Department of City Planning

transferred to the National Park Service. He also constructed the Belt Parkway around the north shore of the bay interlacing the road with ribbon parks and green spaces.

It wasn't until the 1960s that the true ecological value of Jamaica Bay and the harbor estuary were realized. Rachel Carson, the first female employee of the U.S. Fish and Wildlife Service, raised awareness of the sea as a living eco-system in her history of the ocean, *The Sea Around Us*. Water pollution was at an all-time high by the early 1970s. Growing concern and environmentalist clout led to the Clean Water Act signed into law by President Richard Nixon in 1972: "to make the nation's waters safe for fishing and swimming, reduce harmful discharges of pollution, and protect the nation's wetlands." The results are apparent today. Odors, water color, clarity, and overall appearance of the rivers and harbor have changed for the better. It is a far cry from the "oily, dirty, and germy" water Joseph Mitchell wrote of in "The Bottom of the Harbor" in 1951.

Many things were happening simultaneously on the New York City waterfront. Cleaner water and an abandoned waterfront led to people wanting greater access. Harbor events like Operation Sail on the bicentennial July 4, 1976 and the first Fleet Week in 1987 brought thousands to a waterside ripe for regeneration.

In 1973, a cement truck on its way to make repairs on the elevated Miller Highway (West Side Highway) caused a 60 foot section of the structure to collapse near Canal Street. While the elevated roadway had served the needs of the port-related industries on the piers, it had restricted access and obscured views to the river for more than fifty years. The Westway plan for the highways reconstruction proposed in 1974 to tunnel a six-lane interstate through landfill along the shore of the Hudson River and create parkland on top of the structure. The project was steadfastly opposed because of adverse environmental impact on aquatic life and successfully halted in 1986. The Hudson River Park scheme took form in 1992 to create a linear park in conjunction with highway construction. The 550-acre Hudson River Park now stretches five miles from Lower Manhattan's Battery Park Place north to 59th Street. When completed (scheduled for 2008), it will contain 14 public piers, 400 acres of marine sanctuary, four boathouses for non-motorized craft, and numerous new facilities.

Plans to revitalize the lower Hudson River shipping piers on the Lower Manhattan waterfront were first presented in 1966 by Governor Rockefeller. United Fruit (now Chiquita), had occupied the piers until the Hunts Point Market opened in the Bronx. Battery Park City was raised on a 92-acre landfill obtained from the construction of the World Trade Center towers in 1976. The mixed-use complex of housing, office space, marina and parks opened incrementally through the 1980s and 1990s. The development is designed to provide public access along its entire waterfront.

Projects are underway throughout the city that reclaim and open the waterfront for public use and refurbish the remnants of traditional waterfront usage. New waterfront residential developments are required to incorporate waterfront public access into the design. Brooklyn Bridge Park will encompass the waterfront from the Manhattan Bridge through Pier 5 at Atlantic Avenue while preserving a row of old Tobacco Warehouses. In Queens, at Hunter's Point a large swath of land has been transformed to fishing piers and promenades with restored Long Island Railroad gantries as the centerpiece. Donald Trump built 23-acre Riverside Park South in response to community opposition to his planned 13-block-long development over the 75-acre Penn Yards site. The resulting park features a fishing pier and the restored a 90-year-old Grand Central float bridge at the foot of 69th Street.

A Plan for the Waterfront

Most of the waterfront land in New York City is in public ownership. In 1992, the Department of City Planning proposed a land use guide for the entire city shoreline. This Comprehensive Waterfront Plan, subtitled

Reclaiming the City's Edge, presented "a long-range vision that balances the needs of environmentally sensitive areas and the working port with opportunities for waterside pubic access, open space, housing and commercial activity." Over the past decade, the city has amended outdated waterfront zoning laws and has begun to implement many of the plans recommendations.

The Waterfront Plan mapped out a framework where working, recreational and natural waterfront uses coexist. It called for protecting and encouraging water dependent uses, such as maritime support, marina, commercial excursion boating, and water-borne transportation. Six Significant Maritime and Industrial Areas were designated to protect and encourage concentrated working waterfronts, including: The Kill Van Kull in Staten Island from Howland Hook to Snug Harbor; the Brooklyn waterfront from Erie Basin to Owls Head; the Brooklyn waterfront from Pier 6 to Red Hook Containerport; the Brooklyn Navy Yard; the Queens and Brooklyn shores of Newtown Creek; and the South Bronx (Port Morris and Hunts Point)

Today, decisions affecting the future of the waterfront are being played out in neighborhoods throughout New York City. Public meetings and forums invite residents to participate in the planning process. Community Board 197a plans are community action programs to provide a blueprint for shaping future land use issues through increased public awareness and involvement in waterfront redevelopment. Neighborhoods from Long Island City, Queens and Greenpoint, Brooklyn to the Bronx's Hunts Point and Stapleton, Staten Island have developed 197a plans that stipulate local recommendations for redeveloping local waterfronts. The struggles over the Red Hook waterfront exposes some of the vagaries of the process.

Since the dawn of the new millennium, Red Hook has been a public arena for competing land use interests. It is surrounded by water on three sides; the harbor views are spectacular taking in the whole of the Upper Bay. Much of the working waterfront was abandoned in the 1960s and 70s when container facilities were built on the Jersey-side of the harbor. The construction of the Gowanus Expressway and Battery Tunnel cut off the square-mile peninsula from the rest of Brooklyn. It is today a mix of early-19th-century buildings put up to handle trade from the Erie Canal; civil war era warehouses; small manufacturing businesses; the large Red Hook Houses projects (originally built in the late 1930s for dockworkers) where 70 percent of the population lives; and brick row and wood framed houses. Retired NYPD detective Greg O'Connell began buying up derelict and condemned properties here in the early 1980s and restoring them for small business usage. Port-related businesses started to return to the area. The Red Hook Terminal opened in 1981 as the only break-bulk terminal in Brooklyn. In 1989, long vacant Erie Basin was occupied by Reinauer Transportation Companies for a Marine Support Service Center and tugboat berthing. New York Water Taxi made Red Hook its homeport of operation.

In the 1990s residents united to fight a city waste transfer station. Residents then clashed over Fairway's plan to open a giant supermarket in one of O'Connell's historic warehouse buildings at the foot of Van Brunt Street. At the time, the community's need for fresh produce and jobs won out. Today, the real estate market is booming and the areas future holds promise for the first time in four decades. Swedish retailer Ikea is seeking to build a giant box store on prime waterfront land and pave over the old docks of Todd Shipyards to accommodate parking. Todd Shipyards (also known as New York Shipyards) once occupied the 22-acre walled parcel of waterfront that includes the city's largest dry dock and graving dock. The store will attract over 10,000 cars a day to the areas narrow cobbled streets. An alternative proposal has emerged to preserve the yards' maritime use and create a mixed-use community with marinas and public waterfront access. The future of the shipyard property is as yet undetermined. City officials and public housing residents appear to lean toward the jobs and taxes promised by Ikea, while others are hopeful the neighborhood will retain its working waterfront roots.

The story of the Port of New York continues today against a back-drop of constant evolution and renewal. The Port has persisted through the Second World War and the great technological changes of the twentieth century. It has persevered through lose of position as the top U.S. port, short-sited development and the devastating attacks of 2001. Today the Port is experiencing an unprecedented pattern of growth. Ship size and cargo increases are benefiting from new advances in information technology and landside operations that will further impact economies of scale. *A Maritime History* 1941 concludes that the one consistent theme has been the Port's "continuous and vital growth." That theme still holds true today.

Barbara La Rocco is co-founder of Going Coastal, Inc. and the author of *Going Coastal New York City: A Guide to the Waterfront.* Barbara is currently researching her next book for the Going Coastal imprint— *Field Guide to Historic Ships Across America,* due for release spring 2005.

Bibliography

ANTHROPOLOGY AND INDIANS

BOLTON, REGINALD PELHAM. *Indian Life of Long Ago in the City of New York*. New York, 1934.

SKINNER, ALANSON. *The Indians of Manhattan Island and Vicinity*. New York, 1915.

BIOGRAPHIES

BOYD, THOMAS. *Poor John Fitch, Inventor of the Steamboat*. New York, 1935.

SPEARS, JOHN R. *Captain Nathaniel Brown Palmer, an Old Time Sailor of the Sea*. New York, 1922.

THURSTON, ROBERT H. *Robert Fulton*. New York, 1891.

CANALS

EATON, M. *Five Years on the Erie Canal: An Account of Some of the Most Striking Scenes and Incidents, during Five Years Labor on the Erie Canal, and Other Inland Waters*. Utica, N.Y., 1845.

HARVOW, ALVIN F. *Old Towpaths, the Story of the American Canal Era*. New York, London, 1926.

WATSON, ELKANAH. *History of the Rise, Progress, and Existing Condition of the Western Canals in the State of New-York, from September 1788, to the Completion of the Middle Section of the Grand Canal in 1819*. Albany, 1820.

COMMERCE, FINANCE, MERCHANTS, TRADE

BARRETT, WALTER (pseudonym of J. A. Scoville). *The Old Merchants of New York City*. 3 vols. New York, 1889.

MAURY, LIEUT. M. F. *Direct Trade with the South*. (Southern Literary Messenger, Vol. 5.) January 1839.

CORRESPONDENCE, DIARIES, DOCUMENTS, JOURNALS, MANUSCRIPTS, MEMOIRS

BURNABY, REV. ANDREW. *Travels through the Middle Settlements in North America in the Years, 1759 and 1760.* London, 1775.

GRISWOLD, CHARLES. *Letter from Charles Gristwold to Prof. Benjamin Silliman on Submarine Navigation. (The American Journal of Science and Arts,* Vol. 2, No. 2.) Nov. 1820.

HONE, PHILIP. *Diary of Philip Hone, 1828-61.* (Edited by Allan Nevins.) 2 vols. New York, 1927.

JAY, JOHN. *The Correspondence and Public Papers of John Jay.* (Edited by Henry P. Johnston.) 4 vols. New York, London, 1893.

JUET, ROBERT. T*he third Voyage of Master Henry Hudson toward Nova Zembla... Written by ROBERT JUET,* of Lime-house. (See: *Collections of the New-York Historical Society, for the year 1809. Volume I. New-York: Printed and published by I. Riley, 1811.*)

LAMBERT, JOHN. *Travels through Canada and the United States of North America, in the years 1806, 1807, and 1808.* 2 vols. London, Edinburgh, Dublin, 1814.

NEW-YORK HISTORICAL SOCIETY. William Bradford: *Correspondence between New Netherlands and New Plymouth.* Series 2, Vol. 2. New York, 1841.

SAMUELS, SAMUEL. *From the Forecastle to the Cabin.* Boston, 1924.

SHAW, SAMUEL. *The Journals of Major Samuel Shaw, with a life of the author by Josiah Quincy.* Boston, 1847.

VAN LAEK, A. J. F., ed. *Van Rensselaer Bowier Manuscripts.* (University of the State of New York.) Albany, 1908.

HISTORY—GENERAL

FISKE, JOHN. T*he Discovery of America.* 2 vols. Boston, New York, 1895.

MORISON, SAMUEL E. *The Maritime History of Massachusetts, 1788-1860.* Boston, New York, 1921.

ROSEWATER, VICTOR. *History of Cooperative News-Gathering in the United States.* New York, London, 1930.

HISTORY—GEOLOGICAL

DAVIS, HARRY M. *New York's Own Grand Canyon under the Sea.* (New York *Times* Magazine, July 11, 1937.)

MORRIS, FREDERICK K. *The Making of the Valley, a Billion Years along the Hudson.* New York, 1936.

NEWBERRY, J. S. *The Geological History of New York Island and Harbor. New York,* 1878.

HISTORY—NEW YORK CITY

EARL, ALICE M. *The Stadt Huys of New Amsterdam*. (*Historic New York*. First series of the *Half Moon Papers*.) New York, London, 1898.

GOODWIN, MAUD W. *Fort Amsterdam in the Days of the Dutch*. (*Historic New York*. First series of the *Half Moon Papers*.) NY, London, 1898.

GUERNSEY, ROCELLUS S. *New York City and Vicinity during the War of 1812-15*. 2 vols. New York, 1889-95.

INNES, JOHN H. *New Amsterdam and Its People*. New York, 1902.

MORGAN, EDWIN V. *Slavery in New York, with Special Reference to New York City*. (*Historic New York*. Second series of the *Half Moon Papers*.) New York, London, 1899.

STOKES, I. N. PHELPS. *The Iconography of Manhattan Island, 1498-1909*. 6 vols. New York, 1915-28.

WILSON, JAMES G., ed. *The Memorial History of the City of New York*. 4 vols. New York, 1893.

HISTORY—STATE OF NEW YORK

BRODHEAD, JOHN R. *History of the State of New York*. 2 vols. New York, 1859-71.

O'CALLAGHAN, EDMUND B., ed. *Documents Relative to the Colonial History of the State of New York*. 11 vols. (Procured in Holland, England, and France by John Romeyn Brodhead, Esq.) Albany, 1853.

O'CALLAGHAN, EDMUND B., ed. *Laws and Ordinances of New Netherlands, 1638-74* (Compiled and translated from the original Dutch Records.) Albany, 1868.

WASSENAER, NICHOLAS VAN. *Description and First Settlement of New Netherland*. (*Historic van Europa*.) Privately printed. Edinburgh, 1888.

HISTORY—UNITED STATES

ADAMS, HENRY. *History of the United States of America*. 9 vols. New York, 1921.

McMASTER, JOHN B. *A History of the People of the United States*. 8 vols. New York, 1915.

MAHAN, CAPTAIN ALFRED T. *Sea Power in Its Relations to the War of 1812*. 2 vols. Boston, 1905.

ROOSEVELT, THEODORE. *The Naval War of 1812*. 2 vols. New York, 1910.

MISCELLANEOUS

DRISCOLL, CHARLES B. *Doubloons, the Story of Buried Treasure*. New York, 1930.

GRAMLING, OLIVER. *AP, the Story of News*. New York, Toronto, 1940.

KAPP, FRIEDRICH. *Immigration, and the Commissioners of Emigration of the State of New York*. New York, 1870.

PIRACY, PIRATES, PRIVATEERS

COGGESHALL, GEORGE. *History of the American Privateers, and Letters-of-Marque, during Our War with England in the Years 1812, '13 and '14*. New York, 1856.

GOSSE, PHILIP. *The Pirates' Who's Who*. London, 1924.

JOHNSON, CAPT. CHARLES. *A General History of the Robberies and Murders of the Most Notorious Pyrates, and Also Their Policies, Discipline and Government, etc*. London, 1724.

MACLAY, EDGAR S. *A History of American Privateers*. New York, London, 1924.

PORT OF NEW YORK

ALBION, ROBERT G. *The Rise of New York Port, 1815-60*. New York, London, 1939.

HARRINGTON, VIRGINIA D. *The New York Mechant on the Eve of the Revolution*. New York, London, 1935.

McKAY, RICHARD C. *South Street*. New York, 1934.

SHIPS AND SHIPPING

ALBION, ROBERT G. *Square-Riggers on Schedule*. Princeton, London, 1938.

BANK OF MANHATTAN CO., *Ships and Shipping of Old New York*. New York, 1915.

BOWEN, FRANK C. *America Sails the Seas*. New York, 1938.

CALVIN, H. C. & STUART, E. G. *The Merchant Shipping Industry*. New York, 1925.

CLARK, ARTHUR H. *The Clipper Ship Era*. New York, 1911.

CUTLER, CARL G. *Greyhounds of the Sea*. New York, London, 1930.

HOWE, OCTAVIUS T. & MATTHEWS, FREDERICK C. *American Clipper Ships*. 2 vols. Salem, Mass., 1926.

MARVIN, WINTHROP L. *The American Merchant Marine*. New York, 1902.

MORRISON, JOHN H. *History of New York Shipyards*. New York, 1909.

SLAVERS, SLAVERY, SLAVES

APTHEKER, HERBERT. *Negro Slave Revolts in the United States, 1526-1860*. New York, 1939.

DONNAN, ELIZABETH. *Documents Illustrative of the History of the Slave Trade to America*. 4 vols. Washington, D.C., 1930-35.

O'CALLAGHAN, EDMUND B., comp. *Voyages of the slavers St. John and Arms of Amsterdam, 1659, 1663*. Translated from the original manuscripts, with an introduction and index by E. B. O'Callaghan. Albany, 1867.

STEAMBOATS AND STEAMSHIPS

BOWEN, FRANK C. *A Century of Atlantic Travel, 1830-1930*. Boston, 1930.

BUCKMAN, DAVID L. *Old Steamboat Days on the Hudson River*. New York, 1909.

DAYTON, FRED E. *Steamboat Days*. New York, 1925.

MAGINNIS, ARTHUR J. *The Atlantic Ferry*. London, 1893.

MORRISON, JOHN H. *History of American Steam Navigation*. New York, 1903.

Many books, other than those listed, were consulted as well as newspapers, periodicals, pamphlets, state papers, documents, and municipal, state, and Federal publications and reports.

INDEX

Going Coastal, Inc.

Going Coastal New York City, by Barbara La Rocco
(goingcoastal.org $21.95)

The waters surrounding New York City contribute to our happiness and standard of living. Going Coastal, Inc. is a public benefit corporation dedicated to promoting responsible use and public enjoyment of coastal resources. We are at the service of all with similar aims.

Visit us online at www.goingcoastal.org.

Printed in the United States
22349LVS00002B/71-100

9 780972 980319